YOUTH, POPULAR CULTURE AND MORAL PANICS

YOUTH, POPULAR CULTURE AND MORAL PANICS

PENNY GAFFS TO GANGSTA-RAP, 1830–1996

John Springhall

Reader in History
University of Ulster at Coleraine

St. Martin's Press
New York

St. Martin's Press, Scholarly and Reference Division, 175 Fifth Avenue, New York, N.Y. 10010

First published in the United States of America in 1998

This book is printed on paper suitable for recycling and made from fully managed and sustained forest sources.

Printed in Hong Kong

ISBN 0–312–21394–8 clothbound
ISBN 0–312–21395–6 paperback

Library of Congress Cataloging-in-Publication Data
Springhall, John.
Youth, popular culture and moral panics : penny gaffs to gangsta
-rap, 1830–1996 / John Springhall.
p.   cm.
Includes bibliographical references and index.
ISBN 0–312–21394–8. — ISBN 0–312–21395–6 (pbk.)
1. Popular culture—Influence.   2. Youth—Attitudes.   3. Youth–
–United States—Attitudes.   4. Popular culture—United States–
–History—19th century.   5. Popular culture—United States–
–History—20th century.   I. Title.
HM101.S7736 1998
306'.0973—dc21   97–53206
                                                                      CIP

For the members of the south-west London
Gastronomico-Philosophical Society – IN VINO VERITAS

WITHDRAWN

CONTENTS

ACKNOWLEDGEMENTS

I owe a great deal to archivists and librarians for making documents and collections relevant to my research into theatrical, literary, cinematic and comic-book history available and, in most cases, allowing generous photocopying. Special thanks to Clive Hurst, Head of Special Collections at the Bodleian Library, Oxford, for allowing access to 'penny dreadfuls' held in the Opie, John Johnson, and Frank Pettingell Collections. The following libraries and museums also helped with access to special collections used for Chapters 2 and 3: the Boys and Girls House (Osborne Collection) of Toronto Public Library; the Walter Library (Hess Collection) of the University of Minnesota in Minneapolis; the Rare Books Section (Dime Novel Collection), Library of the University of Rochester, New York State; the British Library (Barry Ono Collection); and the Bethnal Green Museum of Childhood (Renier Collection), London. Chapters 1–3 could not have been written without access to the British Newspaper Library in Colindale, London. Russ Cochran of West Plains, Missouri, deserves mention for publishing the unique EC comic-book series once again. Chapter 4 on gangster films would not have been possible without access to the British Film Institute Library in London. Research for Chapter 5 was carried out at the Library of Congress in Washington. Frequent resort was also made to Cambridge University Library, unrivalled as a copyright library with an excellent cafeteria attached. The inter-library loan service of my employer, the University of Ulster at Coleraine, has proved invaluable on the remote periphery and I am grateful to the Faculty of Humanities for granting me periods of study leave and for assisting with travel expenses to the above libraries. I hope the reader will find what follows as pleasurable to read, despite the prosy academic style, as it has been to research.

Distinguished past and present Ulster colleagues, Sean Connolly, Bill Riches, David Pattie, Wally Johnson, Terry O'Brien and Steve Ickringill, kindly read and commented upon drafts which have subsequently made up the chapters of this book. The final stage of preparing the typescript was expedited by Gillian Coward, Rafik L. Mortada, and Joanne Taggart.

The editors of the following journals have given me permission to incorporate in revised form some previously published material: *The Economic History Review, Victorian Studies, History Today, History of Education* and *Victorian Periodicals Review*. The Editors of the proceedings of the 1980 and 1994 annual conferences of the History of Education Society of Great Britain have also given permission to reproduce copyright material.

I have had the great privilege in recent years of trying out some of my ideas in papers given to the Queen's Cultural Forum in Belfast, the History of Education Society, the Victorian Periodicals Society and to Popular Culture Association conferences in both America and England. Research on 'penny dreadfuls' brought me into contact with Kevin Carpenter, Michael Holmes and Mike Saavedra, collectors who are also serious students of the literature. I am indebted for the conversation and companionship of those to whom this book is dedicated, the Colcloughs, the Fishers, the Roberts and the Mazlins, without whom my research sojourns in London would have been much duller. I am also grateful for the long-term support of both my mother and brother. Final-year students taking thematic modules at the University of Ulster at Coleraine on 'Popular Culture' or, more recently, 'Leisure, Sport and the Media', may have wondered over the years why they were hearing so much about the 'penny dreadful'. This book should explain that preoccupation and I am grateful for their forebearance.

Portstewart   JOHN SPRINGHALL
Co. Londonderry
Northern Ireland

INTRODUCTION

In recent years, sensational press reporting of violent crimes committed by and against children has led, periodically, to a host of opinion-makers denouncing 'video nasties' or violence in movies and on television as somehow contributing to a general collapse in moral standards. British Prime Minister John Major told the Conservative Central Council meeting in Harrogate on 6 March 1993 that those who made and distributed films and videos should 'think whether a relentless diet of violence won't have a serious effect on the young'. He was responding to the shocking abduction and murder a few weeks before in Bootle, Merseyside, of 2-year-old James Bulger by two 10-year-old boys, Robert Thompson and Jon Venables. 'UNPARALLELED EVIL AND BARBARIC KILLERS SAYS JUDGE BUT DID HORRIFIC VIDEO NASTY TRIGGER JAMES'S MURDER?' queried a tabloid newspaper headline on the day after their conviction.[1]

In his summing-up, the judge, Mr Justice Morland, introduced an issue not discussed at all during the trial itself by claiming that *Child's Play 3*, a violent American horror video about a malevolent doll, Chucky, that comes to life and kills people, bore some striking similarities to the manner of the attack on the child – 'I suspect that exposure to violent video films may in part be an explanation.' Those seeking a convenient cultural scapegoat, among them the Prime Minister, were undeterred when one of the arresting police officers stated, and a Home Office inquiry concurred, that neither of the boys who were convicted of this terrible crime appear to have watched the video in question. Apparently, Jon Venables' father, with whom he was not living at the time, had recently hired the video. The relationship between the events in the film and the murder of Jamie Bulger were, in any case, extremely tenuous, if not non-existent.[2]

Present-day worries about the impact of crime and violence in the mass media on young people are not without precedent, albeit in a computer age the capacity of new technology to deliver striking visual images has increased dramatically. The upper and middle classes of Victorian England also held exaggerated views about forms of popular entertainment causing

1

not so much individually violent children as more general outbreaks of juvenile crime. Thus on 15 June 1868, a Conservative Member of Parliament, J. G. Hubbard, later Lord Addington, asked the Tory Home Secretary, G. Gathorne Hardy, 1st Earl of Cranbrook:

> whether his attention has been directed to the lamentable amount of juvenile criminality, largely attributable to the spread of cheap publications and theatrical representations of an exciting and immoral character, which corrupt the children of the lower classes, and stimulate them into courses of dishonesty and vice; and, whether the Government will propose any remedy for these growing and most serious evils?

Hubbard's question struck all the correct notes for a moral campaign – juvenile crime, popular culture, moral corruption – but received only a non-committal answer. The Home Secretary took the view that, although cheap serials or 'penny dreadfuls' were 'very bad in character', they were 'merely sensational' and could not be prosecuted, while the 'immoral effects' of cheap theatres or 'penny gaffs' on the young were also much exaggerated.[3] Remarkably few of Gathorne Hardy's successors in office have demonstrated a similar scepticism towards the reported influence on behaviour of young people's chosen forms of commercial entertainment.

This study attempts to illuminate from a social historian's viewpoint not only the fears and anxieties behind criticism of those cultural 'representations' disturbing to mid-Victorian gentlemen such as Hubbard but also, by extension, preoccupations with the portrayal of violence and crime in the twentieth-century mass media. The chapters that follow set out to show that modern-day fears about the supposed moral threat posed to the young by computer games or 'gangsta-rap' have their roots in nineteenth-century anxieties about the 'ill effects' of popular forms of amusement on the 'children of the lower classes'. These concerns stretch in an almost unbroken line through successive 'moral panics' in both Britain and America, once popular culture was transformed into urbanized commercial entertainment from the early Victorian years onwards. A common denominator in the panics excited by each successive technological and commercial innovation was and is their tendency to be consumed by the young, a significant audience for the violent and sexual imagery which for centuries has saturated popular culture. The notion of age differentiation as a key factor determining choice of leisure in the past needs to be given far greater emphasis by the historian than it has so far received.[4]

Patently, sanctimonious adult disapproval of market-based entertainments intended primarily for schoolboys and young, wage-earning customers has a lengthy historical pedigree. Historian James Gilbert refers to the re-occurring attribution of delinquency to a hostile cultural environment as an 'episodic notion'. Belief in the seduction of supposedly innocent, English-speaking youth by popular culture extends over time from at least the arrival of penny theatres in the 1830s to the 'penny dreadfuls' and 'dime novels' of the 1860s and after, from the Hollywood 'gangster films' of the 1930s to the American 'crime' and 'horror comic' books of the late 1940s and early 1950s, from television once sets became widely accessible to the 'video nasties' of the early 1980s and the violent computer games of the early 1990s. The ideo-logues of cultural standards writing in the newspaper and periodical press consistently labelled the antecedents of mass culture directed at a largely urban youth market in the nineteenth century as 'pernicious', 'sensational' or 'wickedly corrupting'. Historical studies might usefully attempt to deter-mine the nature of the interrelationship between the generally unrestrained and melodramatic content of this so-called 'commercial culture', its predom-inantly youthful audience and society's vigilant moral guardians. Campaigns to censor youth's diversions have, in Britain alone, resulted in such anti-lib-ertarian legislation as: the licensing provisions of the Metropolitan Police Act (1839), encouraging the police to close down 'penny gaffs' popular with the young; the Children and Young Persons (Harmful Publications) Act (1955), outlawing American 'horror comics' from Britain; and the Video Record-ings Act (1984) giving the British Board of Film Classification (BBFC) the strict-est powers in Europe to certify and censor purchased home entertainment.[5]

This is the first book to examine, over a lengthy time span, examples of both British and American popular culture that supposedly incited juvenile crime, among other iniquities, and also to test the accuracy of such claims. To understand properly how fears like this have arisen, forms of cultural production need to be studied in relation to other cultural practices and to social and historical structures. The role of individuals, pressure groups and bureaucratic agencies, often involved in a complex and shifting pattern of alliances, supports interest group interpretations of 'moral panics' and social crusades, but only within an historical climate of underlying fears and social anxiety. The chapters that follow focus primarily upon popular or 'commercial culture' in printed, cinematic and stage form that was prim-arily directed at, or consumed by, ordinary urban youth. An attempt is made to contextualize various 'panics' aroused since the 1830s by ephemeral forms of purchased entertainment, locating hostility to the amusements of child-hood and youth within the prevailing construction of cultural values. This present book looks at panics related to gangster movies and 'horror comics'; but for post-1945 American moral crusades against other mass media, one of the few works available is psychologist Steven Starker's *Evil Influences* (1991 edn), a slight book stronger on citing hostile criticism of the media than in assessing its validity.[6]

A more useful short guide to anti-media campaigns is Mark I. West's *Children, Culture, and Controversy* (1988) which supplies American case-studies of censorious adult reactions to dime novels, series books, children's radio programmes, movies, rock 'n' roll, and realistic juvenile novels. West argues that, even after the American Civil War, most forms of amusement that adults purchased for children were predicated upon the romantic idea of childhood innocence. Children themselves often selected cultural forms that contradicted this Lockean ideal and, therefore, made adults feel uncomfortable. Puritanical moral reformers such as New York's Anthony Comstock, who campaigned against 'dime novels', defended the pre-Freudian concept of innocence by arguing that the young were 'seduced' into a fondness for stories that dealt with topics such as violence, crime and sexuality; corrupted by this reading they went on to become juvenile criminals. Hence also anti-Freudian psychiatrist and anti-comic book campaigner Dr Fredric Wertham's *Seduction of the Innocent: The Influence of Comic Books on Today's Youth* (1954) contributed, through the partial use of evidence (see Chapter 5), to an extensive censorship of a primary American communications media. Decades later, an alarmist Christian diatribe, John Fulce's *Seduction of the Innocent Revisited* (1990), excitedly proclaimed 'the unremitting war of comic-book publishers on religion'. The student of censorship pressures in recent years should also consider, along with outpourings from the New Right, film critic Michael Medved's *Hollywood vs. America: Popular Culture and the War on Traditional Values* (1992), a facile but well-publicized attempt to incite 'moral panic' over modern American movies, however well crafted, for disrespectfully attacking religion, glorifying violence and undermining the family. A puerile comedy sympathetic to conventional religion hence rates as a better movie by Medved's criteria than a serious drama which questions faith healing and evangelism.[7]

Moral Panic

'Moral panic' occurs when the official or press reaction to a deviant social or cultural phenomenon is 'out of all proportion' to the actual threat offered. It implies that public concern is in excess of what is appropriate if concern were directly proportional to objective harm. This problematic and much-devalued term was popularized in 1971 by the pioneering studies of Jock Young on the social meaning of drug-taking and in 1972 by sociologist Stanley Cohen in *Folk Devils and Moral Panics: The Creation of the Mods and Rockers*, specifically to represent a press outcry in the early 1960s against rampaging teenage gangs confronting each other at seaside resorts during English Bank Holidays. (As a student I witnessed one such ritual stand-off in Brighton.) In this context, 'moral panic' implied a periodic tendency towards the identification and scapegoating of 'folk devils' (mods and rockers) whose activities were regarded by hegemonic groups as indicative of imminent social breakdown. Panics served as ideological safety valves whose effect was to restore social equilibrium. A classic study of the creation of a British 'mugging' problem in the early 1970s by Stuart Hall *et al.*, *Policing the Crisis: 'Mugging', the State and Law and Order* (1978), is more explicitly Marxist and views this particular 'moral panic' as being manipulated, using veiled racist rhetoric, to divert the working class from united action within a political context of severe economic crisis and rising unemployment.[8]

Moving away from a selective or ideological approach, moral panic theory now embraces American interest group theories. Erich Goode and Nachman Ben-Yehuda's painstakingly dull sociological text, *Moral Panics: The Social Construction of Deviance* (1994), instances how value conflicts between social interest groups result in the manufacture of deviance, such as the Renaissance witch craze, or that for American anti-marijuana legislation in the 1930s. Also, Rob Sindall, writing about English *Street Violence in the Nineteenth Century* (1990), has drawn attention to the newspaper 'panic' in 1856, and again in 1862, over 'garrotte' attacks in London, involving footpads choking their victims. By 1863 any form of street theft accompanied by violence (even jostling) was referred to in the contemporary press as a 'garrotte' attack. These events coincided with a dramatic growth in newspaper circulation, in which 'garrotters' and 'cornermen' were routinely conceived as 'folk devils'. Although street violence was probably on the increase, it was distorted and exaggerated to create sporadic 'moral panics', followed by harsh penalties, throughout the second half of the nineteenth century.[9]

Moral panics over popular culture, upon which this book is focused, can be discerned in Britain well before the steam-driven impact of commercial mass production and technological innovation. Cheap repository tracts, a series of ballads, tales, Bible stories and the like, were underwritten from

1795 by those evangelists known as the Clapham group as striking rather than simply didactic alternatives to broadsides, chapbooks and other 'infidel publications' sold by hawkers. Hannah More and others wrote their Christian tracts as 'an antidote to the poison continually flowing thro' the channel of vulgar and licentious publications', accused of corrupting mechanics, artisans, labourers and children attending the new Sunday schools. With the gradual formation of a mass market through urbanization, rising literacy, the railways and changes in technology, the British experienced some of the earliest examples of panics over the influence of mass culture. Early Victorian showmen, printers, publishers and performers, with their highly developed entrepreneurial sense, flourished precisely because they were alert to the opportunities for profit to be made from the provision of entertainment recently opened up in London and the expanding northern cities of the industrial transformation. They were beneficiaries of market-economy-generated forms of amusement which were frankly commercial in nature, unlike the old communal pastimes, rituals, customs and ceremonies of the village and the small town.[10]

Yet it oversimplifies to portray the changes in printing technology, which gave periodical and serial publishers of various hues their opportunity, as some kind of overnight transition from an oral and story-telling culture to a more passive urban entertainment. Increased literacy brought about a situation where the new printed culture overlay an older oral tradition without, in rural areas, entirely destroying it. Conversely, the commercial possibilities of a juvenile audience for entertaining fiction was recognized well before mid-Victorian entrepreneurs began to target this market. In mid-seventeenth-century England, for example, printed literature for the semi-literate young townsman, schoolboy or apprentice, and for yeoman and servants in the countryside, was actually quite extensive; although only oral culture was available for the non-literate peasant. Chapbook and jestbook publishers clearly thought the young were a group of consumers well worth cultivating. Margaret Spufford provides more direct evidence on the reading of chapbooks by schoolboys in the 1640s and 1650s than for any other social group. She argues that those schoolboys who read popular tales acted as 'mediators' between the culture of the elite and popular culture. The first juvenile magazines did not appear until the late eighteenth century but, like children's books of the time, were intent on improving and instructing rather than simply entertaining the young, thus limiting their appeal. From the 1830s onwards, entrepreneurs set out to attract new mass audiences, adjusted their product to meet market demand, were responsive to new technology and employed so-called professionals, all characteristics which marked them off from their predecessors. The British commercial touchstone for Wombwell's menageries, Astley's circus, nautical dramas, the pantomime, dancing saloons, panoramic exhibitions, cheap theatres and 'penny bloods' was entertainment based upon consumer demand. Many of these profit-driven changes in leisure patterns did not appear in America, France or Germany until 30 or 40 years later, once urbanization and industrialization attained levels comparable to those of Britain.[11]

Whenever the introduction of a new mass medium is defined as a threat to the young, we can expect a campaign by adults to regulate, ban or censor, followed by a lessening of interest until the appearance of a new medium reopens public debate. Each new panic develops as if it were the first time such issues have been debated in public and yet the debates are strikingly similar. This repetitive and spiralling process has been characterized as 'media panic' by Kirsten Drotner, a Danish cultural historian of English children's periodicals. A brief summary of her thought-provoking 1992 essay on modernity and media panics cannot really do justice to its conceptual originality. Using Scandinavian and German examples, she shows how the young have possessed a cultural power in the world of commercial leisure as consumers since the mid-nineteenth century, to the extent that many commercial media are media *for* the young. The technical and cultural competence young people gain as spin-offs of media use pose a potential threat to existing power relations within society. Media panics can help to re-establish a generational *status quo*, that the pioneering cultural position of the young has undermined, by targeting violence or sex in teenage but not in adult forms of entertainment. A basic assumption of media panics is that the media are part of popular culture in opposition to high culture or art and, therefore, in the hierarchy of values they are found wanting. Secondly, media experience and social behaviour are seen as directly linked: in nineteenth-century panics the emphasis was more on social effects, in the last 50 years on psychological ill effects. Thirdly, children and the young are continually defined as 'victims' in media panics, based on an assumed relationship between culture and social psychology that is negotiated through modernity's concept of 'enlightenment', or the necessity to socialize children into the norms of adult middle-class society. Drotner further argues that, through media panics, adults seek to redefine the parameters of enlightenment undermined by the advent of every new unenlightened mass medium.[12]

The 'moral panic' formulation, used here instead because of its overall convenience and familiarity, needs to be interrogated. For while it usefully draws attention to themes of social apprehension and their association with censorship campaigns, it groups all such 'panics' under a single generic heading, representing them as a consequence of some endlessly cyclical feature of media manipulation within a consensual 'society'. Cohen's model is urgently in need of updating to take into account the almost daily construction of panics in the 1990s and a new plurality of 'folk-devil' reactions, including the ability of pressure groups and commercial interests to respond instantly to media demonization of the group they represent through the disparate perspectives of different mass, niche and micro-media, such as consumer magazine titles. Users of the 'moral panic' label have also become obsessed by the debunking notion of 'demystification', like those they accuse reaching a pre-ordained conclusion before examining the precise evidence. 'Moral panic' is one of those deflating phrases used by allegedly impartial sociologists and historians to condescend to excitements among the general populace. It usually comes equipped with research which demonstrates that alcohol consumption was in fact at its peak in the 1870s, or that football hooliganism actually began in 1898. The academic's message is a reassuring one, 'do not worry, we have been here before, your concerns are an ersatz compound manufactured by the media, a few odd bishops, strident voices from the left and the right, moralists and nostalgists of all kinds'. There is a danger of minimizing the contemporary sense of worry and crisis, in other words, by an account of its repetitive and historically relative character. Newspaper readers may be right to feel 'panic' about rising crime levels, for example, and hence undeserving of academic disdain. Despite all these reservations, the term 'moral panic' seems appropriate here, since the following chapters suggest that the sales-driven incentive to frighten newspaper and magazine readers with exaggerated reports about the 'effects' on their children's behaviour of 'sensational' and violent amusements has been with us for some considerable time.[13]

Recurrent adult 'panic' reactions to forms of commercial entertainment that attract the young are underpinned here by the language used to determine the 'social construction' of cultural values and their contestation. This methodology explores the way in which certain tastes, values and hierarchies are established by the academy, literary periodicals and the authorities as 'respectable' or preferential and others not. The way in which culture is constructed is ideological, according to cultural studies guru Pierre Bordieu, and the consequences of discrimination in taste are that aesthetic distinctions become operations of domination and subordination. Cultural consumption is hence predisposed, consciously or not, to fulfil a social function of identifying social differences. Bourdieu, if he were less of a Marxist, might have referred to the legitimation of age variations as well. The process of establishing taste differentials thereby becomes a symbolic weapon in the struggle between classes *and* generations for ideological domination. How cultural and taste hierarchies were established is relevant here because the construction process allowed cultural authorities to amplify social anxiety or rejection over popular culture appealing to the young that threatened established 'good taste'. In this sense, the manufacture of labels such as 'penny dreadful' and 'horror comic' represent the struggle between middle-class moralism and popular demand, assigning taste for the exciting or melodramatic to a permanent lower-class or, as here, juvenile ghetto.[14]

There are instructive parallels to be drawn between concerns now about the mass media and in Victorian and Edwardian times about their more age- and class-based prototypes. In the present century, the media have provided convenient 'targets for identification' by the censorious, and the supposedly baleful influence of television now excites almost as much concern as once did the 'penny dreadful'. As late as 1911, William Groser, an author of Sunday School teachers' manuals, warned that 'penny dreadfuls diffuse subtle poison among tens of thousands of youthful readers'. They brought 'wreckage, and havoc . . . and ruination to hundreds of our brightest and best lads and lasses'. One of the first English middle-class 'cycles of outrage' at nineteenth-century forms of popular entertainment intended primarily for the youth market was directed against the penny theatre – a rehearsal for similar and more recent campaigns. Journalist James Grant was convinced in 1838 that 'a very large majority, of those who afterwards find their way to the bar of the Old Bailey, may trace the commencement of their career in crime to their attendance in Penny Theatres'. The latter had a curious symbiotic relationship with 'penny dreadfuls', another form of almost exclusively juvenile entertainment endemic to several Victorian cities. The continual two-way 'blood' transfusion between gaff melodramas and penny serial fiction, with each attempting to exploit the notoriety gained in the other medium, also has its present-day equivalents.[15]

Finally, as a foretaste of what follows, Chapter 1 will locate penny theatres in the context of the demand for entertainment among the young working-class in cities such as London and will also consider the incessant legal persecution of these so-called 'nurseries of crime'. Chapter 2 looks at cheap juvenile publishing in late-nineteenth-century Fleet Street as a mass-market business. The emphasis will be on periodical and instalment

fiction, its publishers, content and market supply, or the commercializ-
ation of juvenile reading as a mass leisure commodity by entrepreneur–
proprietors. Chapter 3 documents how such 'penny dreadfuls' became
a scapegoat for juvenile crime with reference to late-Victorian trials in
which serials and periodicals found in the possession of young men were
used as evidence of criminal intent. Chapter 4 focuses on the calls for censorship which Hollywood gangster movies provoked in both Britain and
America, largely because of their mass appeal in the 1930s to what were
perceived as the potentially criminal young. Chapter 5 is devoted to
American publication of crime and 'horror comic' books in the late 1940s
and early 1950s with attention given to Dr Fredric Wertham's campaign
against the horror output of New York comic-book publishers and to the
passage through Parliament in 1955 of legislation banning 'horror comics'
in Britain. Chapter 6 offers a short postscript touching on more recent
'moral panics' over aspects of media entertainment, such as 'video nasties',
violence on television, 'gangsta-rap' and the interactive computer-game
scare.

1

PENNY THEATRE PANIC: ANXIETY OVER JUVENILE WORKING-CLASS LEISURE

'Language of the most disgusting kind is uttered, and plans of robberies, no doubt, concocted', claimed a letter to a London newspaper in 1838, urging suppression of the penny theatre 'nuisance'. 'Boys and girls are not only tempted to pilfer from shops, but even to rob their parents that they might have the means of attending these receptacles of vice.' Similar accusations have been levelled in successive decades to condemn forms of entertainment chosen by children and adolescents but disapproved of by adults. Festive mockery in penny theatricals and early penny bloods of 'industrial literacy', or factory work-disciplines and school knowledge, argues Edward Jacobs, citing James Malcolm Rymer's *Varney the Vampyre* (1847), 'functioned as one of the dominant ideologies structuring street culture as a counterculture, and thus constituted one of the major moral threats to the hegemony of the literate, Christian, middle-class values that have come to typify Victorian culture'.[1] What follows will attempt to determine the precise nature of the theatrical entertainments that merit both this recent bold evaluation and also the opening indictment, in so far as their managements, audiences and performances can be reconstructed from tenuous scraps of surviving evidence. Local newspapers, in particular, are a rich source of information that the historian of nineteenth-century popular amusements can ill afford to neglect.

A regular columnist for an East London paper thus reported a visit early in September 1859 to a penny theatre opposite Shoreditch church. 'Asmodeus' observed that 'crowds of boys in waiting for the next performance may usually be seen gathered round its windows, or amusing themselves at

11

the adjacent pump'. The preponderance of juveniles in the audience was quite striking, while the performances 'comprise wizard "business", ventriloquism, and comic duets, and are free from anything objectionable – judged, of course, solely by those on the occasion of our visit'. This local journalist complained, none the less, that the boys were not kept in very good order and made 'unflattering personal allusions to ourselves' because of a refusal to offer his 'tile' (stovepipe hat) for a stage trick by the wizard. Moving on to nearby Church Street, Bethnal Green, 'Asmodeus' visited another gaff that served as a photographic parlour by day. 'We pay a penny, pass along a narrow white-washed passage, and enter a dirty shop fitted with seats rising one above another. At the extreme end there is a raised platform [stage].' The majority of the audience consisted of boys and girls with a precocious, self-reliant sharpness, 'dwarfed, stunted men and women, a peculiar species of the London *gamin*', altogether difficult to reconcile with the idealized Victorian middle-class concept of childhood. Some sleight-of-hand tricks began the stage show, followed by an exhibition of 'laughing gas', in which the audience's invited participation was found by the prim reporter to be most indecorous. 'When in these dens any dramatic piece, however harmless, is played, the actors are sure to be marched off to the police-station. They have been from this very place twice within our memory [see "Police Closure of Gaffs"], but it would seem as if there were impunity for everything else', the columnist expostulated.[2] From this and other press reports, we learn that boys and girls formed the majority of the East End gaff audience, while converted shops were often used to house the shows, also magic tricks and 'laughing gas' were popular (in 1859) and arrests followed if spoken dramas were performed.

The Penny Theatre

The penny theatre or 'gaff' (any public place of amusement was liable to be called the 'gaff' in Cockney or coster slang) was hence generally found in previously vacant premises such as a shop or warehouse taken over for cheap, staged entertainment intended primarily for wage-earning children and adolescents of both sexes aged from about eight to twenty. These unlicensed theatres offered innocuous forms of dancing, singing, pantomime and melodrama, the latter in dumb show or mime after the 1843 Theatre Regulation Act to avoid prosecution for putting on episodes of 'straight' drama reserved for the 'legitimate' West End stage. Police harassment of penny gaffs provided a rehearsal for subsequent campaigns against presumed cultural incitements to criminality, convenient scapegoats to account for the errand boy who robbed his employer or the scullery maid who turned to prostitution.[3]

In 1834, national judicial statistics for the first time seemed to provide solid evidence that 'juvenile delinquents' were at the root of the nation's crime problem. By breaking down the total annual offences by age it could be shown that, while a tenth of the nation's population was aged 15–20 years, this group produced a quarter of known offenders. Historians have queried whether the proportion of juvenile offenders was actually rising and point out that most of the offences of which juveniles were convicted were extremely trivial, none the less an impetus was created that led eventually to the setting up of reformatory and industrial schools from the 1850s to separate young criminals from adult convicts and rescue neglected children from the temptations of crime. Along with these institutional solutions went a search for causes of delinquency that avoided indicting the consequences of the new kind of urban-industrial society that had been built upon *laissez-faire* capitalism. Popular culture was a prime target in this as in any other age, but from the 1830s onwards it was a new, more profit-oriented culture for the people whose origins lay in the same social and economic circumstances that were gradually transforming the nature of the British experience.[4]

Penny theatre performers were liable to arrest as rogues and vagabonds under the 1824 Vagrancy Act throughout much of the 1830s, until a change in the law in 1837 meant that henceforth magistrates at sessions could only indict the owner of a theatre for causing a nuisance. Help was soon at hand for those 'respectable' citizens irritated because of the noise created by patrons leaving or entering penny theatres. The Metropolitan Police Act of 1839, the first since London's regular force was formed by Home Secretary Robert Peel out of the old Bow Street Runners 10 years earlier, created a whole new list of offences that criminalized popular recreational activities, including sledging and kite flying on the public highways. The Act's most significant provision in relation to penny gaffs was the power given to the Chief Commissioner, under written warrant, to order metropolitan police entry into:

> any house or room kept or used within the said district for stage plays or dramatic entertainments into which admission is obtained by payment of money, and which is not a licensed theatre, at any time when the same shall be open for the reception of persons resorting thereto, and to take into custody all persons who shall be found therein without lawful excuse.

In December 1839 the editor of *The Examiner*, a radical newspaper started by Leigh Hunt, expressed sarcastic incomprehension at 'the fury of the law against penny theatres', citing the arrest of actors and members of the audience at an unlicensed theatre in Parker Street, off Drury Lane. 'A whole division of the police was employed in bringing up the theatrical delinquents. This is indeed the vigour of justice on a worthy occasion'.[5]

Pressures on the 'gaffs' at this time were largely the result of a widespread belief that they were somehow linked with an apparent rise in the rate of juvenile crime. In 1841 the report of the inspector of prisons for the north-east district of England cited an examination of nearly 100 boys held in Liverpool prison:

> with the view that the mischievous tendency of such productions [as 'Jack Sheppard'] may be placed beyond doubt . . . that attention may be excited to the subject, and some means may be suggested for the extension and purification of those pleasures which the poorer classes of society are entitled to in the intervals of labour.

Early Victorian prison inspectors, firm believers in 'rational recreation', were convinced that interest in criminal rogues of a past era, such as Dick Turpin or Jack Sheppard, made juveniles into offenders, whereas present-day criminologists would probably argue that their way of life turned these boys towards deviant or violent heroes. From 1839 to 1840, London theatre managers transformed Sheppard, a burglar and jail-breaker (only briefly a highwayman) hung at Tyburn in 1724 aged 21, into a Cockney folk hero (see Appendix I). They were exploiting the magazine serialization of William Harrison Ainsworth's middlebrow 'Newgate novel', *Jack Sheppard* (1839), accompanied with meticulous illustrations by George Cruikshank. The eponymous novel was also dramatized for the 'penny theatres', reaching youngsters excluded from London's minor theatres by admission price and general appearance. The stage play's 'very popularity with juvenile audiences (who might be so easily swayed by its specious morality) was seen as an index of the danger to society in general and to the moral health of the theatre in particular', writes Stephens.[6]

On 17 November 1839, a police court magistrate in south-east London heard that the 'respectable' shoemaker father of 18-year-old Richard John Bayne, arrested for burglary, was convinced that 'bad company' and frequenting a 'penny gaff' in Woolwich had contributed to his son's crime. Characteristically, the ill-informed magistrate, Mr Broderip, did not know what was meant by a 'penny gaff', so the prisoner's father helpfully explained to the Bench that it was an unlicensed theatre in temporary premises popular with the young, 'which he was convinced did serious mischief in the town. The principal attraction was a new version of the adventures of Jack Sheppard, the housebreaker, and the "gaff", as it was termed, was crowded nightly by children. It was here that his son first met Lindsay, the thief'. Mr Broderip recommended that this theatrical 'nuisance' be 'looked after' by the local authorities and was told by the police that measures would immediately be taken for its suppression. The new Metropolitan Police Act gave London's Chief Commissioner of Police power to order the arrest of all those operating an unlicensed theatre.[7]

There was a considerable young working-class audience for theatre of some kind in the new Victorian towns and cities, its size until recently underestimated.

> Just as the growing class consciousness of the middle classes is reflected in their challenge to the established privilege of the Patent Houses and the founding of the Minor Theatres between 1787 and 1821, so the growing working-class consciousness is reflected in the development of 'Saloon' Theatres, penny gaffs and other illegal theatres from the late 1820s onwards,

argues theatre historian Clive Barker. Even if we exclude illegal theatres, and music halls, the percentage of total capacity outside London's West End in primarily working-class areas amounted to half of all places in the city's theatres. Until late in the nineteenth century, 'the vast sub-stratum of working-class theatre, whether performed in regular playhouses, or in saloons, penny gaffs, and fairground booths, dominated [total audiences] by sheer bulk and represented a mass popular entertainment market of considerable proportions'.[8] For at least 60 years, penny gaffs offered cheap commercial entertainment to the urban working-class young who could not afford a seat at the more imposing local theatre/music hall or who preferred the less strait-laced drama which only the gaffs could provide. Penny theatres not only have a great deal to tell us about childhood, adolescence and recreation throughout the Victorian period, but the middle-class opposition to them on moral grounds also helps illuminate the different strategies of social control, however ineffective, available to the municipal authorities.

The Penny Gaff in London

Penny theatres are important for the historian of Victorian working-class and lower-middle-class childhood and adolescence because, in sprawling cities like London, they were a primary entertainment form characteristic of these classes and age groups. 'London life was further distinguished by the presence of a distinct adolescent or apprentice culture whose own traditions mirrored those of their elders', writes Mark Judd of the period up to 1860. 'High literacy rates and the wider availability of cheap printed matter together with the relative weakness of Methodist and temperance movements were further ingredients in a distinctive urban culture and tradition which contrasted sharply with the new cities further north.' London culture was uniquely cosmopolitan. Resident dramatists and cheap fiction authors had to provide a constant diet of entertainment for the huge new youth clientele that roamed the city's streets with a few pennies to spare on amusements. Penny theatres and saloon theatres are the much overlooked commercial harbingers of new mass-entertainment forms, such as the music halls, which did not emerge and flourish until after mid-century.[9]

Penny theatres in London and elsewhere were improvised out of almost any available building space, including empty shops, small stables, sheds, abandoned warehouses or even holes in the ground. Most often, a former shop would serve as an entry-way or waiting room, the storage area behind it as the playhouse itself and the first floor as a gallery. Gaffs found in abandoned shops, the most familiar location, were crammed with rough forms or wooden benches rising in amphitheatrical fashion up to the ceiling to form a cheap gallery, sometimes reached by only a clumsy ladder with light supplied from penny candles. Eminent social investigator Henry Mayhew's vivid description of a mid-century gaff near London's Smithfield can be taken as representative. The front of a large shop had been entirely taken away and the entrance decorated with paintings of the comic singers who performed inside:

> To form the theatre, the first floor had been removed; the whitewashed beams however still stretched from wall to wall. The lower room had evidently been the warehouse, while the upper apartment had been the sitting-room, for the paper was still on the walls. A gallery, with a canvas front, had been hurriedly built up, and it was so fragile that the boards bent under the weight of those above. The bricks in the warehouse were smeared over with red paint, and had a few black curtains daubed upon them. The coster-youths require no very great scenic embellishment,

and indeed the stage, which was about eight feet square, could admit of none. Two jets of gas, like those outside a butcher's shop, were placed on each side of the proscenium, and proved very handy for those gentlemen whose pipes required lighting.

The small gaff stage and the lower seats of the gallery were often on the same level, an arrangement that could occasion fights between actors and audience. In many gaffs, boys and young men sat on one side of the gallery and girls and young women on the other, allowing the former to smoke their 'pickwicks' or short clay pipes. The only musical accompaniment was usually provided by a couple of fiddlers, with the occasional clarinet, flute or ancient piano, while even less money was spent by the thrifty proprietor in hiring scenery and wardrobe.[10]

Sometimes crude pictures of the performers and the bill of fare gave the fronts a gaudy and attractive look, while at night coloured lamps and transparencies were often displayed to draw an audience. One of the least condescending descriptions of a gaff theatre can be found in a 'penny dreadful' serial, *Rags and Riches; A Story of Three Poor Boys* (*c.* 1875), by prolific hack author Edwin Harcourt Burrage. One part issue describes a visit to the 'Crystal Hall', an unadorned penny theatre in late-Victorian Bermondsey, the heart of London's busy docklands. The 'gaff' is nothing better than a shanty erected upon a piece of waste ground behind a public house; the rude narrow walls first covered with a coat of whitewash, 'and coarsely garnished with a few cheap ornamental devices'. The Crystal Hall is described as 'a place much patronised by the youths who were aware of its existence, for the price was low, and the performance of a high melodramatic order'. A crowd of boys stood outside in the street, shouting and whistling, waiting for the door to open. The gaff had 'no glare of gas outside; no blazing stars or magnificent transparencies; nothing beyond a coloured lamp, with the words "Crystal Hall" upon it; which, without the words, would have shone with advantage by a doctor's door'. Burrage also denied places like this were the 'hot-bed of vice' that virtuous gentlemen with £500 a year and a comfortable home were anxious to make them appear. 'It is true that hundreds of lads assembled together, with many a black sheep among the flock; but the majority came, paid their penny, saw what was to be seen, and went home none the worse than they had been before.'[11]

Semantic confusion exists over what can legitimately be labelled a penny theatre. Some contemporary reports equate them with 'singing saloons' or 'concert rooms', usually adjoining a public house, but these were more the seedbeds of the commercial music halls that appeared in the second half of the nineteenth century. A commentator on popular culture in Glasgow creates some confusion by identifying 'gaffs' with portable, canvas-roofed, wooden theatre-booths erected at fair-grounds, some of which, such as those of the great showman John 'Muster' Richardson, were quite sophisticated internally and could seat between one and two thousand at only a penny admission. Yet unlike urban penny theatres, canvas theatre-booths were not normally prosecuted for having speaking plays performed after the 1843 Theatre Regulation Act, so long as a fair was going on nearby and the actors had received the permission of the local mayor to build their pitch. Penny gaffs in built-up areas got around the law by providing mimed drama or singing and dancing, as well as silent pantomime ballets and harlequinades. Authentic gaffs seem to have increased in numbers consequent on pleasure fairs near London and other large cities declining or being forbidden. Many of the performers who had earlier made a living at fairground side-shows moved to the cities and found work on some kind of primitive gaff stage.[12]

The Calvinist editor of the *Morning Advertiser*, James Grant, calculated in 1838 that there were between 80 and 100 gaffs in London about 10 years after their first appearance, insisting that they were 'no better than so many nurseries for juvenile thieves'. Penny theatres were especially abundant in the East End, on the Commercial Road, Whitechapel Road and Mile End Road, with the average attendance ranging from 150 to 200 at each house, few holding more than 400 patrons. Grant gives an overall attendance of around 24,000 per night for all the gaffs in London – a probable underestimate. Large numbers of poor children, often of a semi-mendicant or semi-criminal nature, roamed the capital's streets beyond any form of adult control, offering an ideal 'target' audience for the penny theatre. Journalist James Greenwood, famous as 'the Amateur Casual' after a series of articles on the casual ward of Lambeth workhouse, claimed in the 1860s that within a 5-mile radius of St Paul's Cathedral at least 20 of these 'dangerous dens of amusement' might be found: near Peter Street, Westminster; in the New Cut at Lambeth; in White Cross Street, Southwark; and several between Whitechapel Church and the Ratcliffe Highway. Penny theatres could also be found around Kings Cross, in Tottenham Court Road, in Shoreditch and, south of the Thames, in the wide thoroughfares making for Lambeth, Blackfriars, Waterloo, Southwark and London bridges. Penny theatres were not restricted to London, where they were sometimes called 'penny dookies' or 'dukeys', but could also be found in Manchester, Birmingham and other large urban centres. In Glasgow they were called 'geggies' and in Liverpool appear to have been associated with low sailors' dives. Thus 13-year-old Robert Lorraine, who later acted in the West End of London, made his debut in 1889 on a stage erected in a Liverpool 'dive', or one of a long chain of inter-communicating cellars in the quayside of the docks. Two fresh plays were performed here every night, knocked out of old melodramas, topical murders and 'penny dreadfuls', with Lorraine playing as many as four different parts in each.[13]

London was unusual in that, unlike the factory cities of the industrial north, there was little demand for child and teenage labour until late in the nineteenth century. 'It appears probable that there is less demand for the labour of children in the Metropolis than exists in either manufacturing towns or in the country generally. The vast number of pauper children in London is as melancholy as it is remarkable', asserted the Poor Law Commission at the end of the 1860s. There were an estimated 30,000 homeless youngsters in London at this time, the sum total of the city's homeless of all ages in more recent years. Street children enaged in trading, begging, thieving and coster work (itinerant street-market selling) and were likely to spend what little spare time and money they possessed on cheap distractions like the penny gaffs. The latter were therefore at their peak, in terms of audience appeal, when the labour demand for children and youths in London was at its weakest. It awaited compulsory school attendance from the 1870s onwards to reduce the size of the large pool of juvenile and child unskilled labour, and even this measure only served to concentrate its supply chiefly in the teen years. The recruitment of large numbers of adolescents into short-term unskilled work with few prospects, the so-called 'boy labour' problem, is not really prominent in London much before the 1880s, by which time the penny theatre was in decline as a cultural force. Once these 'blind-alley' occupations (errand and office boys, machine minders, printers' devils, van and warehouse boys) began to absorb a greater share of the teenage labour force in an expanding commercial and distributive centre like London, wages and employment prospects for adolescents showed temporary signs of improvement which served to reduce the appeal of cheap makeshift entertainments like penny gaffs.[14]

Gaff Audiences

The respectable householder's fear was that a typical customer queuing up for admission to a penny theatre, waiting to gain entrance between performances, might be the kind of young thief without shoes and stockings that Henry Mayhew's collaborator in *London Labour and the London Poor*, John Binny, described as loitering among the street stalls in the New Cut, Lambeth. Regulars at penny gaffs in Somers Town were described by the police in 1859 as 'young thieves and prostitutes, whose morals are still further vitiated by the scenes nightly enacted at these sinks of infamy and vice'. The interrogation of a police witness before the 1866 Select Committee on Theatrical Licences offers a fairly definitive rebuttal to this kind of loose allegation:

> COL. STUART: What is the class of people who go there?
> INSPECTOR RICHARD REASON: I should think there is a great number of the criminal class, and some of the children of the working classes.
> MR LOCKE: The boys do not pick one another's pockets while they are there I suppose? – No, I suppose not.
> MR LOCKE: And when they are inside, they are not picking other people's pockets? – No.
> MR LOCKE: Therefore it keeps them out of mischief? – Yes.

Collapse of police witness, perhaps, for at this point the Chairman judiciously changed the subject to that of dancing saloons. In 1858 George Godwin, radical editor of *The Builder*, described a remarkably law-abiding gaff audience: 'we saw no impropriety then, or on any other occasion'. The young men present were all dressed in short velveteen coats, cord trousers, caps and showy neck-ties – traditional coster wear. Their female companions were dressed in decorative cotton–velvet 'polkas', a fashionable woman's jacket, and wore dowdy feathers in their crushed bonnets, normally reserved for Saturday nights out.[15]

James Greenwood also identified those who attended London gaffs as coster boys and girls, from 8 or 9 to 16 years old, as well as errand boys or girls employed in small East End 'outwork' industries. 'We saw few on any occasion who seemed over twenty years of age', confirmed Godwin, 'excepting one or two broken-down old men, who strangely contrasted with those surrounding.' Unlike Greenwood, he saw more boys of 'elder growth', young mothers with infant children in their arms, a few very young girls and numerous youths of from 16 to 20. The usually observant Mayhew noted from his own visit to a gaff that patrons, with few exceptions, were all boys and girls whose ages ranged from eight to 20. Unlike most commentators, he also noted that above three-quarters of those pouring out through the lobby after the first 'house' was over were women and girls, the rest consisting chiefly of 'mere boys'. Out of 200 present he counted only 18 adult men. The location of this gaff in a broad street near Smithfield and Mayhew's probable attendance on a market day may account for the excess number of females present, or the performance may have held some unspecified appeal for the ladies. For most middle-class commentators, teenage boys, 'the great patrons of such places', were preponderant over a small number of girls in the audience. Penny theatres in London had their most passionate following among poor, out-of-work boys, young labourers, errand boys, shop boys and girls, milliners' girls, apprentices and the ubiquitous costers.[16]

The young men waiting to gain entrance outside a typical London gaff of the early 1850s smoked short pipes, joked about or whistled an accompaniment to a small band playing current dance tunes in order to lure customers inside. Yet the behaviour of their female companions excited scandalized comment from a censorious Mayhew because they 'stood laughing and joking with the lads, in an unconcerned, impudent manner, that was almost appalling'. Some of them, he went on, 'when tired of waiting chose their partners, and commenced dancing grotesquely, to the admiration of the lookers-on, who expressed their approbation in obscene terms, that, far from disgusting the poor little women, were received as compliments and acknowledged with smiles and coarse repartees'. Observations such as this encapsulate much of the mid-Victorian moral reformer's objection to the non-childlike precocity of street-raised, independent-seeming, working-class youngsters, or 'the worldly-wise little factory girls' who came to be amused at the penny gaff. 'The rows of brazen young faces are terrible to look upon. It is impossible to be angry with their sauciness, or to resent the leers and grimaces that are directed upon us as unwelcome intruders, some have the aspect of wild cats', wrote Blanchard Jerrold of his descent into a penny gaff in Whitechapel, accompanied by artist–engraver Gustave Doré. 'The lynx at bay has not a crueller glance than some I caught from almost baby faces.' Matthew Browne was also suspected of being a 'spy' at the Rotunda in Blackfriars Road, 'though I hummed nigger tunes, and jested with my neighbours, in order to put them as much at their ease as possible'.[17]

Recent theory suggests that more attention should be paid to the role of the audience in shaping or determining the nature and composition of theatrical performances. The eagerness and rapt concentration of the penny theatre audience were often alluded to by sympathetic middle-class observers such as George Godwin. 'Dancing of the most vigorous description is highly relished', he pointed out, 'as also are feats of strength, legerdemain, &c.; and it is remarkable how great an attraction chemical experiments have. The exhibition of laughing-gas, galvanism, &c. has been, and still is, a standard portion of these exhibitions.' Galvanism, or the use of electric current to produce spasmodic shock effects in a member of the audience, was widely popular in mid-century gaffs. The emphasis on pseudo-scientific 'chemical experiments' which, like sleight-of-hand tricks or legerdemain, involved inviting audience members from the pit to come up on stage, suggests that the gaffs of the 1850s not only encouraged audience participation but positively welcomed it as part of the entertainment. Primly unsympathetic journalists reporting these shows were often offended, on the other hand, by audience volunteers performing tumbling tricks or by the 'indecorous' results of applying laughing-gas to young people who seemed 'to lack all proper restraint'.[18]

Gaff Management

Several interesting details about the management of penny gaffs were provided in 1838 by James Grant, most of his information coming from commercial enterpreneur Hector Simpson who, at this stage in his career, was the proprietor of cheap theatres in Tooley Street, near London Bridge, and in Queen Square, Westminster. 'Have you seen Simpson's Place of Amusement, Vine Yard, Tooley Street. Where the Old may laugh, the Young may sigh, The Student improve, the Romantic cry' ran a contemporary playbill advertising, for a penny admission: 'HARLEQUINADES, Serious Pantomime, BALLETS, Duetts, Glees', plus dogs Carlo and Lion for 'the Lovers of CANINE SAGACITY'. Simpson went on, after his penny theatres were closed down by the police, to a far more prestigious career as the producer of pantomimes at Covent Garden Theatre, where he was well known as a great 'dog-and-bear man'. By mid-century he had also become proprietor of the Albion Saloon in Whitechapel which put on lavish staged entertainments for the local working class. Simpson told Grant that one shilling and twopence per night for six or seven pieces was good pay for gaff actors and actresses, albeit tenpence a day or five shillings a week was the more common rate. He was also not averse to explaining how, by abandoning the players, he managed to avoid payment altogether. By the mid-1850s the pay of a gaff actor varied from two shillings and sixpence to three shillings a night, for which they were expected to sing at least two songs at each of the three nightly shows besides acting in a sketch. The general pay for clowns at this time, according to one of Mayhew's informants, averaged from one pound to 25 shillings weekly, rising during the Christmas pantomime season to 30 or 35 shillings for shows which could last from an hour and a half to an hour and three-quarters, three times a night. In general, penny-circus clowns appearing at fairs outside London could earn more than those in acting-booths, the so-called canvas actors. On Boxing Day, penny gaff clowns in pantomime played to as many as 16 houses or from 3000 to 4000 people, beginning at 11.30 a.m. and finishing at midnight.[19]

Simpson explained that rentals of empty properties taken over for a gaff varied according to the size and conditions of the premises, but that the average cost in the late 1830s was 15 shillings per week. Most proprietors were careful to sign separate bills with the lessees, so that if ejected they could claim repayment. One press report suggested that owners of penny theatres could amass large sums of money – some as much as £1000 in 5 years. Profit and loss calculations are speculative, but one full gaff performance with 200 in the audience paying a penny, or twopence for a box, would almost reimburse the proprietor for half the wages of four actors, a fiddler and the weekly rental, if we overlook the cost of scenery, costumes, upkeep and new productions. These latter costs could be kept to a minimum. 'The expense of putting on a new piece on the stage is not more than a pound and that includes new scenery', claimed one of Mayhew's interviewees, a strolling actor, 'they never do such a thing as buy new dresses. Perhaps they pay such a thing as six shillings a week for their wardrobe to hire the dresses. Some gives as much as ten shillings, but then, naturally, the costume is more showy.'[20]

An enterprising gaff proprietor like Simpson had to be experienced at taking advantage of contemporary crimes, particularly a sensational and juicy murder. Thus the famous 'Edgware murder' of 1836 whereby Hannah Brown, who took in washing, was killed then dismembered by her intended husband, James Greenacre, a much-married bankrupt, proved quite a windfall when dramatized for London gaffs and played to capacity houses for at least 10 months after the crime had taken place. Such pieces were typically advertised by a hand-lettered placard outside the theatre, since printed handbills were considered too costly. Grant provides one such placard of the 'Edgware murder': 'FOR THE BENEFIT OF MR. TWIG, On Tuesday next will be performed the Grand National Dramar OF GREENACRE, or THE MURDER OF CARPENTER'S BUILDINGS.' The equally notorious 'Red Barn murder' of 1827–8, the gruesome slaying and burial in Polstead, Suffolk, of country maid Maria Marten by her seducer, prosperous farmer William Corder, remained popular as a play until the demise of penny theatres. Indeed, the latter showed quite a remarkable taste for 'horrible murders' and as soon as a press account came out it was not long before a piece embodying the most lurid incidents was 'got up' for representation on the stage. It was to amuse the youthful clientele of penny gaffs that the popular Victorian taste for melodramatic, rather than horrific, murder assumed its crudest, most colourful forms.[21]

From the 1850s onwards, the expanding juvenile audience for the 'penny dreadful' was another consumer demand which could also be satisfied in dramatized form. Typical of such productions was *The Groans of the Gallows, or The Hangman's Career*, based on a serialized penny work, probably *Life and Recollections of Calcraft the Hangman*, which was put on at a gaff in Whitechapel, 'for everything about a hanging was always a hit'. The actor who played Calcraft, the public hangman, recalled that the piece was very successful and ran for 3 weeks, drawing in 'a deal of money.' Colin Henry Hazlewood (1823–75), resident dramatist at the imposing Britannia Theatre, Hoxton, in East London, made a career of translating to the stage popular 'dreadfuls' like *The Work Girls of London* (1865), a 'women-in-peril' tale (see Chapter 2). Dramatized 'penny dreadfuls' such as this found their way not just to gaffs but also to the Surrey, Britannia, City of London, or Standard theatres in East London. The gaff proprietor, noted James Greenwood in 1869, 'at once perceives a chance in the modern mania that pervades the juvenile population for a class of literature commonly known as "highly sensational"'. Greenwood devotes several pages to describing another dramatized penny number, *Gentleman Jack, or the Game of High Toby*, an equestrian spectacle with real horses and a carriage, performed in dumb show at a Whitechapel gaff. Errand boys who had their appetites whetted by reading in 'penny dreadfuls' about the Black Highwayman, Spring Heeled Jack or Jack Sheppard could see them brought to life, playing to crowded houses nightly, on the penny gaff stage. While playsmiths snatched up a popular 'dreadful' and transferred it to the stage, Fleet Street's scribblers reciprocated by promptly seizing upon a successful stage melodrama and turning it into a weekly-part serial.[22]

Gaff Performances

The great similarity of the kinds of popular entertainment to be found in theatres, gaffs, streets, tents and halls allowed versatile performers and managers to shift from one venue to another with frequency and ease. On any given evening, early-Victorian penny gaffs, in imitation of the respectable London theatres, would perform one principal piece, either dramatic, balletic or spectacular, usually a combination of all three; then a shorter play, an interlude or selected scenes from a classic; and finally a farce to conclude the bill. Sometimes two full-length dramas and a song would be put on together, or a string of variety acts was substituted for the second play. The entertainment on offer at a penny gaff contemporary with the 1839 Police Act can be gleaned from cheap publisher Edward Lloyd's serialized *Oliver Twiss* (1838–9). This semi-plagiarized version of Charles Dickens' Newgate novel was written under the pseudonym 'Bos', thought to be Thomas Peckett Prest, and ran to more than twice the length of its original source. The Lloyd penny serial also dealt with levels of working-class society untouched by its more famous progenitor. Thus in one chapter, young Cockney thieves Bill Swankey (the Knowing Cove) and Jack White have put off returning to the haunt of Solomons, their Fagin-like Jewish fence, when, not far from Petticoat Lane in Whitechapel, their attention is attracted by a poster advertising that evening's performance at a local gaff. The conversation that follows offers a satirical yet affectionate portrait of the old-style penny gaff, before the passing of the 1843 Theatres Act prohibited spoken drama on its boards. '"Strike me lucky if I don't go in there Jack", exclaimed Master Swankey, as soon as he had read the bill from top to bottom. "Here's a reg'lar tragedy, a comic song, a pass de dux, and an 'arter piece, and all for two pence".'[23]

Bill Swankey's companion, who has forgotten his schooling since taking up thieving, asks for the programme at this Whitechapel gaff to be read out aloud:

> 'Vell', returned the other boy, 'the first piece is called "The Bandit of Blood, or the Poisoned Dagger", arter which a Comic Song by Mr. Muggins, then a dance, and the whole to conclude with a laughable farce, called "Giles Scroggins' Ghost"'. 'What a plummy lot for twopence', observed Master White as his friend concluded. 'And they're all on 'em such prime h'actors – sich reg'lar out and outers', answered the Knowing Cove.

Jack is then assured by Bill Swankey that the performance will be brief: '"I've seen three ghostesses, four murders, two castles burnt to the ground, and a comic dance, all done in little better than half an hour; – and done in prime style, too, I can tell you, my boy".' The show turns out to be even briefer than expected because several policemen leap onto the unlicensed stage in mid-performance and arrest the actors, starting a stampede by the 500-strong audience for the exit doors, 'each struggling, pulling and hauling, to see which should get into a place of safety first'. The assembled cast, meanwhile, 'attired as they were in their tawdry costume were conveyed to the station-house there to pass a few uncomfortable hours, until the time should arrive next morning where their cases were to be heard by the magistrates'.[24]

Penny theatres and their audiences were a popular topic for the tribes of journalists, sensation seekers, moral reformers and would-be sociologists, who inflicted their often unwelcome attentions upon the poor of East London in the wake of Henry Mayhew. Their essays or magazine articles were chiefly intended to titillate or amuse a middle-class reading public rather than to offer accurate observations of what actually took place on stage. An exception could, perhaps, be made for the German journalist Max Schlesinger whose collected *Saunterings In and About London* (1853) offered a vivid appraisal of the performance in a small gaff near Drury Lane popular with young labourers and apprentices. The manager or 'director' first climbs on to the stage by a ladder to excuse 'some small deficiencies' in the theatre and make profuse apologies for the non-arrival of famous singers and actresses ('Jenny Lind has sent me a message by my own submarine telegraph, asking for an extension of her leave') and then vanishes through a trap-door. Two performers now come on to the stage, 'dressed in character' as an Irishman and a Scotsman, to play some national airs:

> and while thus engaged strip themselves of every particle of their outer clothing and appear as American planters. Some one from below hands up a couple of straw hats. . . .They then go to the back of the stage and return with an unfortunate 'African'. The part is played by no less distinguished a person than the director himself. His face is blackened, he has a woolly wig on his head, and heavy chains on his wrists and ankles; and to prevent all misunderstandings, there is pinned to his waistcoat an enormous placard, with the magic words of 'Uncle Tom'. . . . The planters produce a couple of stout whips and belabour the African's back until the negro, exclaiming 'Liberty!', 'Liberty!' breaks his fetters and turning around with great deliberation descends into the pit. Exit the two planters, each with a somersault.

The director's defiance of his placard's reference has been interpreted as part of the gaffs' mocking response to the restrictions imposed upon them by the licensing laws, 'a particularly topical dramatization of gaff culture's own rebellion against disciplinary literacy'.[25]

Harriet Beecher Stowe's celebrated novel of slave life, *Uncle Tom's Cabin, or Life Among the Lowly,* first appeared as a serial in *The National Era* in 1851 and was published as a book in the following year, quickly becoming world famous and having a powerful effect in promoting the cause of slave emancipation. The above hastily improvized penny gaff piece crudely, but no less significantly, implies widespread sympathy for emancipation among the London working-class audience. Schlesinger's account also refers to a chauvinistic piece based on the contemporary fear of invasion by Napoleon III, the newly proclaimed Emperor of the French, who is repelled from props depicting the chalky cliffs of Dover by a sailor boy kicking him back into the pit. Taken together, these pieces indicate the spontaneity and topicality of the mid-century gaff programme, as well as the bufoonery and boisterous humour of its representation.[26]

Liverpool journalist Samuel Phillips Day, writing in 1858 of a Saturday night visit to penny theatres in south London, was already firmly convinced of the immoral and profane nature of such entertainment, 'where the drama is vilely caricatured by low actors and actresses reeking of beer and tobacco'. After paying his penny entrance fee to a gaff near Blackfriars' Bridge, he walked down a long, filthy passage to the pit which was crammed with dirty and untidy boys, plus a few men and girls of the 'lowest class', making a deafening noise and wreathed in tobacco smoke. A series of 'low' tumbling tricks were performed by volunteers from the audience to uproarious laughter, next a comic vocalist played the role of a crossing-sweeper, followed by *poses plastiques,* such as Samson and the Lion, 'some of which brought the Holy Book into ridicule'. During the interval the intrepid reporter paid an extra penny to get a box, all of which were filled with boys, 'somewhat better dressed than below but still of the lowest class, a few smoking short clay pipes'. A mimed play about the ever-popular Jack Sheppard followed, nearly 20 years after his first gaff appearance, and was greeted with 'unrestrained enthusiasm'. There was a rush from the lower house when the drama was over, several boys being carried on the shoulders of others. Then the journalist moved on to a gaff in the New Cut, Lambeth, where he paid twopence for a box and sat among a slightly better audience of 'the labouring and lower classes'. A comic ballet was followed by 'out of tune and harsh' singers, applause, then an 'improper' comic song sung by 'a lean, shabbily dressed young man' for a few pennies thrown onto the stage. The principal performance was another mimed version of 'Jack

Sheppard' which, as always, drew crowded houses. Phillips Day reiterated the orthodox view that gaffs were frequented by gangs of young pick-pockets and prostitutes, claiming 'nothing, I apprehend, can have a more injurious effect upon the minds and morals of the community than such representations'.[27]

Early gaffs of the 1830s which were observed by journalists such as James Grant, and whose handbills can be found in the Frederick Burgess collection at Harvard, tended to specialize in rather extravagant repertoires in imitation of the legitimate theatre, featuring ballets, comic songs, optical illusions, farces, melodramatic scenes from current plays and 'dog pieces' or animal acts. They were also responsive to the audience appetite for juicy murders re-enacted on stage, as well as the requisite Christmas panto-mimes and harlequinades. A comparable wave of reporting penny theatres by unsympathetic middle-class observers such as Greenwood and May-hew, conspicuously outside the class and age group for which they were intended, does not appear for another 20 years. The programmes of the gaffs have changed over the intervening period, particularly following the 1843 Theatres Act which made spoken drama illegal on their unlicensed premises.

The emphasis in accounts of gaffs in the 1850s and 1860s is hence less on melodrama, with the exception of mimed versions of stories such as that of Jack Sheppard with which the audience was already familiar, and more on audience participation through singing on stage, dancing and tricks using the up-to-date wonders of electricity and laughing-gas. The popularity of galvan-ism and 'chemical experiments' suggests that gaff proprietors were eager to exploit new scientific developments for commercial profit. Some of the old staples remain but young audiences seem to have become more tolerant of amateur performers, more prepared to go up on stage themselves, and less inclined to watch lengthy dramatic pieces performed in dumb show. The strong communal aspect of theatre-going in working-class areas converted the offerings on stage into part of a wider age-group experience, indicating how urban popular culture had not yet become dominated by professional entertainers performing to largely passive consumers.

Police Closure of Gaffs

Prosecutions of unlicensed penny theatres had their peaks and troughs in the nineteenth century which tended to relate to how far perceptions of increasing juvenile crime or changes in theatrical licensing laws encouraged police action. There is evidence of a police 'crack down' on gaffs taking place in London after the 1839 Metropolitan Police Act, the 1843 Theatres Act, and the 1854 Select Committee Report on Public Houses and Places of Public Entertainment, with its recommendation that no public theatrical or musical performances should be allowed without a licence. Nearly all of the penny gaffs in London were licensed by the local magistrates, if at all, for music and/or dancing only. So performances of unlicensed theatrical pieces were particular targets of the police until, reported George Godwin on 5 June 1858, 'all attempts at what may be called theatrical exhibitions have been stopped; and the amusement offered now consists chiefly of the singing of popular street songs and negro melodies in characteristic costumes'. Journalists liked to poke fun at the bathos of gaff performers arraigned while still in costume with the added bonus, as will become evident, of a chance to deflate the pomposity of custodial police officers.[28]

Early in 1859 a complaint against 'unlawful theatricals' in Church Street, Bethnal Green, had been made to the sitting magistrate, Mr Hamill, at Worship Street Police Court, near Finsbury Square in Shoreditch. As a result, Superintendent Steed had gone along to the unlicensed gaff premises referred to and taken all the performers into custody. The audience, greatly alarmed, were allowed to leave. In evidence, witness Sergeant Cleary said that he had attended this gaff several times in impenetrable disguise and, questioned by Hamill, described the entertainment on offer in some detail:

WITNESS: Once I saw the 'Robber's Wife' played; but last night it was a new piece, called 'The Profligate Nephew or, The Disinherited'.

MR HAMILL: You were one of the audience, I presume?

WITNESS: I was a dustman with a black eye, and I paid one penny admission.

MR HAMILL: What did you see?

WITNESS: The first thing was a song, 'Paddy on the Railway', then there was a sailor's hornpipe, by a lady in tights; then there was the laughing gas that did not affect anybody; then there was . . .

MR HAMILL: Come to the legitimate. Was there any acting? Who was the profligate nephew?

WITNESS: This gentleman; and this was the Count; and this was Ralph the Reckless, a most determined villain. The lady was the Count's beloved wife, Alice; and this gentleman was the old one.

Losing patience, the magistrate asked Sergeant Cleary whether there was any dialogue, since the bill of fare stated *The Profligate Nephew* to be a 'ballet' and a breach of the 1843 Act would render prosecution more likely. The policeman then ponderously outlined the dialogue of the drama which revolved around a dissipated Count who, to avoid being disinherited, hires Ralph the Reckless to waylay and murder his old uncle.[29]

The piece came to an abrupt close after the murder as Sergeant Cleary then stepped on to the stage and 'collared the Count', while upon a given signal his superintendent and an inspector with 12 policemen forced an entrance and secured the rest of the cast. The magistrate could not resist intervening here:

> MR HAMILL: The dustman secured the Count?
>
> WITNESS: Yes, sir. I thought he was the worst of the lot; but just as I got hold of him, 67H, my brother officer, collared me. He thought I was one of the 'dramatis personae'.
>
> MR HAMILL: Well, the piece certainly turned out tragically.
>
> WITNESS: It was a melodrama, sir. There was comedy in it, for this gentleman was one Peter Pop, a beadle or policeman, who had a scene with this other lady, his sweetheart, 'Sally come up', in the kitchen.

Having established the use of scenery, make-up, theatrical costume, and the absence of a licence, even for singing, Hamill remarked that he would certainly put a stop to all such places that were brought to his notice, 'as they were calculated to effect irremediable mischief with the youth of both sexes.' The defendants promised never to offend again and were allowed to depart, promising to keep the peace for the next 3 months, at least in relation to spoken drama. The magistrate also congratulated Sergeant Cleary whose 'apt sketch and immobile countenance during it, rendered every attempt to preserve gravity totally impossible'.[30]

The plight of actors arrested for performing in unlicensed premises was often less amusing. Mayhew relates how some mid-century strolling players who had been performing a plagiarized version of *Oliver Twist* on private ground at Lock's Fields, Walworth, outside the legality of a fair, had to 'treat' a local policeman with porter and money every night. Despite this precaution they were still put into prison for acting without a licence. 'It was something like a penny a-piece for the policeman, for we were rather afraid of something of the kind happening.' The actors in this particular troupe were arrested and marched off to the local police station, 'we were in an awful fright when we found ourselves in the police cell that night'.

They were then taken from Walworth to Kennington Lane, where they were to appear before the local magistrates. Windows full of people waited to see the players come out of police custody in their stage clothes, laughing and pelting the arresting officers with vegetables from a nearby greengrocers, one actor catching a severe blow by accident from a turnip. Those who could not pay the 20 shillings fine imposed served for 2 weeks on bread and water at Kingston, Surrey, in their full theatrical dress, picking oakum and making mats. Mayhew's transcript still resonates with the unhappiness of their situation:

> It was very hard, I thought, putting us into prison for getting our bread, for we never had any warning, whatever our master may have had. I can tell you, it was a nail in my coffin, these fourteen days, and one of us, of the name of Chau, did actually die through it, for he was of a very delicate constitution, and the cold laid hold of him. Why, fellows of our life and animation, to be shut up like that, and not allowed to utter a word, it was dreadful severe.

The same canvas theatre actor or 'mummer' pointed out that there were very few penny gaffs in London where performers could speak. 'In fact, I only know one where they do. It ain't allowed by law, and the police are uncommon severe. They generally play ballets and dumb acting, singing and dancing, and such-like.' The police themselves complained that magistrates could not close gaffs because it was difficult to get evidence of spoken dramas being performed, justifying the need for disguise or other such subterfuge, as in the Bethnal Green case.[31]

'Many people consider them [gaffs] very objectionable, inasmuch as they induce boys and girls to steal the entrance money', explained the long-serving Chief Commissioner of the Metropolitan Police, Sir Richard Mayne, to the Parliamentary Select Committee on Theatrical Licenses in 1866. He had visited several gaffs but had 'very seldom found that there was anything that the police could interfere with.... No doubt there are thieves there and young girls who are prostitutes, but their conduct is unobjectionable in the place itself.... I may be a little lax, but I am rather for allowing performances than restraining them.' This more tolerant official view, that the gaffs were best left alone to provide harmless amusement for the juvenile poor, is not really borne out by evidence of the continued closure of penny theatres, albeit taking place more as a result of formal complaints by the 'respectable' than because of police-initiated prosecutions. Hence the Lord Chamberlain's Office received several complaints in the spring of 1868 about the Garrick Theatre in Leman Street, next door to Whitechapel police station, temporarily a penny gaff and thus evading the licensing laws, where 'no respectable person can pass without being Annoyed by Boys and Girls of the lowest order, who congregate in crowds round and near the Building'. A police report was requested which gave the persons attending as about 400 nightly, chiefly boys of the poorer class, many from 10 to 12 years of age. There were two evening shows, the first one finishing about nine and consisting of melodramas such as *The Crock of Gold* and *The Pilot's Grave*, together with comic, sentimental and negro singing, acrobats on the flying trapeze, performing dogs, and clog and hornpipe dancing. Blanchard Jerrold and Gustave Doré visited the Garrick a few years later, in 1872, when it seems to have resumed its former elevated status, despite losing audiences to the Standard Theatre at Shoreditch. They arrived during a performance of *The Starving Poor of Whitechapel*, a play evidently with considerable local appeal, for 'at the moment of our entry the stage policemen were getting very much the worst of a free fight, to the unbounded delight of pit and gallery'.[32]

In August 1868 ten people were arrested for performing dramatic pieces in another unlicensed gaff termed the 'Eastern Alhambra' and run by the Collins family opposite Limehouse Church in the Commercial Road. A formal complaint had been made to the Chief Commissioner by the 'respectable' inhabitants of St Anne's parish. Sir Richard Mayne, notwithstanding his testimony to the 1866 select committee, issued his warrant for the supression of the 'nuisance', and the arrest of the proprietor and the *corps dramatique*. Edward Worels, the Division Superintendent, went along with several police officers to the gaff, a room 60 feet long and 20 feet wide, with an 'orchestra', stage and scenery. There was an audience of about 120, principally consisting of boys, who were soon dispersed. Six of the prisoners were in theatrical costume, the elder Collins and his son, playing on harp and violin, formed the 'orchestra.' The wife of the younger Collins was in a box taking money. On a previous evening, police constable Thomas Cliff had gone along to the Eastern Alhambra out of uniform with his son to collect evidence of plays being staged and they paid a penny each for admission. Regrettably, a farce called *A Policeman's Difficulties* was being performed, in which the 'policeman', who was in uniform, courted a cook. This was followed by a 'grand romantic drama' called *Herne the Hunter*, presumably based on the 'old tale' that Shakespeare refers to in *The Merry Wives of Windsor*, IV, iv. Those arrested acted different parts and one Abrahams, a photographer, was selling refreshments. The elder Collins told the police that he had been 20 years on the Limehouse stage and was not aware that he was doing wrong and had never been interfered with before. The police court magistrate, Mr Paget, believed penny gaffs 'a great nuisance' that 'contaminated the morals of the young, and led them on to vice.' The younger Collins, who appeared to be proprietor, manager, and treasurer of the gaff, was bailed at £100 and two sureties of £50 each to keep the peace and be of good behaviour for 6 months. The other prisoners were to enter into their own recognisances in the sum of £20 each to appear and receive judgement when called upon. If the outcome of such trials was catastrophic for all concerned, with performers fined or imprisoned and gaffs closed down, theatre historians can take some comfort from trial reports such as the above having preserved something of the flavour of what took place on stage.[33]

Melodrama and the Popular

The melodramatic or 'sensation' style which gaff plays, legal or otherwise, invariably adopted arose because this had become the ascendant mode of expression in Victorian popular culture, exemplifying a kind of romantic and extreme diathesis, invariably crude, sentimental and conventional, with strict attention to Manichean opposites, poetic justice and happy endings. Moral antithesis was rarely expressed in terms of the drama of changing human relations, but rather through the absolute dichotomy of a benign Jack Sheppard versus a totally evil Jonathan Wild (see Appendix I). Melodrama was by no means attractive exclusively to working-class audiences, as evidence from the Birmingham theatre confirms. It was also the dominant repertoire of much of nineteenth-century British life and thought, invading the language of political, economic and social discourse. Rapidly industrializing and expanding cities, which saw the emergence of a new kind of capitalist mass entertainment, were fractured along polarized class lines. Melodrama was very often the only common meeting place of middle-class and working-class cultural trajectories, contributing to the institutional and aesthetic formation of 'the popular'. Cultural historians have taught us that if 'the popular' is claimed as a point of social cohesion, it is also contested, fraught with tension, struggles and negotiations. Thus bourgeois ideology, as reflected in cheap literature, is encountered only in the compromised forms of popular culture it must adopt in order to provide some accommodation for opposing working-class values. There are also areas of space between different class cultures, where values such as self-help and thrift become part of a negotiated version of middle-class culture and ideology.[34]

It has been argued that melodrama became the standard ethos of Victorian modes of entertainment, with an audience extending across class boundaries, because it signified the popular dramatic culture re-entering into general view with rapid urbanization and the emergence of working classes in towns. Melodrama may well have had some progressive political aspects as a dramatic style, but generally speaking it reinforced concepts of patriotism, Dickensian domesticity, *laissez-faire* and an unequal society. In effect, as the social backgrounds of gaff playwrights and managers, as well as 'penny dreadful' authors, editors and publishers, might suggest, commercial entertainment for working-class juveniles operated within primarily middle-class ideological constraints. The consensual values re-commended by the authors of cheap plays and serialized fiction, if not consistently practised by their less savoury characters, were nearly always those of orthodox Victorian morality, as reinterpreted through the conventions of melodrama. Cultural hegemony was secured not simply by the obliteration of an 'authentic' working-class culture, but through the latter's articulation to bourgeois culture and ideology. The cost of obtaining consent to society as presently ordered was that so-called Victorian or middle-class values were not imposed in a pure form but were themselves reshaped by the need to accomodate those of the subordinate classes.[35]

The received historical view of Victorian penny theatres presents them, almost uniformly, as a sordid product of slum life, the cheapest and lowest of theatrical shows. According to a distinguished American literary critic writing in 1970:

> The London slums had many of these squalid entertainments, con-
> ducted by actors, singers, and dancers in the last phases of drink and
> decrepitude who performed to unruly audiences... composed almost
> exclusively of costermongers, street boys, and their girls. The atmos-
> phere of these resorts, which besides specializing in reputedly obscene
> songs and dances were known to be meeting and recruiting places
> for apprentice criminals, attracted the condemnation of moralizing
> students of urban life and the constant attention of the police.

Yet not all gaff actors were rendered incapable by drink or senility, nor were performances excessively devoted to 'obscene songs and dances', and it clearly exaggerates to portray gaff audiences as almost entirely

made up of costermongers or juvenile criminals. The evidence that
penny gaffs were 'hotbeds of vice in its vilest forms' or, as Blanchard
Jerrold put it, 'the place where juvenile poverty meets juvenile crime', is
not very convincing and more a reflection of the mid-Victorian revival of
evangelical puritanism among the middle classes than of any noticeable
impurities in popular forms of entertainment. What offended Victorian
reformers and moralists alike was that gaffs signified an autonomous
working-class youth subculture over which they exerted only sporadic
control. Penny theatre performances, at least in this sense, *did* represent a
threat to the literate, Christian, middle-class values that typified Victorian culture.[36]

Changing trends in the dominant cultural hegemony, in other words,
were probably more responsible for the words of a street song performed at
a gaff being labelled 'obscene' or 'improper' than the actual verses themselves. Even the perceptive editor of *The Builder* was not entirely immune to
such influences from the surrounding social culture: 'A year ago, the performances at penny theatres consisted of singing, dancing, and a short
piece, generally of a melodramatic kind; or, in the season, a sort of pantomime: *in some instances, the words of the songs were broad and improper.* Since
then, however, the police have overlooked them; many have been closed'
[my emphasis], wrote George Godwin in 1858. After being 'overlooked'
by the police, singing and dancing in the gaffs took on a greater refinement,
as popular leisure forms adapted to the bourgeois urban folkways of mid-
Victorian England. The entertainment at penny theatres which Godwin
took pains to see, 'although not instructive, had not of itself any immoral
tendency'. He stressed the good behaviour of the gaff audience and felt
that, although open to improvement, penny theatres did 'more good than
harm' among the young.[37]

Decline of the Gaffs

Penny gaffs lingered on as a primitive form of juvenile working-class entertainment in the East End of London until the turn of the century, despite
police harassment. After the demise of gaffs as all but a folk memory, they
were sometimes bathed in a hazy, nostalgic glow which the following 1953
attempt to recall 'A Victorian Street Scene' in the East End on a Saturday
night exemplifies:

The Christmas revival of *Maria Marten* may recall to many people memories of the Victorian street entertainments, for this lurid old melodrama could once be seen at the cost of only one penny in the 'penny gaff' of the Whitechapel Road, a hundred yards or so from the Pavilion Theatre. The 'gaff' was a converted shop, and it was one of the features in the long stretch of fun fair and market along the broad pavement of Whitechapel Road and the Mile End Road to the Paragon music-hall.... *Maria Marten* was only one of the items in the repertory of the 'penny gaff', where versions of *Sweeney Todd* and *Uncle Tom's Cabin* were also given. Performances were irregular – they began as soon as enough passers-by had been gathered in to pay their pennies. If business was good, the melodrama would be shortened so as to get in as many houses as possible, and no show would have been complete without the old stage illusion known as 'Pepper's Ghost'. The grand finale of *Maria Marten* was intensely popular, especially when the murderer Corder was shown in the condemned cell with a vision of the body of Maria.

The popularity of melodramas like *Maria Marten* and *Uncle Tom's Cabin* in the gaff repertoire, and the abbreviation of performances in order to put on an extra 'house', are already familiar from contemporary accounts of penny theatres, evidence of how popular forms of leisure received much of their strength and vitality from the experience of the past and from continuities over time in the culture of the urban poor.[38]

The death warrant of the majority of penny theatres in cities such as Liverpool, Glasgow and London was sealed not by the tightening up of the largely unenforceable theatrical licensing laws but by changing audience tastes and a general improvement in living standards. Gaffs gradually disappeared with the advent of well-paid errand boy jobs for school-leavers and the rapid expansion of a cheaper music-hall entertainment in the 1880s and 1890s. Rising real wages and compulsory schooling removing large sections of the audience were hence among the most significant contributory factors in the gradual disappearance of the penny theatre. Slowly, the leisure patterns of modern urban British society were beginning to take on an identifiable shape and, in this sense, penny theatres were important as the much overlooked precursors of new forms of mass entertainment such as the music hall. Yet the marks of 'respectability' and 'rationalisation' which the music halls adopted, more for sound commercial reasons than a desire to disseminate middle-class values, were never a prominent trait of the penny theatres. Curiously, the first introduction many urban working-class children had to the silent cinema was through yet another version of the 'penny gaff': derelict shoprooms which in the early 1900s were used to show primitive early cinematograph films. The next two chapters look not at the cinema, whose gangster pictures are the focus of Chapter 4, but at the 'penny dreadful' whose popularity among British youth both paralleled and was sustained by that of the penny theatre.[39]

2

'PENNY DREADFUL' PANIC (I): THEIR READERS, PUBLISHING AND CONTENT

'The mid-nineteenth century witnessed an extraordinary literary and social revolution with the birth and enormous popularity of the Penny Dreadful', declared George Speaight, historian of the English toy theatre, as long ago as 1946. 'It is much to be hoped that this fantastic episode in our literature will soon receive the historical study it deserves.' Not long after, E. S. Turner, in his classic work on generations of British boys' periodicals, *Boys Will Be Boys* (1948), devoted several chapters to an engaging overview of 'penny dreadfuls', acknowledging it would have been possible to fill his book with an account of them alone.[1] The temptation was resisted, partly because the number of his readers who could remember following the adventures of such as Jack Harkaway, Turnpike Dick and Cheerful Ching-Ching had by 1948 become rather finite. Turner's infectious humour, compelling use of quotation, and underlying affection for these old storypapers, makes these chapters as readable now as when they first appeared in print nearly 50 years ago.

Most works since Turner to deal with those popular juvenile texts broadly, if imprecisely, known as 'penny dreadfuls' have been glossy illustrated books or compilations with a minimum of explanatory text.[2] The ensuing account may be more solemn than Turner's but attempts to be equally informative. This chapter defines 'dreadfuls', places them in the historical context of the new juvenile mass market, explains the economics of cheap publishing in and around London's Fleet Street, and then shows how 'low-life' London and women-in-peril instalment novels exemplify the thematic preoccupations of Victorian melodrama. The next chapter looks at periodic 'moral panics' incited over criminal trials that were intended to demonstrate how reading 'dreadfuls' had corrupting 'effects' on the impressionable young and questions whether such charges had any verifiable basis.

Routinely mentioned by nineteenth-century literature specialists in stark contrast to more elevated fiction, 'penny dreadfuls' are often excoriated but seldom read or critically discussed. They represent what most late Victorian and Edwardian juveniles actually *chose* to read, as opposed to the improving 'reward book' literature which adults in power over them felt that they *should* read. Together with earlier 'penny bloods' they were forerunners of the vast output of popular fiction as commercial entertainment that is traditionally associated, from the early 1890s onwards, with the Harmsworth brothers and what became their Amalgamated Press. A literary and historical assessment of the wide-ranging field of mass-circulation juvenile serial and periodical fiction carelessly labelled 'dreadfuls' is long overdue. The interest of such truly popular writing is diminished neither by the neglect which it has received from literary scholars nor by its general inaccessibility except in special collections.

In creating and shaping the beginnings of a commercial market for literature that aimed primarily to entertain, 'bloods' and 'dreadfuls' inaugurated, and were the first great expression of, the modern era of fiction as mass entertainment. Such ephemeral reading reflects in coded melodramatic discourse the aspirations and fears of a class-, age- and gender-structured British society, while providing insights into the tastes, fantasies and potential role models of the generations brought up on this literature of the streets. 'We had not even known of the existence of these [penny] papers, and yet there they were, going forth into the hands of hundreds and thousands of readers, all of whom were being more or less instructed in their modes of life and manner of thinking by the stories which were thus brought before them', wrote an amazed Anthony Trollope in 1870, after buying drinks for a poor, Cambridge-educated, hack writer who bemoaned the meagre rewards of the cheap fiction business. The author of the Barchester novels, like other middle-class observers, chose to exaggerate the moral and pedagogic influence of such reading on its largely juvenile audience.[3]

Defining the Penny Dreadful

In 1836 the French newspaper *Le Siècle* started *le roman feuilleton*, or the novel specifically written to be serialized in a daily newspaper. This was to inspire a new style of writing interminable sagas, for issue in weekly instalments by the popular press, that had an important influence on the development of fiction for the English working classes in the 1840s. The serial-novel idea was rapidly taken up by other competing French papers, recruiting writers such as George Sand, Eugène Sue, Honoré de Balzac, Jules Janin and Dumas père. This great outpouring of French popular fiction, with a situation left in suspense at the end of each part, was liberally translated to provide material for English 'penny bloods' and publications for the people such as *The London Journal* (1845–1912) and *The Family Herald* (1842–1940). The viability of cheap publishing was confirmed by the rotary steam-printing press, the removal of paper taxes and declining paper costs. The French *roman feuilleton* also had a great influence on George William MacArthur Reynolds (1814–79), best-selling English author of long-running serialized novels (see below). Poorly paid hack writers of 'bloods' and 'dreadfuls' in London followed the *feuilleton* style to make up the requisite pages, breaking up their prose into short independent paragraphs, their conversations into mere phrases and melodramatic exclamations. This gave a patchy look to the page and a certain jerkiness to the narrative which was not assisted by each weekly part running on directly, sometimes in mid-paragraph, from where it had left off in the previous issue. 'As long as the paragraphs are short, the incidents sensational, the conversation high-flown, and the end of all things a marriage, the grammar may be bad, the plot preposterous, the characters wooden, and the anticlimax persistent', according to Talbot Baines Reed, the boys' school-story author.[4]

Lengthy serialized fiction only became the primary reading matter of the German working classes in the 1870s and into the 1880s. The *kolporta-geroman* or 'colporteur novel' was a delayed but probably independent German response to the same kind of social and economic conditions that had stimulated the development of popular fiction in England and France, particularly the enormous latent demand for simple and eventful reading matter among the newly urbanized German workforce. Cheap instalments of the latest *heftroman,* or part-issue novel, were sold in largely urban areas by door-to-door salesmen and wandering book peddlers. A similar commercialized urban culture had developed in Britain decades before, when workers flocked from rural areas to London and the new industrial cities. In the heyday of German serialized novels, each chapter sold separately to the worker or artisan for ten pfennigs, recalling both the English 'penny bloods' of the 1830s onwards and their 'penny dreadful' successors, yet there is no evidence that *kolportageroman* were at all consciously based on English models. German cheap fiction consisted of violent and blood-thirsty tales of ghosts, bandits, murders and crimes, or mysterious scandals with contemporary settings, particularly those involving European roy-alty. The success of serialized fiction in Germany was determined as much by the way in which it was marketed as by its content; for example, free copies of opening chapters were designed to lure people into subscribing to and paying for all the subsequent instalments. Cheap mass-produced litho-graphs and other prizes were also offered as incentives to the potential read-ers of 'colporteur novels'.[5]

The equivalent to 'penny bloods' in an urbanizing America were 'dime novels' published in series or 'libraries', usually Western or detective stor-ies complete in each monthly or fortnightly part and sold for a dime (10 cents). 'Half-dimes' or 'nickel weeklies', addressed to a more juvenile mar-ket from the 1880s onwards, were closer to the English 'penny dreadful'. Fifty years earlier a number of American firms had started publishing cheap 'yellow-back' or 'yellow-covered' novels, known from the colour of their paper wrappers. These derived almost entirely from contemporary British popular or middlebrow fiction, such as revamped Gothic novels and imitations of Walter Scott, Charles Dickens, 'Captain' Marryat and William Harrison Ainsworth. Escapist serialized novels for immigrants and working-class Americans first appeared in cheap, mass-produced 'story weeklies', printed on newly introduced rotary steam presses, such as *Uncle Sam, The Star Spangled Banner, Saturday Night* and *The New York Weekly*. After 1860 they shared the cheap fiction market with 'dime novels' which first reprinted serials from the weeklies or story papers then made use of the same writers and popular characters (see Appendix II).[6]

The generic term 'penny dreadful', applied so indiscriminately to a whole range of English popular fiction, no longer has much exact currency as a descriptive historical term. It was originally used as a blanket term of condemnation by magistrates, journalists, clergymen and school-teachers, to designate penny-part serials and cheap weekly periodicals, devoted mainly to tales of historical adventure or contemporary mystery, illustrated with vivid woodcuts, which held a particular appeal for working-class youth. One of the earliest official appearances of the term 'penny dread-ful' is in the 1874 edition of John Camden Hotten's *Slang Dictionary*, as an expressive term for those penny publications which 'depend more upon sensationalism than upon literary or artistic merit for their success'. Recent work on narrative has drawn attention to usage of terms like 'sensation' and 'sensationalism' as highly problematic, since they could be used as a means of rejecting what were implicit class criticisms in popular writing, acting as

·

part of an emergent 'respectable discourse' deflecting the attacks of the radical press or serial fiction on middle-class cant or aristocratic infidelity. That publishers of cheap serials also exploited these terms to promote their own wares seems to have eluded the theorists. The more self-evidently pejorative and habitually misleading 'dreadful' label was constructed largely by middle-class journalists in order to amplify social anxiety or 'moral panic' over the latest commercial innovation directed at the young. Accordingly, 'penny dreadful' is used here, within inverted commas, to represent the profusion of melodramatic and exciting, but otherwise harmless, serial fiction published in instalment, periodical and complete-novel form that, from the 1860s onwards, found a new following among the increasingly literate young. Although librarians and educators have ill-advisedly continued to use the term 'penny dreadful' until quite recently, the genuine article effectively died out in the aftermath of the First World War.[7]

An adequate all-embracing definition of 'penny dreadful' is made difficult, despite the above attempt, because there are at least six different meanings which can be distinguished from its usage in popular vocabulary. (1) As a general term of abuse for cheap weeklies or 'sensation' fiction of any description throughout the nineteenth and early twentieth centuries. (2) To describe highly coloured, criminal or Gothic penny-issue novels of the 1830s and 1840s, such as those issued by Edward Lloyd from Salisbury Square in weekly or monthly parts, and (3) their successors directed towards a more juvenile market, culminating in the Newsagents' Publishing Company (NPC) serials of the 1860s. (4) As a definition of penny magazines, or the cheaper weekly boys' periodicals appearing from the mid-1860s onwards, particularly those associated with Edwin Brett (1828–95) or the Emmett brothers, and (5) of the long-running serials published weekly in such boys' journals, and (6) also, if successful, in separate weekly parts and later in collected shilling volumes.[8]

Whilst recognizing that 'dreadful' has been used to embrace all these contingent forms of publication, 'penny blood' is applied here to the earlier serials for working-class adults associated with publisher Edward Lloyd (1815–90) and author G. W. M. Reynolds. 'Penny dreadful' is reserved solely for their counterparts from the 1860s onwards, addressed specifically to a more youthful and also generally working- or lower-middle class audience. Hence the absence from these pages of such Lloyd penny favourites as Fleet Street's demon barber Sweeney Todd or the grotesque masked avenger Spring-Heeled Jack. Both have been dealt with at length elsewhere and, although eventually put out in revised form for juveniles, do not qualify as 'dreadfuls' under the above definition. Significantly,

Henry Mayhew ends his well-known section on the reading habits of London's mid-century costermongers by pointing out that a taste for works 'relating to Courts, potentates, or harristocrats', such as Reynolds supplied, was fast replacing 'tales of robbery and bloodshed, of heroic, eloquent, and gentlemanly highwaymen, or of gipsies turning out to be nobles.' Yet the publishers of highwaymen, pirate and rags-to-riches stories, of the kind that 'now interest the costermongers but little, although they found great delight in such stories a few years back', were to find new customers mainly among the urban young.[9]

'Penny dreadfuls' of the 1860s onwards were hence the inheritors of more adult-orientated 'penny bloods', convoluted serial novels about Gothic villains, pirates, highwaymen, thieves and murderers. Like them, 'dreadfuls' were sold weekly in penny parts, each part consisting of eight pages of octavo-sized text, printed on fairly good straw paper in double columns of eye-straining type, minion or brevier, and embellished with a lurid front-cover wood engraving. Lengthy serial publication required as wide a range of characters as possible, some of whom could then go off on their own adventures, eventually to be reintegrated into the main plot. The introduction of disparate narrative 'tracks' which come together through chance was a literary device quite often found in 'penny dreadfuls.' Bloods and 'dreadfuls' had their largest sale in London, the major market at every level, but manufacturing cities such as Manchester, Liverpool and Birmingham also took considerable quantities. One of the most 'disreputable' companies publishing 'dreadfuls' in the 1860s was financed by a syndicate of 'respectable' London newsagents. Some serials had an average weekly sale of only 10,000, but the most popular, such as the long-running *Black Bess; or, The Knight of the Road* (1863–8), could expect to sell some 30,000 or 40,000 copies weekly. The shrewd entrepreneurs introduced below who published 'dreadfuls' in the vicinity of Fleet Street frequently used promotional schemes to assist sales. When a new serial began, for example, the first two numbers in a bright red or yellow wrapper were sold for the price of one and, with the collusion of wholesalers, free samples were inserted into copies of rival cheap periodicals. Posters and handbills at newsvendors helped spread the message of a new title, as did advertisements on the wrappers and in the margins of other serials by the same publisher. Coloured illustrations were given away in early issues, while competitions and lottery prize distributions were also organized to boost sales. Readers were not entirely passive consumers, however, since serialized novels would be abruptly terminated should their weekly instalments fail to sell. The 'penny dreadful' business was, to this extent, customer led, with readers exercising positive choice over the wide range of material which they were being offered.[10]

'It is hard to think of these [penny dreadfuls] as forming a part of the stream of children's literature, and it is also harder to be objectively critical of them', wrote a Canadian Professor of Librarianship in 1951, commenting disdainfully on the poor style, inappropriate illustrations, generally careless make-up, and wretched standards of the more 'sensational' journals. Such cultural aloofness towards so-called 'dreadfuls' is no longer shared by those scholars interested in the leisure activities of Victorian and Edwardian youth. For at least half a century, stories and periodicals so labelled were the favourite reading of a probable majority. Literary critics have perhaps avoided reading this kind of mass fiction, with only a few exceptions, because its purposes were primarily commercial rather than artistic. They have also been deterred because the weekly parts of these despised texts, when reissued complete in bound volume form, take up hundreds of double-columned pages. The social historian's concern is as much with creative management as creative writing, with the business of publishing cheap juvenile fiction for the urban 'masses', rather than the ersatz 'popular' fiction reaching a largely middlebrow audience that the literary academy tends to focus upon. This chapter and the next concentrate on popular serialized forms of low-life London, women-in-peril and highwayman stories, excluding for reasons of space other categories of 'dreadful', such as historical-adventure stories, school stories, Robinsonnades, rags-to-riches stories, and pirate stories.[11]

The Juvenile Market for Commercial Fiction

What eventually replaced customary forms of pre-industrial popular recreation was not a cultural vacuum but a profit-based, commercial-entertainment culture more attuned to the less violent, more literate and slightly less drunken, younger generation of mid- and late-Victorian society. Widening dissemination of print led to the transformation of popular cultural experience and from the centre of this transformed culture there emerged, from the 1840s onwards, the beginnings of a new mass-produced print culture. Cheap serialized novels or 'penny bloods' were purchased or borrowed by the urban working class, appealing to a semi-literate audience brought up on the *The Newgate Calendar* (1773 and various editions), a five-volume compilation of criminal lives named after both the notorious London prison and the court document listing those awaiting trial at the assizes.[12]

Mass markets open to capitalist competition for profit had clearly been shaped by England's massive population expansion of the early nineteenth century; some historians prefer to talk of urban evolution rather than industrial revolution as characteristic of this period. One of the earliest mass markets to develop was that for cheap reading matter, created primarily through serial publication, followed by newspapers and weekly magazines. 'Mass circulation journals became as central a feature of the industrialization and urbanization of Britain as did its coal, iron and textile industries', claims an historian of the didactic *Penny Magazine* (1832–45), arguably the first British mass-market publication. The large proportion of young people in London and the manufacturing cities, made up of working-class boys and girls with only a few pennies to spend and middle-class children with parents willing to spend far more, was a primary component of the new expanding consumer market. Young people's urge to read for excitement and entertainment flourished as never before in these anonymous yet bustling and eventful new urban surroundings.[13]

Economies of scale deriving from the English age structure made the publication of juvenile fiction into a sound mid-Victorian commercial proposition. At the 1861 census of England and Wales 4,038,000 were aged between ten and 19 years of age out of a total population of 20,067,000, comprising a potential juvenile reading public of more than 20 per cent of the total. The inclusion of all those children below the age of ten gives an additional 5,045,000, making a combined 45 per cent of the total population under the age of 20. A hundred years later only under 30 per cent of the English population were aged below 20. The enormous growth of Victorian cities, a result of population growth, rural migration and industrialisation, containing populations with an insatiable desire for amusement, made it increasingly profitable to commercialize the leisure of even the poorer and younger sections of British society. The spread of youth literacy in the new, and fast expanding, urban-industrial areas vastly increased the pool of potential readers.[14]

Widespread literacy in even the poorer sections of the British population, it is now generally accepted, had existed prior to the advent of universal, compulsory education. Urban-industrial change, which had increased the adult reading public by at least five-fold, also greatly expanded the pool of potential juvenile readers. In the early Victorian period, more than half the younger generation could at least sign their names and probably had a minimal reading ability. By the 1860s, when the serialized 'penny dreadful' was at its peak and before the advent of state elementary education, it is quite possible that at least two-thirds of working-class children in England had received some kind of schooling. The combined efforts of dame and private day schools, Sunday schools and denominational day school systems, factory and workhouse schools, and schools sponsored by working-class organizations, had ensured that the great majority of working-class children either received some education or, as David Vincent puts it, 'were at least in a position to form some estimation of what they were missing'. Forster's 1870 Education Act and its successors did not create the mass juvenile reading public, rather they filled gaps and levelled up the degree of reading attainment already achieved. The impact of technical and commercial innovation was not limited to the publication of cheap serials, but the insatiable desire for entertainment certainly provided a firm motive for learning to read. 'The exercise of the imagination was the greatest and most persistent incentive for gaining a command of the tools of literacy, and their first and most satisfying application', argues Vincent. 'Without the chapbooks and broadsides, and later the penny dreadfuls and the cheap reprints, rather more than 5 per cent of the population would still have been illiterate by the time compulsory education was finally imposed'.[15]

By 1871 nearly 30 per cent of London's population was aged between five and 20 years, the largest concentrated target group for the 'penny dreadful'. During a period of rising real wages, the demand for 'boy labour', or well-paid but unskilled errand-boy jobs, was a special characteristic of the economy of late-Victorian London. Small-scale production methods combined with chronic under-employment meant a greater work opportunity for those in their teens, since many employers used adolescents to bring down the wage levels which adults could attract on the London labour market. There was no single large industry in the metropolis, of course, and as a commercial and service centre London provided fewer openings for skilled artisans than Birmingham, but there were numerous workshops, small factories and daily markets, while many trades had a fringe of casual labour. All required a mass of unspecialized 'boy labour' to work as printer's devils, machine minders, warehouse-, van-, shop- and office-boys. Contemporaries identified the youth in these urban occupations, together with schoolboys, as among the most insatiable readers of the 'penny dreadful'. This may account for the appearance in the mid-1860s of instalment novels celebrating *The Wild Boys of London* (1864–6), *The Poor Boys of London* (1866?) and *The Work Girls of London* (1865), oft-reprinted serials about low-life crime and mystery that would have held a vicarious appeal for young metropolitan readers seeking a romantic escape from uneventful daily lives.[16]

With a growing mass readership to draw upon, the 1860s and 1870s hence produced some of the most striking cheap serials of all, deliberately targeted at the young. 'The romantic love-element disappears and is replaced by lurid crime and violence, by heroes who are highwaymen or thieves, by settings of Newgate or the lowest slums of the cities', claims one brief survey of the field. Cheap engravers, speculative printers and wholesale newsagents, assisted by rotary printing presses, cheap machine-manufactured paper, improved transport and rising literacy, seized upon the opportunity to market a consumer product which this particular audience at this particular moment in time demanded. As a result, these entrepreneurs unleashed a middle-class 'cycle of outrage', equating the reading of 'penny dreadfuls' with the commission of juvenile crimes (see Chapter 3), that concealed a fear of popular taste and values.[17]

'"I wish I know'd as much as you, Dick. How did you manage to pick it up?"' asks one of the eponymous Wild Boys of London of the well-mannered young hero of this notorious weekly serial. '"Mother taught me most, and I read all the books I can get"', he replies. '"So do I; sich rattling tales, too"', interjects the street waif. '"The Black Phantom; or, the White Spectre of the Pink Rock. It's fine, it is; somebody's killed every week, and it's only a penny". "That is not the sort of book I mean"', says the snooty hero. '"Mother does not like me to read them". "Why?" "She says they have a bad influence". "Who's he?"' asks the perplexed Wild Boy.[18] The preceding lines of dialogue from *The Wild Boys of London: or, The Children of Night. A Story of the Present Day* not only suggest an element of beguiling self-parody but also indicate the firm arrival of a new commercial popular culture of 'rattling tales' aimed directly at the young working- and lower-middle classes in London and the expanding industrial cities of mid-to late-nineteenth-century Britain.

The actual readers of serial novels such as *The Wild Boys* are difficult to identify with any real precision and even contemporaries were reliant on generalized speculation. The cultural principles of use by 'penny dreadful' readers are even more difficult to ascertain. Self-made autobiographers from working-class families readily admit to reading Edward Lloyd's serialized 'penny bloods' in the 1840s, yet none can be found openly confessing to a taste for late-Victorian 'penny dreadfuls.' The latter were read, as a rule, claimed a hostile reporter in 1873, 'by ignorant shop and office-boys, young apprentices and factory hands, and by, perhaps, a small number of school lads.' A columnist in *The Bookseller* 5 years earlier was convinced that 'dreadfuls' were written for one small class of readers only: 'boys without education or domestic ties, little street Arabs who could be seen at corners painfully spelling through the latest weekly parts of their favourite serials'. This hardly accounts for weekly sales of 30,000 to 40,000 for the most popular serials, circulated among several readers and later loaned out in volume form by small shopkeepers, suggesting an actual audience approaching 100,000 per penny issue. Monthly sales of Charles Dickens' best-selling *Pickwick Papers*, at an expensive one shilling for each part of 32 pages, reached a maximum 40,000 copies at their peak in 1836.[19]

Small newsagents, tobacconists and stationers supplying cheap juvenile serials were located in the courts and alleys of the East End of London, or what were dubbed the 'lowest parts' of Manchester, Birmingham and other manufacturing towns. 'You will find', said one London bookseller in 1867, 'that the blood-and-murder stories are generally sold at the lollipop and toy-shops, and that respectable newsvendors don't deal in them'. Upon being pressed, however, the same retailer confessed to stocking at least six well-known 'dreadful' titles in his own shop.[20] The limited vocabulary, repetition and range of plots in these weeklies undoubtedly catered for the partially educated reader who could only pick out a few words. Yet they also reached adolescents closer to the well-spoken protagonist of *The Wild Boys* than to the homeless orphans of the title. Sons and daughters of skilled working men and clerks could vicariously enjoy the adventures of boy thieves, actresses and criminals from the comfort of outwardly respectable suburban homes.

Much of the middle-class 'moral panic' directed at 'penny dreadfuls' derived from apprehension that their own sons and daughters were as much at risk from contamination as the children of the urban poor. 'It [penny fiction] is creeping not only into the houses of the poor, neglected, and untaught, but into the largest mansions; penetrating into religious families and astounding careful parents by its frightful issues', warned Lord Shaftesbury in 1878, addressing the Religious Tract Society (RTS). Alexander Strahan, publisher of *Good Words for the Young* (1869–77), was sternly pessimistic about the possibility of rescuing poor children from the lure of 'this horrible garbage'. He was equally alarmed at 'the gradual spread, upwards in what is called the social scale, of this sort of trash. Any observant person may notice low newspapers and low periodicals in houses of a pretension which would seem to point to something a great deal better.' Earlier, crusading journalist James Greenwood – whom we have already met visiting penny gaffs – had depicted the voracious 'penny dreadful', like the fabled vampire of legend, already having 'bitten your little rosy-cheeked son Jack. He may be lurking at this very moment in that young gentleman's private chamber, little as you suspect it, polluting his mind and smoothing the way that leads to swift destruction'. *The Boy's Own Paper* (*BOP*), published by the RTS from 1879, was primarily intended as a virile Christian alternative to such 'pernicious' reading.[21]

There is some evidence that secular, cheap periodicals, also dubbed 'dreadfuls', were read by middle- and lower-middle-class, as well as by working-class, children and adolescents. Edwin Brett's long-running *Boys of England* (1866–99) was a recognized favourite with boys of all social classes. The necessary adjunct is that 'dreadfuls' were virtually the sole reading material of working-class boys, whereas their middle-class coevals were able to enjoy both popular and more elite forms of juvenile literature. Hence George Sampson, a future school inspector, feasted on 'harmless' dreadfuls such as Deadwood Dick, Jack Harkaway and Sweeney Todd, whilst maintaining his affection for the parent-approved *Boy's Own Paper*. Glaswegian J. A. Hammerton, who in the 1900s worked for Northcliffe and Arthur Mee on *The Children's Encyclopedia*, confessed to adolescent reading of Charles Fox's *The Boys' Standard*, *Ching-Ching's Own* and other 'dreadfuls' of the late 1880s, but also owed ultimate allegiance to the *BOP*. 'Not that I could have been consciously critical of the crudities of such stuff as Sweeney Todd, Three-String Jack, or Spring-Heeled Jack, my taste merely made me more partial to informative reading', he smugly explains in his autobiography. On the whole, the majority of 'penny dreadful' readers were drawn from the ranks of the working and lower-middle classes, that section of the community least likely to parade their juvenile reading habits before a wider public in subsequent autobiographical form.[22]

Girls and young women were also among the audience for 'penny dreadfuls', despite the emphasis upon boy heroes with whom the male reader could more readily identify. Viragos were occasionally represented, such as Elmira, the female pirate, or May Turpin, the queen of the road, but they were invariably dependent upon heroic males to rescue them from perilous situations. Women in 'penny dreadfuls' were, none the less, allowed a more independent, even aggressive, role than could be occupied by the polite middle-class heroines of most adult three-decker novels. In 1868 *The Bookseller* drew attention to several 'especially sensational' penny numbers, such as *Rose Mortimer, or The Ballet Girls' Revenge* (*c.*1865), which were specifically written, in the editor's estimation, for servant-girls and seamstresses (see below). *The Pretty Girls of London* (*c.*1867) was another, a 'highly exciting and not too modest story', of which, regrettably, no surviving copies can be traced.[23]

Other titles considered of feminine appeal at this time were *Black-Eyed Susan,* a novelization of Douglas Jerrold's famous 1829 nautical stage melodrama, and cheap reprints of Mrs R. M. Roche's *The Children of the Abbey* (1796), a favourite Gothic romance. The tendency of such stories, according to *The Bookseller,* was bad, if not actually demoralizing, 'albeit suggestive rather than descriptive of evil'. In 'dreadfuls', 'the delusive charms of illicit love, intrigue, and exciting incident are made far too prominent'. Vice was at least censured in the three-volume 'sensation novels', written for and read by middle-class women in the 1860s, whereas in penny serials it was 'glossed over in such a way as makes readers rather admire the temptation and yearn for the *excitement of guilty pleasures,* than listen to the moral which may or may not be enforced' [my emphasis]. Stories that provoked vicarious enjoyment among female readers were clearly beyond the tolerance of even the broad-minded editor of *The Bookseller.*[24]

Thus a new phase in the history of British popular culture opens with the advent of various forms of mass-produced entertainment in London and the growing industrial centres. Critics have been convinced ever since that this meant a qualitative change for the worse. The new mass culture would spread, it was thought, like a contagious disease, if arbiters of cultural values did not take a stand. Hence the anonymous author of an *Edinburgh Review* essay on 'The Literature of the Streets' [1887] was horrified at the enormous range of penny instalment novels, reprinted magazine serials, and penny novelettes that accompanied the vast outpouring of juvenile periodical fiction:

> There is now before us such a veritable mountain of pernicious trash, mostly in paper covers, and all 'Price One Penny': so-called novelettes, romances, tales, stories of adventure, mystery and crime; pictures of school life hideously unlike the reality; exploits of pirates, robbers, cutthroats, prostitutes, and rogues, that, but for its actual presence, it would seem incredible.

Yet judgements of the value of cultural forms are notoriously subjective and what the snobbish essayist viewed, collectively, as 'pernicious trash' have been seen more recently as open to symbolic interpretation. Stories of school life might appear, for example, as subversive or 'hideously unlike the reality' because they offered an exaggerated representation of generational and social conflicts.[25]

The Publishing and Marketing of Dreadfuls

The market for commercial printing increased rapidly from the mid-nineteenth century onwards, making the publishing trade generally into a significant aspect of London's commercial development. Railway distribution, the penny post and a growth of government spending, all helped to raise the scale of demand for print to an entirely new level. Periodical and newspaper publishing, in particular, saw a vast expansion in the second half of the century, owing to the enormous increase in circulations made possible by the rapid spread of literacy and the repeal of the so-called 'taxes on knowledge'. Removal of the advertisement duty (1853) and, in particular, the stamp duty on newspapers (1855) made possible the mass-market penny press. When the paper excise duty was at last repealed (1861), slashing the cost of paper, over half of the nation's printers could be found in central London. The capital also led the way in a gradual steam-driven, technical revolution of the printing process, hence in 1856 the afore mentioned Edward Lloyd became the first British publisher to install a Hoe rotary press, dramatically increasing the speed of printing his long-running *Lloyd's Weekly Newspaper* (1842–1902). In 1862, following repeal of the paper duties, Lloyd's miscellany was reduced to a penny and printed from stereotype plates. Both machine-manufactured paper and cheaper paper-making materials also helped bring cheap fiction before a mass urban audience.[26]

In the 1860s, a decade of phenomenal cheapness for publishing, numerous small firms in or near Fleet Street began to redirect their penny fiction sales towards the fast growing youth market; aggressively preceding the major commercial publishers in the lucrative field of juvenile literature by several years. Only the rewards anticipated in the late 1860s from Forster's 1870 Education Act led firms such as Macmillan, Routledge, Nelson's and Longman's to set up their own juvenile departments. By the early 1880s, over 900 new juvenile books were being issued annually and 15 secular boys' periodicals were competing simultaneously. In that juvenile publishing became a steady source of industry to the flourishing book and magazine trade, the 'penny dreadful' business made a little-acknowledged contribution to the atomistic business world of the metropolitan economy. There are striking parallels with the seedy British back-street publishing houses that for a decade after the Second World War, in the temporary absence of American competition, churned out million-seller paperback thrillers, science fiction and Westerns, with alluring covers (see Appendix III).[27]

The adult audience for gothic and romantic instalment fiction, or the Edward Lloyd-style 'penny blood', had begun to drift away from mid-century, with the advent of cheap Sunday newspapers and weekly illustrated magazines now carrying serialized novels. 'Naturally people who read such romances have ceased to take an interest in them since they found that the penny weeklies gave them three or four times as much matter of the same character for the same price', according to critic Francis Hitchman. A form of entertainment recently abandoned by adults was to be appropriated, and in the process transmuted, by a younger age cohort. Thus the literary craft industry scrutinized here was set up in and around the City of London's Fleet Street as a positive response to a new market opportunity, in an age of rising youth literacy, for manufacturing juvenile fiction. Produced in its late-Victorian heyday by a bohemian, underpaid, yet highly productive workforce, the 'penny dreadful', broadly defined, became by far the most alluring and low-priced reading available to ordinary youth; at least until the advent in the early 1890s of future newspaper magnate Alfred Harmsworth's price-cutting 'halfpenny dreadfuller'.[28]

The area in and around late-Victorian Fleet Street was honeycombed with the offices of boys' weeklies and serial publishers, operating on too small a scale to be included in the census of production. Several were also busy wholesale newsagents, putting out juvenile weeklies almost as a sideline. The Emmett brothers ran Hogarth House in St Bride's Avenue and later in Bouverie Street; Charles Fox, who took over their business, was based in Shoe Lane, then Red Lion Court. Edwin John Brett managed the 'Boys of England Office' at 173 Fleet Street, overlooking St Bride's churchyard. John Allingham published from Fetter Lane; Charles Shurey was based in Caxton House, Gough Square; and Henry Vickers at the corner of Drury Court. A former Fleet Street errand boy, who in the late 1880s spent his pocket money on highwaymen stories purchased direct from these adjacent publishing offices, recalled that Edwin Brett's busy office, by then removed to Fetter Lane, was crammed from floor to ceiling with bound volumes and penny numbers, with about six men and boys employed serving and packing. The premises were presided over by a rather stern-looking Brett, 'who appeared more like an ordinary mechanic than a publisher'. His enormous stock of 'penny dreadfuls' was enough to make any boy's mouth water, to say nothing of 'a tempting display of the Brett firm's coloured covers which adorned the office window'. Charles Fox managed his business with only one assistant, frequently serving over the counter at Shoe Lane himself, in one of the cleanest and tidiest of all the publishers' offices. The buildings, courts and alleys from which these small publishing and distribution outlets operated were either demolished next century or incorporated into the erection of huge newspaper publishing offices between the two world wars.[29]

Publishing cheap fiction was, first and foremost, a commercial business, unlike other Victorian mass entertainment forms, such as organized spectator sports, that for long resisted maximizing their profits. Ex-cavalry man George Emmett, for example, confessed to writing his 'Shot and Shell' adventure series primarily to increase sales of Hogarth's *The Young Englishman's Journal* (1867–70). 'Remember', he told fellow editor–proprietor John Allingham, 'every additional thousand copies, beyond a certain number, represents an extra sovereign profit per week'.[30] George and his brothers were not well-intentioned philanthropists eager to win converts to either religion or improving literature, unlike the clergymen who edited juvenile weeklies generously subsidized by the Sunday School Union and the RTS. Neither were publishers of 'penny dreadfuls' entirely mercenary or philistine businessmen, for several of them wrote serial stories or provided engravings for the boys' journals of which they were managing editors. Magazine proprietors who were popular story tellers as well as editors, publishers, wholesale newsagents and distributors, were clearly more versatile than the average Victorian businessman.

John Allingham, George Emmett and Edwin Brett, established toilers in the field of low-priced juvenile publishing, regularly commuted to their City of London offices from homes in comfortable residential suburbs like East Dulwich, Peckham Rye and Holloway. Despite a sometimes unconventional, even radical, youth, they probably thought of themselves as 'gentlemen' driven by either chequered careers or drink into a demeaning form of commerce. Yet 'penny dreadful' publishers did their best to maintain a respectable facade, in order to achieve status and recognition within the existing social order, perhaps envying the careless bohemian life-style of their more profligate employees. For London was crowded with penny-a-line writers, underpaid journalists, eccentric well-bred scribblers, improvident artists and despised plagiarists. The maximum price usually paid to authors for serial penny novels in 1868 was two guineas for a sheet of eight double-columned pages, the length of an average weekly instalment, the minimum only 15 shillings, or a few shillings more than the average weekly wage of an ordinary labourer. Cheap fiction writers commonly lived in the many courts or squares off Fleet Street itself, in lodgings around the Gray's Inn Road, or further out in unfashionable London suburbs. Together, these underpaid hacks provided satisfyingly rousing entertainment for generations of English children and adolescents.[31]

The City of London's prolific output of cheap juvenile fiction from the 1860s onwards exemplifies the ability of those blessed with sufficient entrepreneurial spirit to capitalize on a rising market demand among the young for entertaining and adventurous fiction. Schoolboys, errand boys, office clerks and young men in the numerous small workshops devoted to skilled or semi-skilled trades, endemic to a large commercial and business centre like London, thrilled to the ebullient, cliff-hanging exploits of heroes such as the Wild Boys of London, Spring-Heeled Jack, Charley Wag, Jack Sheppard and Turnpike Dick, the Daring Highwayman. 'In format, illustration, content, and popularity, [penny dreadfuls] were matched only by the rise and influence of the comic book in the mid-twentieth century', writes Sheila Egoff. 'This was the beginning of mass-media publishing for the young and of the syndicated writer.' If newly educated readers made the slightest attempt to employ their literacy skills, it would be to glance at a broadside, a 'penny blood', or some later form of cheap fiction such as the 'penny dreadful'. 'The field of the imagination', confirms David Vincent, 'presented the most direct engagement between capitalism and the use of literacy.' Interestingly, former Chartist sympathizer Edwin Brett concealed control of his earliest boys' papers behind the euphemism of 'a capit alist' to suggest the anonymous support of a wealthy company proprietor. Plant-owning craftsmen like Brett, desirous of becoming middle-class businessmen, set out to meet the demand from boys (and some girls) in their teens for entertaining fiction. The latter, rather than improving fact, offered the most certain return on investment for newly equipped printers and engravers with an entrepreneurial flair who wanted to enter the popular market and benefit from economies of scale.[32]

The Newsagents' Publishing Company

By 1867 Brett had become the sole proprietor and managing editor of the serial publishing side of the Newsagents' Publishing Company (NPC), accused by a journalist of being 'the foremost of the gang whose profit is the dissemination of impure literature'. This firm rapidly inherited the dubious mantle of Lloyd's Salisbury Square publishing house, initiating, according to another hostile critic, an 'era of the greatest general depravity, as well as literary wretchedness, in the history of periodical fiction'. The News Agents' Newspaper and Publishing Company was registered and incorporated as a limited company on 10 April 1862 for the purchase, sale and

publication of newspapers, pamphlets, journals, magazines, serials and periodicals. A nominal investment capital of £5000 was divided into £1
shares, but by 1865 less than a tenth of the stock had been taken up by sub-
scribers, of whom the majority were London newsagents. The NPC's registered office was at 147 Fleet Street, next to the well-known Cheshire
Cheese tavern, and newsagent A. W. Huggett was officially identified as
both secretary and manager. In this exalted capacity, he probably acted as
a wholesale agent rather than a supplier of cheap fiction for, according to
The Bookseller, a reliable source, 'the novels themselves are usually the
property of speculative printers or inferior engravers.' This may explain
why Brett, himself a mediocre engraver, only appears in the official returns
as a small £3 shareholder. If he held the rights to several NPC instalment
novels, he would have had a much more substantial interest in the business.
Although not struck off the Companies Register until 1882, it can safely be
assumed that the NPC had ceased active trading by 1870, when they failed
to submit a stockholding return.[33]

The NPC may have acted as a wholesale newsagent, but its chief claim
to ignominy among moralizing Victorians was that it churned out at least
three dozen penny-weekly novels, such as *The Boy Detective, or the Crimes
of London* (1865–6?); *The Dance of Death; or, the Hangman's Plot* (1865–6);
and *The Skeleton Horseman; or, the Shadow of Death* (1866). The anonymous
or pseudonymous writers 'principally engaged in the production of this
literary garbage', *The Bookseller* informed its readers, were Vane Ireton
St John, Samuel Bracebridge Hemyng, J. R. Ware, Charles Stevens,
W. Thompson Townsend and John Cecil Stagg. Serial publication, more
than any other form of mass publication, enabled a publisher to forecast
sales with some assurance. A successful serial attracted readers by its title,
eye-catching front-page engravings and general reputation, until buying
and reading it became a matter of habit, often formalized in a regular
order to the local newsagent. The sale of one number was also a more
certain guide to the print run for the next issue than the sale of one edition
of a book was to the sale of the next. In London, NPC serials sold like
wildfire to children, teens and some adults, from small newsagents and
stationers, tobacconists, lollipop and toy-shops, sweetstuff vendors and
small chandler's shops in the courts and alleys of Westminster, Lambeth,
Bethnal Green, Shoreditch, Stepney, Shadwell and Rotherhithe, also
passing 'through the hands of countless juvenile readers from the regions
of Bermondsey and Whitechapel, to Bell-street and the Edgware-road'.
The most popular NPC instalment titles sold 30,000 or more weekly
copies, eventually reaching retail outlets in the poorest areas of Manches-

ter, Birmingham and other manufacturing towns, or were lent out in volume form for twopence a week from circulating libraries carried on at the same premises.[34]

The NPC's healthy profits, according to one account, helped Brett launch *Boys of England* (1866–99), his most successful and long-running boys' weekly. Another source claims that Brett, low in funds, had to ask some publishers' agents to advance him several hundred pounds in order to float the new boys' paper. Firm evidence does not survive, for it was not Brett's custom to keep account books, being satisfied so long as he found a good balance in the bank at the end of the year. The actual profit margins of 'penny dreadful' publishing must remain speculative at best, but a tentative attempt to calculate the NPC's production costs can be made using surviving fragments of information. These calculations refer to accounting costs rather than economic costs, or paper, printing and writing payments considered as recorded costs only. A more rigorous cost analysis, identifying opportunity costs and external effects, for example, requires much better documented company records. None the less, we do know that machine-made paper was fast reducing the costs of printing and a strong North African grass, esparto, had been introduced as a cheap substitute for rags in British paper-making. Thus the average cost for a ream of paper with a maximum of 500 sheets, which in the 1840s was 24 shillings taxed, had been reduced with the repeal of paper duty by more than half to about ten shillings.[35]

Several sources repeat that an NPC author was paid, at the most generous, 50 shillings per number, which cost another 50 shillings to set up in type and was printed for five shillings per 1000, while the wholesale price to the retail trade was another 50 shillings per 1000. These rounded cost figures have a certain suspicious symmetry. In 1868 *The Bookseller* claimed, with probably more accuracy, that copies of NPC serials were sold wholesale at the rate of sixpence or sixpence halfpenny for a dozen of 13 copies – a more generous trade discount of from 38 to 41 shillings per 1000.[36] One week's unsold copies were exchanged on a sale or return basis for a similar number of the current issue, making serial 'dreadfuls' quite an attractive proposition to the newsagent. On a rough estimate, at a maximum print run for a single title of 30,000 weekly copies, requiring one folded sheet each, the NPC would pay about £30 sterling for 60 reams of paper, plus £12 and 10 shillings for author and printer costs. This means that, on the more likely estimate of wholesale prices, each NPC title would have to sell more than two-thirds of its maximum print run to retailers, principally in London, if Brett were to clear his initial capital outlay. Reprint costs were cheaper and more profitable, of course, saving on both author and typographic expenses. The NPC did not divulge its circulation figures but, if the maximum print run for a single title were sold to the retail trade, the firm would net about £ 60 per title per week, excluding running costs and stock dividends.[37] The NPC appears to have been raided and closed by the police around 1870, by which time it was only issuing reprints of popular titles. Edwin Brett had already moved on, transferring to 173 Fleet Street and giving his publishing business a new name: the 'Boys of England Office'.

Low-life London Dreadfuls of the 1860s

Poorly paid Grub Street hacks writing for the growing juvenile audience rarely originated their own literary forms; most of their stories were adapted from an earlier generation of adult 'penny bloods'. One noteworthy exception was a commercial variation on the Tom Brown or English boarding-school story, pioneered in 1867 by George Emmett's serial 'Boys of Bircham School' in *The Young Englishman's Journal* and characterized by jocular violence, xenophobia and crude horseplay. The present author has written elsewhere about the 'penny dreadful' antecedents of Charles ('Frank Richards') Hamilton's Greyfriars and St Jim's stories, their creators and the contemporary 'panic' such irreverent school stories incited among clergymen and head teachers. Here our immediate focus will instead be on how a formula pioneered by Pierce Egan's *Life in London* (1820–1), with its colourful accounts of Corinthian Tom, Bob Logic and Jerry Hawthorn's peregrinations among the capital's sporting low life, was adapted, via the exciting melodramas of Sue and Reynolds, for instalment-novel 'dreadfuls'. Penny-a-line authors had learnt that macabre and exciting fare could be cast just as successfully in contemporary as in historical dress, thus providing an accessible version of Gothic for the young working class.[38]

'There were in London and the large manufacturing towns of England hundreds of boys out of whom constant drudgery and bad living had ground all that spirit of dare-devilism so essential to the enjoyment of the heroes of the [Dick] Turpin type, but who still possessed an appetite for vices of a sort that were milder and more easy of digestion', claimed James Greenwood, attempting in 1873 to explain the appeal of a certain class of 'dreadfuls' among young males:

It was a task of no great difficulty when once the happy idea was conceived. All that was necessary was to show that the faculty for successfully defying law and order and the ordinations of virtue might be
cultivated by boys as well as men, and that as rogues and rascals the same
brilliant rewards attended the former as the latter. The result may be seen
in the shop window of every cheap newsvendor in London – 'The Boy
Thieves of London', 'The Life of a Fast Boy', 'The Boy Bandits', 'The
Wild Boys of London', 'The Boy Detective', 'Charley Wag', 'The Lively
Adventures of a Young Rascal', and I can't say how many more.

Greenwood estimated that 'upwards of a million of these weekly pen'orths
of abomination find customers' and was certain that more respectable
youths were among them. Ironically, despite inveighing against the NPC's
'penny packets of . . . poison', Greenwood had agreed to provide serialized
stories for Brett's *Boys of England* in 1868, presumably unaware of its
editor's shady past.[39]

Other contemporary observers noted the heightened sense of melodrama which pervaded low-life fiction, while the speed with which the
material was written, produced and presented, seemed entirely appropriate to the bustle of urban streets. Authors of London low-life tales and
mysteries suffused the commonplace with dramatic encounters, conveying extremes of emotion and fortune through concrete detail of daily life.
They often worked through a 'rope' plot which moved forward parallel
strands of stories which are secretly being wound together, usually through
the agency of coincidence. Such serials were generally faithful to a recognizable urban landscape, despite their increasing absurdity of incident,
gruesome details and sentimentality, making them almost an exemplar of
Victorian stage and literary melodrama. Low-life 'dreadfuls' also contained anachronisms, frequently depended upon attenuated one-sentence
paragraphs to meet their requisite column inches, and rarely reached beyond melodrama for their literary effects. 'The main reliance of the publishers now is on unnatural and violent incidents thickly crowded and
developed by dialogue that runs on with a rattle like the stick of a London
boy drawn along a row of area-railings', it was claimed of middlebrow 'sensation fiction' in 1867, in a marvellous characterization equally appropriate for low-life 'dreadfuls'.[40]

Probably the most notorious of all nineteenth-century popular narratives was Eugène Sue's *Les Mystères de Paris* (1842–3). Its hero – Rodolphe,
Prince of Gerolstein – fights a private war against crime, is superhumanly
clever, rich and powerful, and secretly manipulates the other characters.

The flood of English serial publications which took the city low-life theme and adapted it extensively for a largely juvenile audience were chiefly inspired by the extraordinary success of an anglicized version of Sue's exciting *feuilleton* bestseller. G. W. M. Reynolds' long-running serial *The Mysteries of London* (1845–50), the most successful penny-issue work of its time, was written in a commercial style that juxtaposed the radical with the thrilling and was soon selling nearly 40,000 weekly copies. This was followed, after the author's acrimonious break with publishers George Stiff and George Vickers, who continued the third series with other writers, by Reynolds' even lengthier *The Mysteries of the Court of London* (1848–56). Through these melodramatic serials, Reynolds was to become arguably the most widely-read English author of the nineteenth century for, unlike many radicals and socialists who came after him, he was not hostile to the 'vulgarity' and Manichean dramas of popular culture. Reynolds updated the Gothic novel by casting it in modern dress and setting it with great precision in familiar, present-day London locales that highlighted his shock effects, unveiling lurid criminal conspiracies which took place just behind the scenes. The creation of a good and a bad brother, Richard and Eugene Markham, and a professional criminal, the Resurrection Man, around whom a huge assembly of characters from different social backgrounds converged, gave some coherence to the first series of *The Mysteries of London*. 'Into the central plot Reynolds keyed thinly disguised historical facts, statistics, Mayhew-like surveys and biographies, and editorial comment on social conditions. [*The Mysteries*] exchanged city houses for gothic castles, slum cellars for dungeons, and financial extortioners for the evil count or monk', writes Louis James. 'Romance was becoming politicized'.[41]

For reasons of reader-identity, boys were themselves made the central characters of the new generation of urban thrillers. The anonymous authors of the NPC's London stories hence placed youthful heroes in highly dramatic and often incongruous situations which took place among sordid and criminal milieux in the lower reaches of London society. Hence, *The Wild Boys of London*, whose notoriety exceeded that of any other NPC 'dreadful', depicts in serialized form, and with some grasp of urban vernacular, the often violent and lurid adventures of a gang of street urchins who run the gamut of delinquencies from piracy to lynching. The first edition in the mid-1860s was published in 103 weekly parts of eight double-columned pages each, making a combined total of about 800,000 words, or ten times the length of the average modern thriller. The interest for young working-class readers, such as errand boys and street sellers, was considerable because *The Wild Boys* effectively glamorized their existence ('the adventures of our hero are only such as they themselves may know') yet promised to 'satisfy the keenest appetite of those who love sensation' without resort to 'sanguinary improbability'. The hero, Dick Lane, is the son of a previously sober and industrious Lambeth bricklayer who has taken to drink after being led astray when his union calls an unnecessary strike, and his *alter ego,* Arthur Grattan, has been brought up by a poor schoolmaster but is, in reality, the kidnapped son of Lord Wintermerle. Befriended by the Wild Boys, Dick is better educated than his companions and only driven by circumstances, 'the effect of strikes and drinking', to make a living on the streets.[42]

The street-arab gang of the title hatch their mischief 'round a fire in their haunt beneath the sewers of London', somewhere near London Bridge pier, from whence they fight off ruffians, salvage corpses, and traffic in stolen goods. Above ground, they come to grips with thieves, murderers, kidnappers, incompetent policemen and grave-robbers, not to mention child-stealers. '"Twelve years ago"', says the wicked heir to a vast fortune, '"you, at my instigation, stole a child, the son of Lord Wintermerle. You were instructed to proceed to London, and place the infant in the hands of those who would rear him in obscurity, and never let him know the secret of his birth".' The speaker, invoking hyperbole, '"would deluge the world with blood if necessary"' to keep his property and title. Nemesis approaches in the unlikely guise of an avenging gang of fashionable young men called the Night Avengers of the Iron League: 'That such leagues are in existence is no fiction. . . . the Freemasons and their brotherhoods are proof of this.' Scattered throughout the serial is the odd Reynolds-like radical sentiment:

> Wandering through the busy streets, Dick could not help thinking it strange that in the midst of a city where there seemed plenty for all and to spare, there should be people dying of absolute starvation. He had yet to learn that those who have most wealth give least of help. He had not lived long enough to know that the poor have no friends save those they find among their own class.

Yet this penny serial's ringing denunciations, imputing wickedness to those of high degree, jostle uneasily alongside random abuse of trade unionism ('a crew of interested idle harpies who fattened on the artizan's starvation'), caricatures of Irish Fenianism, and a general anti-semitism. Together with a melodramatic approach to violent crime, this *mélange* permeates the uneven picaresque narrative.[43]

The front page illustrated engravings for each issue of *The Wild Boys* acted as an evident allure. Harry Maguire's rather stilted drawings featured selected Wild Boys swinging mischievously on a Chinaman's pigtails; battering an old Jewish fence whom they have suspended upside down on a rope; and voyeuristically watching a girl ('Hearthstone Ned witnesses the Punishment of Mildred'), naked to the waist, being flogged by her uncle. That ingredients of sex and violence have always been a commonplace in popular culture, no less in prudish mid-Victorian England, is evident from passages such as the following: 'On the first landing lay the body of the servant-girl in her night-dress. She was nearly naked in fact, for her scanty covering had been torn off in the struggle for life. A knife was sticking up to the hilt between her breasts, and her body was lying in a pool of gore.' The blood-and-thunder excesses of popular staged melodrama, prominent in East End theatres, are also apparent in places: 'Then he staggered out, shrieking loud in desperate horror, with his hand upon his forehead, and his eyes starting from their sockets. "Blood!" he whispered, hoarsely; "red, red, red hot blood, dropping from the ceiling, trickling down the wall. Blood on the floor, on my forehead – everywhere, all blood. Help! help! There has been murder done! Help! help! Oh! horror!".' These garish excerpts taken out of context are untypical because the plot mechanics necessary to arrive at an exciting stage in the narrative, and the requisite 8000 words per issue, led to frequent padding with over-indulgent, formula intrigues whose relevance is often uncertain. 'At times', wittily reported E. S. Turner, 'the scene shifted to a mutinous convict ship, or to the Australian bush, but sooner or later the writer would return, nostalgically, to the sewers of London.' An NPC sequel soon appeared, set in the heart of Eugène Sue territory, replete with murders in nearly every weekly issue, and alluringly titled *The Wild Boys of Paris or, The Mysteries of the Vaults of Death* (1866). 'French waiters always knock; and not only knock, but wait to enter until summoned', the anonymous author informed readers gratuitously. 'English waiters do not always employ such discretion'.[44]

What offended pious adults most about London low-life 'dreadfuls' was the precocious independence and potency of their boy heroes, together with their implicit challenge to the generational *status quo*. 'Middle-class Victorians found in these adolescent rebels an uncomfortable contradiction to their romantic and nostalgic images of childhood purity and innocence, inseparable from a state of weakness and dependence', writes Marjory Lang, a specialist on mid-Victorian children's periodicals. 'Literature exalting the cheeky, capable juvenile hero they felt to be especially dangerous to their own well-protected children.' Hence the notoriety attracted by a best-selling serial with a notable subtitle, *Charley Wag: The New Jack Sheppard* (1860–1), the sixth number of which featured a provocative cover engraving by Robert Prowse. This shows a grinning Charley fleeing confidently down the Strand in London with a stolen goose and two bottles of rum, hotly pursued by a policeman brandishing a truncheon, and urged on by a smiling crowd. A dog scampering alongside Charley is also in possession of a stolen goose, while a notice on a nearby wall offers £500 for the boy burglar's capture. Charley Wag perhaps represents a reassertion of the trickster figure from the festive, oral tradition setting out to mock the restraining disciplines of an urban-industrial culture. More prosaically, commentators in contemporary literary reviews profoundly feared the seditious effect which the representation of homeless boys 'cocking a snook' at authority might have upon impressionable, young working-class readers.[45]

Charley Wag, an unwanted child, is early on flung into the Thames by his mother, then fortuitously rescued by an old eccentric, Mr Toddleboy, 'who spent his life in a fog of gin and tobacco.' There are parallels here with the opening chapters of Harrison Ainsworth's *Jack Sheppard* (1839), referred to in Chapter 1 as a literary source for numerous stage plays. Charley is offered to the workhouse by his saviour but, on rejection, left on the doorstep of an elderly, religious spinster, Miss Pamela Andrews, of Montpelier Square; a comic figure anticipating Miss Clack in Wilkie Collins' *The Moonstone* (1868) who was also given to religious bigotry and the distribution of tracts. When Mr Toddleboy first names the foundling, hoping he will prove a popular character, a so-called 'printer's note' cannot resist adding that, 'if a sale of 40,000 of Number 1 of his adventures proves his popularity, he is so'. Sales figures on this scale would have pleased even Reynolds in his heyday. Charley Wag grows up into a high-spirited and uncontrollable young man, 'pugnacious, great at punching heads and bunging up eyes', a cigar-smoker at 13 and a 'regular rascal' where a pretty girl is concerned. One of these, Lucinda, he rescues from the debauchery of the Duke of Heatherland, premier of England, 'who is always scheming to oppress and grind down the already over-oppressed and ground down working classes'. From small-scale burglaries, Charley works his way up to become the most successful thief in London, breaking into the Bank of England and, after numerous plot twists, being wrongfully arrested for murder. *Charley Wag* can be placed firmly within the narrative structure of Reynolds' *Mysteries of London*; its facetious comic passages, on the other hand, owe a common mid-Victorian debt to an omnipresent Charles Dickens.[46]

Cheap serials of metropolitan low life such as *Charley Wag* clearly repay consideration, dealing as they do so vividly with 'the other half' or residuum of London's East End poor explored by contemporary journalists such as Henry Mayhew, George Godwin and James Greenwood. The melodramatic plots of these 'dreadfuls' were often interspersed with descriptive passages which, bearing in mind their exaggerated effects or broad comedy, can sometimes provide useful information about the life and leisure of mid-Victorian London's street people. Thus a whole range of sub-Dickensian characters who make their living on the streets are introduced in one unusually well-written 'dreadful', *The Poor Boys of London, or Driven to Crime: A Life Story for the People* (*c*.1866), brought out in only 12 parts by the Temple Publishing Company, in all probability managed by Edwin Brett's ex-partner, William Laurence Emmett. The unknown author reveals an intimate acquaintance with cockney slang, excelling that of many a contemporary novelist: ' "Met Ikey Belsea, the sheeny and tossed him for browns, and he got the whole blessed lot. I got a tanner out on him, though, and went to the gaff".' [Met Ikey Belsea, the Jew, and tossed up for halfpennies with him, and he won them all. I borrowed sixpence from him, though, and went to the penny theatre]. Among the urban flotsam encountered by the hero are Whitechapel Dick, a cheap Jack (travelling hawker), who gathers a large crowd by selling 'wonder cures' or patent medicines and Shakespeare Dick, or Richard the Third, who gains 'a precarious livelihood by reciting stirring passages from the immortal bard's works, which he mixes up according to his fancy. Shakespeare Dick was never without a wooden sword which he flourished about during every performance – ' "A 'orse, a 'orse; my kingdom for a 'orse".'[47]

A drunken labourer encountered by the Poor Boys in a public house orders a pint of dog's nose, a mixture of gin and beer; 'in a word he was the kind of man who could drink lots of beer and sing "Rule Britannia!" at a free-and-easy, and go comfortably home with a black eye'. A red-bearded police detective, Richard Grant, who employs shoeblack boys as 'watchers', is an interesting creation, perhaps modelled on Dickens' Inspector Bucket. Yet the Bosker, an articulate burglar, with accompanying bandy-legged bulldog, is riled by the patrician sarcasm of the chief villain, Eastlake, to repudiate stage and Dickensian parallels:

'Bah', said the Bosker, smiling in scorn, 'that style of prate is stale. The aristocratic villain, always cool, refined, and devilish, is out of date; he belongs to tradition and the stage – so does the Bill Sykes type of my class. You affect to treat me as a barbarian brute – a mere thing to be hired and paid'.

'Indeed, we grow interested – this is an age of progress – we hear an eloquent burglar', Eastlake replied with a sneer.

The 'aristocratic villain' was to survive as a cultural archetype, despite this disclaimer, for many years to come. The author of *The Poor Boys* could not conceal ultimate reliance upon the hackneyed plot device of the lost orphan, heir to a fortune, fallen among young street thieves and beggars, while in the background a mysterious stranger plots his downfall. Francis Hitchman, a Victorian literary critic notably harsh towards the 'penny dreadful', none the less believed that this was a 'tale of slightly loftier pretensions [than other 'dreadfuls'], in the course of which the author displays his acquaintance with casual wards, thieves' kitchens, and criminal resorts generally, and uses such descriptive and dramatic powers as he possesses to extenuate the offences of the "poor boys" who, in his own phrase, are "driven to crime".'[48]

Verisimilitude within an imaginary framework was not only a badge of the low-life serial, for a convincing portrayal of London life had also become one of the dominant themes in Victorian stage dramas performed concurrently in the 1860s. On the stage London represented a 'city of dreadful night' in which the village *ingénue,* male or female, becomes caught up in a vicious circle of urban poverty, sexual depravity, drink or gambling. Hence the popularity of melodramatic 'low-life' plays like Dion Boucicault's *The Streets of London* (1864) and Watts Phillips' *Lost in London* (1867). Neither before nor since, argues theatre historian Michael Booth, has the great metropolis exercised such a hold on the imaginations and dreams of English theatre audiences. Crowd scenes and large expensive sets with adjustable moving scenery were commonplace. Paying customers for stage melodramas set in contemporary London, whatever their gender, age or class, expected to see a life-like and detailed picture of the city in which they lived, faithfully recreated before their eyes. Low-life London 'penny dreadfuls', in this respect, both reflected and reinforced current cultural trends.[49]

These penny serials can also tell us something about the sordid subculture of crime and violence in mid-Victorian London, depicting contemporary character types and occupations in some detail, as well as the seedy gaiety of the city's pleasure haunts, such as Cremorne Gardens, the Haymarket and Highbury Barn. A heavy-handed NPC tale of preordained moral retribution of more adult appeal, *The Jolly Dogs of London or, The Two Roads of Life* (*c.*1866), opens with three drunken young scoundrels singing 'Slap! Bang! Here We Are Again, What Jolly, Jolly Dogs Are We!' – tracked down as the popular refrain from *lion comique* Arthur Lloyd's contemporaneous music-hall song. As is so often the case, the prologue strikes a highly moralistic tone:

> The intent and purpose of the present bold, thrilling, and sensational romance is pure. The object is to contrast the meanness and wretchedness of criminal life, the madness and misery of 'fast' life, and particularly the folly, vulgarity, and profligacy of 'Jolly Doggism', with the peace, happiness and comfort of honesty and steadiness. The chief incidents are really true, though strung together in the form of an intensely exciting work of fiction.

This bears little relation to the actual contents, for the anonymous author misses no opportunity to revel in fleshly metropolitan pursuits. *The Jolly Dogs* follows a conventional melodramatic narrative which tells how escaped criminal Richard Renshaw returns to haunt and blackmail his former companions in crime. '"No more of the past; not a word, Renshaw! You shall not torture me by these dark allusions to the wretched past! I am shaken in nerve, enfeebled in brain, heart-broken. I am whirled on and on to a gulf, down which I must plunge inevitably!"', cries one histrionic victim unavailingly. Murder follows at the illuminated Cremorne 'Pleasure' Gardens in Chelsea, a notorious mid-Victorian haunt of prostitutes and free-spending swells.[50]

Some links can be made between the values and behavioural norms represented in this mass commodity fiction and the forms of contemporary historical experience. Most of the serials examined above exemplify the eventual triumph not of working-class but of bourgeois or petit-bourgeois values. Good breeding, bourgeois individualism, and property ownership are seen to bring rewards, whereas the communal sharing of *The Wild Boys of London* leads only to imprisonment or a life of crime. London low-life fiction worked within the parameters of a melodramatic discourse which functioned primarily through middle-class ideological constraints. The principals of cheap fiction were usually 'respectable' young men or women denied their rightful patrimony through the machinations of sinister upper-class figures, while the device of placing a patrician hero or heroine unrecognized in an ordinary working-class family made it easier for the average reader to fantasize their own unmerited disinheritance. Circumstances may change abruptly for the central figures, but their polite upbringing ensures that they will remain at a permanent distance from the proletarian milieux in which they unexpectedly find themselves. Thus *Poor Jack, the London Street Boy* (*c*.1866), discovering he has been adopted, leaves home to find his genuine parents and embarks on an exemplary self-improving career as a crossing-sweeper. '"There has been many a bright man raised from the gutter, and if I should be one of the fortunate boys who become great I shall have no one to thank but myself"', he congratulates himself in advance of his metamorphosis.[51]

Samuel Smiles-style self-help virtues are also positively endorsed in George Emmett's self-explanatory *Charity Joe: or, From Street Boy to Lord Mayor* (*c*.1875), as well as in John Bennett's *The Life and Career of a London Errand Boy* (*c*.1865), in which the poor but honest hero is sent to work for a venal firm of rag merchants in Smithfield before reaching a more elevated position in society. The readers of cheap fiction were thus inducted into a negotiated version of bourgeois values which, over time, helped to assure their consent to the prevailing social order. English low-life serials may have reflected 'mechanic accents', with roots in a genuine urban dialect, but they offered little real challenge to dominant middle-class norms. Significantly, the central characters in low-life serials were invariably compelled only by the vagaries of melodramatic plotting, rather than through choice or class position, to associate themselves with colourful characters in the lower and criminal reaches of London society. Perhaps this mirrored the careers of their downwardly mobile creators, who all too often finished up in cheap lodgings dying of excessive alcohol consumption. Such popular fiction can, however, be deconstructed to illuminate the 'shock of actuality' – recognizable scenes and characters in contemporary guise – as opposed to the less plausible Gothic or historical-romance serials which converted another time and place into accustomed melodrama.[52]

Women-in-Peril Dreadfuls

The NPC and other cheap publishers also sought to appeal to Victorian factory girls, shop assistants, milliners and domestic servants through the seemingly inexhaustible appeal of the literature of aristocratic seduction, arguably a metaphor for the exploitation of the poor by the upper classes. '"No, no! a long and glorious career of profligacy and dissipation is still in store for me!"' Count Lerno reassures himself, following a threat to his reputation, in the London Romance Company's *Rose Mortimer, or, The Ballet-Girl's Revenge* (*c*.1865). This was judged by one literary trade paper 'a sensational tale of love and intrigue, illustrated with suggestive woodcuts, representing the abduction of the heroine at the stage-door of the theatre, and similarly exciting subjects'. Hence, after Rose's successful performance as the Queen of Beauty in a Boxing Day pantomime, the Count carries her resisting, and still in ballet costume, to his carriage. The kidnapped girl is taken to a large house in that part of London's Fulham, lying west of Walham Green, supposedly known as 'Dead Man's Land'. Lerno confesses that he is master of the house and seeks to make Rose its mistress. "Count Lerno", said Rose drawing herself up to her full height – "Count Lerno, sooner than agree to your degrading proposals I would kill myself".'[53]

The wicked and lecherous aristocratic villain such as Count Lerno was a stereotype from early-Victorian 'penny bloods' resuscitated in the 1860s by the authors of women-in-peril stories. '"Tut," was the cruel answer',of Lord Dundreary in *The Work Girls of London, Their Trials and Temptations* (1865), '"do you think I have nothing to do but to marry every girl who wishes to father a child on me? I tell you all I will do for you is to give you some money, but I never want to see you again: as for the brat, never let me hear of it!"' The opening chapters of *The Young Ladies of London; or, The Mysteries of Midnight* (1867–8) introduce the sinister Count Lewiski, man about town, who entraps rich gentlemen visitors to the wicked metropolis, using as bait the beautiful Emma Langton, his mistress, once a happy farmer's daughter. This titillating NPC serial's frontispiece depicted the Haymarket district of central London, notorious for its prostitution. Once near Petticoat Lane, Lewiski is transformed into Edward Lewis, 'the keeper of several lodging-houses and brothels in the east-end of London; a shrewd fellow, who had amassed a considerable sum of money by his dishonest and filthy calling'. Great play is made with the vulnerability of exploited seamstresses in the area as a means of sketching in local colour: poor, pale, weak girls with half a dozen shirts to finish, paid only ninepence for 18 hours of toil to support children or a dying mother. By the late 1860s victimized East End seamstresses had become part of a sentimental and safe iconology, their usage evident since the radical journalism of the 1830s. The real conditions of East London's huge casualized labour force, characterized by low wages, irregular employment and foreign immigration, are never directly confronted in penny fiction. Any radical sentiment is both subordinated to and subverted by the melodramatic plot. In *The Young Ladies of London*, the Count employs one Ghastly Gaskill to drug then kidnap unsuspecting girls who are then put to work in his Haymarket seraglio – '"another poor wretch doomed to fall a victim to your accursed toils"'cries Emma unavailingly.[54]

The over-heated and hyperbolic opening chapters of *The Outsiders of Society; or, The Wild Beauties of London* (c.1863) are devoted to the unscrupulous and licentious Lord Vineyard – 'a proud name in "Burke's Peerage" sounded well in the eyes of the world; but if people only knew the infamy attached to it!' He adopts the tragically orphaned, 'well-proportioned' Lydia Wilson and lavishes money upon her in order to satisfy his evil designs, leading the ruined girl to attempt suicide by throwing herself off Westminster Bridge. In Harry Hazleton's *Fanny White and Her Friend Jack Rawlings: A Romance of a Young Lady Thief and a Boy Burglar* (*c.*1865), published by George Vickers, great play is made with the attempted seduction of the sedated heroine, Fanny White, a music-hall dancer, by an old Palmerston-like roué, Lord Crokerton, in yet another isolated house at Fulham. Miss Fanny is 'a spanking, bouncing young wench – beautiful enough, in all conscience, to excite the desires of the most cold-blooded' yet also, 'as strong as a young bull. Voluptuous, graceful, pliant, and muscular. She could love and languish; but, when her blood was up, she could scratch and bite.' Thus the redoubtable yet erotic heroine, recovering from the effects of a drug, makes short work of the 'horrible old rascal' who had set out to seduce her. 'Then, as he strove once more to seize her, she doubled up that pretty fist of hers . . . and dealt my Lord Crokerton such a terrific right-hander on the nose, that it spread him out flat upon the floor, where he lay, bleeding and gasping, a sight pitiful to behold.'[55]

Women-in-peril and low-life stories appear to have inherited an earlier London-based radical–populist demonology, once again exemplified by G. W. M. Reynolds, which cast titled landlords living off their rents and property, rather than the new entrepreneurial middle-class, as the chief exploiters of the labouring poor. 'Given the current emphasis on the continuing importance of the aristocracy throughout the nineteenth century, Reynolds should perhaps be reclaimed as someone who was trying to define the real nature of the Victorian state', suggests Rohan McWilliam. Equally, in 'penny dreadfuls', it was usually the rich aristocrat, hardly ever the grasping capitalist, who set out to assail the virtue of the modest heroine, 'as though temptation and immorality were only to be found in wealthy neighbourhoods and lewd thoughts were the special and particular property of noblemen and "swells", with rent rolls of ten thousand a year', commented *The Bookseller* astutely in 1867. Assumptions like this were, of course, as much part of the ideological baggage of the thrusting, upwardly mobile, middle-class businessman, with his Manchester-bred intolerance for aristocratic privilege and unearned wealth, as of the downwardly mobile penny novelist. The popular literature of seduction evaded the reality of sexual assault within the working class in Victorian times, as measured by the possibly irrelevant standards of historical accuracy, for

very few unmarried mothers or victims of rape fell prey to genuine aristocratic villains. Perhaps the theft of poor men's daughters by profligate aris-
tocrats symbolized the betrayal of the working class by their elite rulers,
investing the public rhetoric of class struggle with personal and emotive
images of women's sexual oppression. This kind of writing also contributed to a wider rhetoric of the poor as weak and passive victims who
needed to be protected by kindly middle-class paternalists.[56]

Closing Remarks

'Penny dreadfuls' aimed primarily at juveniles did not reflect or create a
dissentient working-class culture, despite Reynolds' earlier success at com-
bining melodrama with social criticism; at most they were read in unwit-
ting rebellion against middle-class moralizing and polite standards of taste.
To suggest that, because sections of the sprawling and inconsistent *Wild
Boys of London* deal with explicitly *political* themes of slavery and Fenianism, the police were incited to smash its printing plates on the excuse of
preventing 'corruption of the young' by indecent literature (see Chapter 3),
tends to idealize youthful reading of these serials as, in part, an 'act of col-
lective resistance' matched by their content. In the final analysis,
'dreadfuls' and 'bloods' were a form of popular entertainment written *for*
rather than created *by* or emerging (directly) out *of* the people. Little real
attempt was made by their bohemian *déclassé* authors to explore the realities of working-class life and culture before the rapid descent into a stylized
and exaggerated fiction that employed all the stereotyped characters and
heightened effects familiar to the audiences of London's East End theatres.
On the other hand, penny-part fiction was not simply a means of disseminating ruling-class propaganda amongst subordinate classes. The need to
put stories into a melodramatic form which potential readers recognized
and enjoyed, emphasizing the predominance of plot and action over characterization, had an effect on any message which it was intended to trans-
mit. Otherwise such writing would not have become so popular.[57]

   With roots in a real vernacular, some aspects of the people's culture are
preserved in the 'penny dreadfuls' of the 1860s, yet they offer little real
challenge to middle-class norms. Hence the most common feature of cheap
serial fiction is the eventual triumph of a bourgeois or petit-bourgeois victim over an aristocratic villain and the assumption of his or her rightful
inheritance. There is no real challenge to the political or social order in

low-life 'dreadfuls', notwithstanding their commercial derivation from
the popular works of republican authors such as Reynolds and Sue. Far
from recommending the values of a criminal or oppositional subculture,
'dreadfuls', as Wilkie Collins wrote of the serials found in penny journals,
managed somehow to combine 'fierce melodrama and meek domestic sentiment.' Current work on narrative theory tells us, apparently, that the
manner ('fierce melodrama') of the telling is not just a stylistic addition, but
can work to modify a story's apparent values. Otherwise, the subtext of
'dreadfuls', like that of seventeenth-century ballads and chapbooks, appears primarily conservative, steadfastly maintaining orthodox beliefs
through fidelity to the sentimental language of popular discourse. The author of the most popular highwaymen serial of all time, *Black Bess*, which is
reputed to have sold over two million copies through 30 years of constant
reissue, claimed in defence of his creation's moral probity that:

> in no place will vice be found commended and virtue sneered at; nor will
> any pandering to sensuality, suggestions of impure thoughts, or direct
> encouragement to crime be discovered; neither are there details of se-
> duction, bigamy, adultery, and domestic poisonings, such as are indis-
> pensable ingredients of our popular three-volume novels.[58]

3

'PENNY DREADFUL' PANIC (II): THEIR SCAPEGOATING FOR LATE-VICTORIAN JUVENILE CRIME

Some attention has been given by social historians to both crime and popular culture as independent variables in the past, but few attempts have been made to look at the interchanges between the two. Victorian middle-class moralists were less scrupulous and hence their attempts to link delinquency with the reading of cheap fiction. The most vociferous critics of new forms of entertainment for the young were recruited from the ranks of the expanding professional middle class and the intellectual clerisy rather than from the manufacturing or business middle class. 'Boys and girls reared in the cellars and garrets of large cities' were accused in 1865 by Harriet Martineau, political economist and champion of middle-class values, of reading a literature of 'animal passion and defiant lawlessness'. She went on, echoing a familiar complaint, 'lives of bad people, everything about banditii anywhere, love stories from any language, scenes of theatrical life, trials of celebrated malefactors, love, crime, madness, suicide, wherever to be got in print, are powerful in preparing the young for convict life.' If compulsory elementary education from the 1870s onwards did not lead working-class school-children towards the high ideal of self-improvement, comments Joseph Bristow, 'then it would appear to have abandoned them to the supposedly corrupting influence of penny fiction'.[1]

Did 'penny dreadfuls', by glamorizing criminals, make crime attractive to youthful audiences? Miss Martineau's thesis, shared by many in authority, that cheap fiction for working-class juveniles encouraged and even instigated delinquency, will be fully addressed in what follows. The questions an historian asks of a past age are, of course, determined by the analogous issues of his or her own present. 'Anyone who reads what is said . . . about the entertainment offered to the children of the towns, about the way Jack Sheppard and similar heroes bulked large in their lives whilst they did not know more respectable heroes, must hear the echoes of the modern discussions which were in the author's mind as he wrote', confessed crime historian J. J. Tobias in 1967. Uncovering a long history of adult censoriousness concerning young people's entertainment struck a familiar chord for Tobias alongside recent memories of the British campaign to ban 'horror comics' (see Chapter 5) and the perennial debate about violence on television. His pioneering work on crime and industrial society in the nineteenth century none the less exaggerates the impact of Victorian penny reading on the young, because of excessive reliance on parliamentary 'blue books', such as the hearings of the 1852 Select Committee on Criminal and Destitute Juveniles, which promote the standard middle-class 'panic' over aspects of popular culture.[2]

The main focus of this chapter will be on reports of English criminal trials, extending from local police courts to the Old Bailey, that inferred a connection between juvenile crime and the reading of 'penny dreadfuls'. Where possible, generalized scare stories of crimes supposedly caused by the reading of 'dreadfuls' have been traced to a specific court room source. Misrepresentation of the dangerous effects of such highly stylized and melodramatic fiction on the young suggests that Victorian reporters, magistrates, policemen and watch committees preferred to target a convenient cultural scapegoat for outbreaks of delinquency, rather than lend credence to more fundamental social and economic explanations. In any event, the peak period for press reporting of the harmful effects of the 'penny dreadful' on susceptible youth in the last quarter of the nineteenth century has been linked by modern crime historians to an unexpected statistical decline in juvenile larceny rates. Official and press reaction to cheap fiction, on the evidence presented here, tells us more about adult middle-class impressions of working-class youth culture than about the actual dimensions and causes of juvenile crime. Middle-class observers, with few exceptions, came to exaggerate or distort the nature of popular reading so as to nurture due chagrin at the disappointingly escapist fruits of a working-class literacy that they had themselves helped to nourish.[3]

Across the Atlantic, rising Irish and southern European immigration into America from the late-nineteenth century onwards meant an ever-expanding urban working population. In response to such new markets for entertaining reading, cheap popular books like the 'dime novel' were sold at newstands, station kiosks and on the trains themselves. Intended mainly for young adult readers, 'dimes' flourished between 1860 and 1885. They were also read by shopkeepers, local professionals, clerks, small farmers and their families but they were not part of a wide and inclusive middle-class culture. 'Dime novels' were part of the popular culture of the 'producing classes', argues Michael Denning, centering on admiration for the 'honest mechanic' and the virtuous 'working girl'. Smaller folio-sized 'half-dimes' or 'nickel weeklies', gaining in popularity in the 1880s, were deliberately aimed at a larger replacement market of adolescent boys and girls. 'The most ardent class of patron . . . are boys', said an 1879 observer describing 'the traffic on publication days'. The predominant audience for 'dimes' was found, therefore, among literate, mobile and entertainment-starved young adults, until the advent after 1880 of 'half-dime novels', story papers and libraries directed more explicitly at boys and girls living in the cities and mill towns of the north-east and west of America. Yet 'half-dimes' were not intended as children's literature because the bulk of story-paper readers were young craftworkers, factory operatives, labourers and servants, internally divided by gender, embracing German and Irish immigrants but excluding blacks and Chinese. Such reading matter was the commercial product of a growing industry employing as authors relatively educated professionals, such as journalists, teachers or clerks.[4]

Anthony Comstock (1844–1915), a name synonymous with American prudery, portrayed 'half-dimes' as 'corrupting the young, glamorising criminal behaviour', and as responsible for the 'fearful increase of youthful criminals in our cities in recent years'. A prodigious moral crusader, Comstock was secretary and chief special agent of the New York Society for the Suppression of Vice (NYSSV), bankrolled by the Young Men's Christian Association (YMCA) and multi-millionaire J. P. Morgan, in which capacity he campaigned until his death in 1915 to put 'dime novel' publishers out of business. Under the Federal Anti-Obscenity or 'Comstock' Law of 1873, the NYSSV lobbied strenuously to suppress cheap fiction, tightening restrictions on the second-class postage rate and arresting publishers sending 'pernicious literature' through the mails. Comstock kept records of all those he arrested, with details of occupation, aliases, nature of offence, inventory of stock seized, and subsequent prosecution. Several Irish newsstand dealers along New York's Broadway indicted by Comstock for selling 'stories of bloodshed and crime' were imprisoned until bail could be raised. While the career of a 'vice ideologue' such as Comstock cannot be taken as fully representative of late-nineteenth-century American culture, he was still part of a much larger reforming and temperance endeavour which obtained the support of both rural-puritan and urban-philanthropic groups. The NYSSV's major campaign against 'half-dime' novels centred on the western outlaw stories of the late 1870s and early 1880s, such as those featuring Jesse James (see Appendix II), converging with the Post-master-General's threat to remove the economic privilege of mailing un-der 'second-class matter' from publications not meeting with Comstock's approval. This assault on American freedoms met with surprisingly little unfavourable publicity, as compared to Comstock's more ludicrous cam-paigns against 'obscenity' in painting and statuary.[5]

The 'Penny Dreadful' as Scapegoat

In England there was a continuing debate about the effects of nine-teenth century criminal romances glamorizing Claude Duval, Dick Turpin, Jack Sheppard and other heroes of crime. Late-Victorian intellec-tuals, in particular, were highly critical of cheap forms of printed fiction intended primarily for the young which they categorized as 'sensational'. The process of establishing taste differentials in effect became a symbolic weapon in the struggle between classes and generations for ideological domination. Understanding how cultural hierarchies were established has as much of an application to 'penny dreadfuls' as to any other form of deni-grated popular entertainment. Thus construction of this derogatory label in the 1870s, to encompass English cheap printed instalment fiction and boys' weekly periodicals reaching a predominantly lower-middle and working-class audience, signified anxiety over juvenile reading among the ideologues of cultural standards writing for the newspaper and periodical press. 'Dreadfuls' were the ultimate in 'bad taste'.[6]

'When it is remembered that this foul and filthy trash circulates by thou-sands and tens of thousands week by week amongst lads who are at the most impressionable period of their lives', anguished literary critic Francis Hitchman in 1890, 'it is not suprising that the authorities have to lament the prevalence of juvenile crime'. Nominated as 'filthy trash' were such oft-reprinted Charles Fox titles of the late 1870s as *Spring-Heeled Jack, or the Ter-ror of London, Sweeney Todd, the Demon Barber of Fleet Street, Turnpike Dick, Three-Fingered Jack, the Terror of the Antilles, Jack Sheppard, Broad Arrow Jack* and *Captain Macheath, the Prince of the Highway*. A deep suspicion of mass fiction also long persisted among unbending Tory evangelicals, such as factory reformer the 7th Earl of Shaftesbury. In apocalyptic mood, he warned a meeting of the Pure Literature Society in 1868 that if 'pernicious' juvenile literature went on unchecked, within four or five years, 'they would see such a development of infidelity and profligacy, and of everything that was subversive of society and antagonistic to religion, as to terrify them to their hearts core'.[7]

'The police-court reports in the newspapers are alone sufficient proof of the harm done by the "penny dreadfuls"', according to an editorial in the first issue of *The Halfpenny Marvel*, a new boys' weekly started by Alfred Harmsworth in 1893 to undercut his rivals:

> It is almost a daily occurence with magistrates to have before them boys who, having read a number of 'dreadfuls', followed the examples set forth in such publications, robbed their employers, bought revolvers with the proceeds, and finished by running away from home, and installing themselves in the back streets as 'highwaymen'. This and many other evils the 'penny dreadful' is responsible for. It makes thieves of the coming generation, and so helps fill our gaols.

Harmsworth, later Lord Northcliffe, found it convenient to endorse the 'moral panic' scenario linking 'penny dreadfuls' with crime for sound commercial reasons, sanctimoniously offering a 'healthy' antidote to their 'poisonous' influence with his own, equally improbable, boys' weeklies.[8]

Cheap serialized fiction and weekly periodicals were accused of provoking the commission of juvenile crimes ranging from theft to murder. Such allegations will be tested here through close analysis of specific legal attempts to identify delinquent acts with the reading of 'penny dreadfuls'; thereby creating a 'moral panic' in the public mind linking popular culture with a complex phenomenon such as disaffected urban youth. Periodic 'moral panics' related to fear of the latter temporarily involved a much wider section of society than those active in censorship campaigns. A reductionist cause-and-effect argument that impressionable youth would necessarily imitate criminal acts dramatized on stage or fictionalized in weekly serials was commonplace in this period. In part this was a Platonist paradigm of art influencing life inherited from the eighteenth century, but it was also a Victorian middle-class 'panic' reaction to supposedly rising urban crime rates, coincident with a vast outpouring of cheap entertainment for the new proletariat. Working man Thomas Wright was more sceptical, pointing out that 'the admiration for things criminal of the boy-readers of the "dreadfuls" is abstract and theoretic, not practical and imitative'.[9]

Is it possible to ascertain the power of 'penny dreadfuls' either to entertain or corrupt? Focusing merely on the critical reaction to popular icons immortalized in print, such as Jack Sheppard and Spring-Heeled Jack, reveals much about Victorian middle-class attitudes towards youth, crime and popular entertainment, but little about the actual culture which inspired such moral disapproval. A content analysis of 'penny dreadfuls', on the other hand, in terms of their cultural conventions, symbolic codes and linguistic discourse, cannot alone prove or disprove sweeping claims that popular fiction had the power to corrupt innocent youth. Instead, what follows approaches how the label 'penny dreadful' was constructed from above by middle-class journalists, and came to be equated with juvenile delinquency, by drawing on the public reporting of selected criminal prosecutions. An urbanized and commercialized popular culture was on trial here as much as the youthful defendants.

The Campaign against Highwayman Dreadfuls

'Give me a highwayman and I was full to the brim; a Jacobite would do, but the highwayman was my favourite dish', recalled novelist Robert Louis Stevenson of his Edinburgh boyhood reading in the 1860s. 'I can still hear that merry clatter of the hoofs along the moonlit lane . . . and the words "post-chaise", the "great North road", "ostler", and "nag" still sound in my ears like poetry.' Yet in 1874 James Greenwood urged his fellow scribblers to use their pens lance-wise 'in assaulting and killing the hideous dragon that, in the shape of "Boy Highwaymen" and "Knights of the Road", of late years has been nestling with our boys, growing every day more daring and pestilential.' Highwaymen titles were singled out, in what was otherwise an all-embracing indictment of the 'penny dreadful', because they offered an heroic and romanticized image of criminals on horseback successfully defying ineffective Hanoverian law officers.[10]

'No doubt it appears, at first sight, the name was gained by highway robbery', ran a vindicatory advertisement for a new Hogarth House edition of *Tyburn Dick, the Boy King of the Highwaymen* (*c.*1878). 'This is quite a mistake, as the hero was a young nobleman, but, being in the way of his high-born mother's schemes, the unnatural parent used every means within her power to drive her handsome son to commit crime, and in this she was aided by the celebrated thief-taker Jonathan Wild.' The contents of *Tyburn Dick* were further extolled by this handbill, denying sordid criminal motives, as romantic adventures set in a vanished age. Certainly the anonymous author studiously avoids reference to the squalor, greed, blood and violence of real Newgate crime. Instead, the reader is offered conventional melodrama, or 'the life and exploits of an unfortunate but gallant young nobleman, who was hounded almost to the gallows by his unnatural relatives, and who, after many struggles, regained his position and estates, thus entirely defeating his enemies'. Romantic and chivalric, the stereotyped highwaymen in 'penny dreadfuls' represented no real threat to social hierarchy, for these heroic adventurers were typically idealized gentlemen, even noblemen. There is abundant evidence that highwaymen were indeed of a higher social and educational level than other eighteenth-century criminals, but parsons' sons and aspiring artisans featured more often than dispossessed noblemen.[11]

Popular highwaymen serials published by the Newsagents' Publishing Company (NPC) made several appearances in court as the specific instigators of juvenile crime. In May 1868, for example, a boy of 14 was charged before the Worship Street magistrate in Finsbury, north-east London, with the heinous crime of having stolen two sacks from his employers. The arresting officer, Inspector Fife, discovered on the prisoner, besides the stolen property, issues of Edwin Brett's long-running *Boys of England* and reprints of the NPC weekly instalment series *Tales of Highwaymen; or, Life on the Road* (1865–6), 'both referring to the achievements of notorious malefactors, which were invested with alluring colours of heroism and magnanimity'. The unfortunate accused was sent to prison for a fortnight on hard labour and Mr Ellison, the magistrate, recommended that steps be taken by the Inspector to prosecute the appropriate printer. 'It was greatly to be wished that something could be done to suppress such publications, which are quite as mischievous in their way as the particular kind of books contemplated by Lord Campbell's [Obscene Publications] Act are in theirs.'[12]

Rather than being a Newgate-Calendar-style compendium of sordid real-life criminal biographies, in actuality *Tales of Highwaymen* was entirely imaginary. It contained such far-fetched continuous stories as 'Captain Macheath, the Daring Highwayman and the Black Rider of Hounslow'; 'The Shadowless Rider; or, The League of the Cross of Blood. A Mystery of the King's Highway'; and 'Black Hugh; or, the Forty Thieves of London'. There is a strong reliance upon excessive Gothic elements, typical of the NPC 'dreadful' in the mid-1860s, rather than the fully realized iconography of the highwayman tale evident in publisher Edward

Harrison's best-selling *Black Bess; or, The Knight of the Road* (1863–8). This voluminous serial of 254 weekly parts featured the adventures and narrow escapes from Tyburn of Dick Turpin, Tom King, Claude Duval and Jack Rann (Sixteen-String Jack), readers not being satisfied with one highwayman, despite the fact that Turpin lived in the early-eighteenth century and Duval in the mid-seventeenth. *Tales of Highwaymen* looked back to the Lloyd-style 'penny bloods' of the 1840s, as well as forward to serials for the young such as Aldine's *Dick Turpin Library* (1902–9) which presented the highwayman as some kind of admirable and charismatic Robin Hood figure.[13]

'Captain Macheath' from *Tales of Highwaymen* is an innocuous historical melodrama that opens at a masquerade ball held in early-eighteenth-century London's Vauxhall Gardens. On the way to her carriage, Lady Ellen Wayne is almost robbed of her jewels by the devilish Black Rider of Hounslow, until interrupted by the 'daring' highwayman's convenient arrival, sword in hand. '"Captain Macheath", said the Black Rider, as, mad with pain and baffled in his purpose, he glared at his antagonist, "we are deadly foes from tonight; beware of me, and take care of her. The Black Rider never forgives".' The hack author was anxious to pad out his material with extraneous diversions, so there follow several retrospective chapters devoted to Neapolitan beauty Lulinne's experience of kidnapping at the hands of Italian brigands, a popular theme in mid-Victorian escapist fiction. She is eventually taken by brigand chief Signor Adriani, a confederate of the Black Rider, to a deserted house in Highgate. Macheath is soon in hot pursuit. '"Come, gentlemen, to the haunt of our foes. This will be a night of blood, for we go to a den of savage wolves"', he cries.[14]

A reissue of *Tales of Highwaymen* was also to figure prominently in the court reports of an 1872 office theft in the Gray's Inn area of central London. Seventeen-year-old Joseph Bennett and his younger confederate, George Constable, were charged at Bow Street petty sessions (magistrates courts) with breaking and entering. George Wyatt, the chief clerk of Messrs Wigg and Oliver, a firm of architects in Bedford Row, Holborn, stated that, arriving at work, he had found Constable there before him. The boy clerk, on going to his desk and attempting to open it, claimed that his drawer had been cut into and robbed of five pounds and ten shillings. Suspicious circumstances led to the police suspecting Constable. The arresting officer, Police Constable Chamberlain, in his testimony to the court, appeared to regard the accused boy's reading of highwaymen tales as almost synonymous with criminal intent:

Yesterday afternoon about 4 o'clock, I went to 7 Bedford Row. I saw Mr. Wyatt in the office. Mr. Wyatt asked me to look at the drawer in the table. Constable was present. I asked Constable for the key. He said, 'I have it; I took it home with me'. Amongst the papers [in the desk] were some numbers of a weekly publication called *Tales of Highwaymen; or, Life on the Road*, with coloured and other illustrations. I said, 'That looks bad to read such things as these'. He touched me on the arm and said, 'Come outside, I want to speak to you'. I went on to the landing with him, and he said, 'I have been tempted to do this by reading the tales, and by a young man named Bennett, clerk to a solicitor in Furnivals Inn. He was in our office and saw the money and asked me to take it, adding that if I did not he would round on me and tell my master something. I believe he broke in last evening about seven o'clock. I knew he was going to do it, but I have not seen him since'. I took him into custody.

Guilt was inferred from mere possession of *Tales of Highwaymen* ('That looks bad to read such things as these'). Constable, despite obvious intimidation ('tell my master something'), may well not have participated in the actual theft, making it difficult to see the direct relevance of his reading habits. On the other hand, the young clerk's reported confession ('I have been tempted to do this by reading the tales') bears all the familiar signs of an attempt to mitigate a crime before a credulous law officer by shifting the blame onto popular entertainment.[15]

Literary critic Francis Hitchman, intent on linking the reading of cheap highwaymen stories with actual criminal behaviour, was easily deceived by testimony such as the above:

An errand boy or an office lad is caught in the act of robbing his master – 'frisking the till', embezzlement, or forgery. In his desk are found sundry numbers of these romances of the road, a cheap revolver, a small stock of cartridges, and a black mask. A little pressure brings out the confession that those 'properties' have been bought by the youthful culprit with the intention of emulating the 'knights of the road', the tale of whose exploits has fascinated him. It is necessary, for the sake of other lads in the same employment, to press for a conviction, and the boy is taken off to prison, to come out a passed recruit of the great army of crime.

'Penny dreadful' authors had a ready response to such simplistic indictments: 'Let not the "Life of Robin Hood" fall into the hands of such a one, or, sure as fate, Sherwood Forest would be his destination, with a bow and arrows for his stock-in-trade.'[16]

The contemporaneous report of a county court hearing, headed 'A Desperate Highwayman', also proferred the titles of some popular highwayman serials used in evidence by the prosecution. A youth of about 19 named Purdue had been arrested in rural Berkshire for daylight robbery. By trade a house painter, this 'modern Jack Sheppard' was caught wearing a mask and carrying a pistol. The so-called 'highwayman' had presented the pistol at his victims and, under threat of blowing out their brains if they raised an alarm, had stolen their watches and money. Eventually, a young victim held Purdue by the waist after a scuffle and brought assistance, whereupon the thief was lodged in the county lock-up at Speenhamland, the village which gave its name to the late eighteenth-century parish 'outdoor relief' system. The local constabulary, having discovered that their prisoner 'kept company' with a girl in service at Newbury, collected from her a quantity of penny serials left in her safe-keeping by the accused, among them reissued weekly parts of the long-running Dick Turpin serial *Black Bess* and its less popular sequel *The Black Highwayman* (1866–8), both credited to Edward Viles. Local law officers also found portraits of Turpin, masked in the style Purdue adopted, and a coloured engraving, of the kind given away free with the first two issues of penny serials, captioned: 'The Black Highwayman and Captain Hawk Rescuing the Countess of Blacklake'. This alone proved damning because the obviously impressionable Purdue had apparently told the victims of his three robberies that 'if any one desired to know who had stopped them, it was "Captain Hawk"'. Purdue's evident taste for 'penny dreadfuls' was probably not as crucial a determinant as the above incriminating evidence might suggest, given that other possible motives for his crimes, such as seasonal unemployment, were excluded by both police and judiciary.[17]

In the second weekly part of *Black Bess*, its anonymous author, now thought to be hack writer John Frederick Smith (1803–90), defended the highwayman story against criticism that 'the narration of such incidents as pertain to a highwayman's career, would tend to make the thoughtless endeavour to imitate them'. He pointed out that bold highwaymen who cried 'Stand and deliver!' were essentially figures from the past who had become as redundant as the stagecoach in the new age of the railway. How could anyone be ridiculous enough, in present-day society, to attempt to emulate their deeds? For the highwayman story was a chivalric romance about a vanished era, the courageous hero went about like a knight-errant redressing social wrongs in the course of adventures among high and low.

The truth was that 'those persons whose ordinary life is monotonous and void of incident, devour with avidity all tales of wild and wonderful adventure, for the simple reason that they present so vivid and remarkable a contrast to the routine of their own existence'. Penny fiction provided a cathartic fantasy escape from law-abiding everyday lives pursued in school, office, warehouse and workshop. Besides, someone like Purdue, who was weak-minded enough to think he could imitate the highwayman of fiction, 'would be just as likely, after reading some romance of chivalry, to don a suit of armour, and set out in quest of adventures like Don Quixote'.[18]

Prosecution of *The Wild Boys*

The only hard evidence of a major prosecution against a specific 'penny dreadful' unrelated to a juvenile crime was that brought against *The Wild Boys of London* by the Society for the Suppression of Vice (SSV) under the obscenity law. The SSV was founded in 1802 by orthodox churchmen not, as commonly assumed, by William Wilberforce and the Clapham Sect, largely to prevent the publication of blasphemous, licentious and obscene books and prints. It bore no relation to the New York society associated with Anthony Comstock. Late in 1877, a Mr Collette, the revivified SSV's current solicitor, applied at Guildhall police court before Alderman Sir Andrew Lusk to take out a summons against the Shoe Lane, Fleet Street, printers of *The Wild Boys*. This was a reprint put out by publisher George Farrah a full 13 years after the serial's first NPC appearance. Charges were made under Lord Campbell's Obscene Publications Act of 1857, one of the great monuments to militant morality in mid-Victorian England which was also used in the 1950s to eradicate Hank Janson paperbacks popular among young adult males (see Appendix III). Police Inspector Peele and several police constables, acting at the Society's direction, had already visited 11 newsagents and seized upwards of 4000 copies of the serial's weekly parts. Collette, in making his application, claimed rather imprecisely that 'at its first start the publication appeared to be perfectly moral, but after some numbers had been published, a very immoral story appeared, which became worse as the numbers progressed'. Sir Andrew said he had read one or two passages from the publication referred to, 'and they were fearful. The prosecution was a very just one, and he thanked the Society for the Suppression of Vice for taking it up.'[19]

No sooner were the objectionable passages pointed out to the printers than they offered to give up the stereotype plates, recall all the numbers possible, 'and do all in their power to stop the publication of such trash'. The summons against them was consequently withdrawn. The SSV's case against the newsvendors was heard at Bow Street police court where the magistrate, Mr Flowers, declared that 'while the offending items were not so openly obscene as the books generally brought to this court under Lord Campbell's Act still, perhaps, they were even worse in their effect, for they were sufficiently well written as not to excite the same disgust the other books did'. Nearly all the defendants conveniently agreed with the magistrate that the serials should be destroyed, declaring with suspicious rectitude that had they had time to read them and find out the nature of their contents, they would never have sold them in the first place. These summonses were, with one exception, settled by the newsagents each paying two shillings costs.[20]

The exception was an unconventional newsagent named John Wells from 76 Theobalds Road who took issue with the police over the infringement of his trueborn English liberties, indignantly refusing to have the serial destroyed, 'on the ground that he was not going to be treated like a child, that worse books were sold every day, and that he was a respectable man'. The magistrate told him he could not be respectable if he sold indecent books and his case was adjourned, pending the outcome of yet another summons taken out at Guildhall against the proprietor and publisher of *The Wild Boys of London*. Eventually, solicitor Collette told Alderman Lusk, just before Christmas 1877, that neither of these gentlemen had put in an appearance in court but that a letter had been received from them, indicating that they would agree to follow the example of the retail tradesmen and consent to the destruction of their publication. Accordingly, newsagent Wells was alone recalled to Bow Street and told that if he still refused to follow suit then the case would be sent for trial.[21]

A Dickensian exchange now took place between the magistrate and the newsagent which is worth citing in full, if only because its comic absurdity could have graced either the trial of Bardell and Pickwick or, a century later, the court of Beachcomber's Mr. Justice Cocklecarrot:

MR. FLOWERS: Well, Mr. Wells, what do you say now?

DEFENDANT: I wish, first of all, to apologize for my unseemly behaviour last week.

MR. FLOWERS: Oh, that's nothing.

DEFENDANT: Oh, but it is. It was my first appearance in a police court, and I felt the injustice of my case. You, I believe (*turning to Mr. Collette*) say you represent the society. Which society? What society?

MR. COLLETTE: Never mind.

DEFENDANT: But I do mind. Are you the treasurer? Are you the committee? Are you the chairman? What is your system?

MR. DOUGLAS, THE CLERK: Keep the man quiet.

DEFENDANT: But I have suffered severely through a false report getting into the paper. Who is the Reporter of this Court? Where is the penny-a-liner who sent such an account to the *Daily Telegraph*? and *Reynolds's*, too! I am suprised at the proprietor of such a respectable newspaper as *Reynolds's Newspaper* copying such a report from the *Daily Telegraph*.

MR. FLOWERS: If you don't mind you'll have it all down, and will have to complain of the penny-a-liner again.

DEFENDANT: And this man, too, who represents the Society of Donothings. He has done nothing; for I hold in my hand Lord Campbell's Act, which says – Did you ever (*turning to Mr. Collette*) have a man in your employment named Matherim?

MR. FLOWERS: This has nothing to do with the case.

DEFENDANT: What I was going to say is that *The Wild Boys of London* has been sold for 12 years. What has this man been about all that time? I have had these books bound in cloth for 10d. for a woman who wanted to keep them for the benefit of her family. I admit it is filthy, but it is classical (*loud laughter*). In the Bible you will find the same things.

MR. FLOWERS: Oh I see what this means now.

DEFENDANT: Yes, and in scores of books. The publisher in Shoe Lane wants to square it.

MR. FLOWERS: If you go on much more I shall have you removed from court.

DEFENDANT: Then burn them!

MR. COLLETTE: And will you promise not to sell any more?

DEFENDANT: I wouldn't sell such filthy things! (*laughter*)

MR. FLOWERS: I am very glad to hear you say so.

DEFENDANT: Quite right. I'm always glad to take your advice, your worship. You told me once that alcohol was the deadly drug of the country, and I took your advice and have been a teetotaler ever since. (*laughter*)

MR. FLOWERS: Very well, then, pay the 2s. costs.

DEFENDANT: Oh, not that sir; I have only 2s. in my pocket and I promised to take my children home 6d. worth of oranges.

MR. FLOWERS: You must pay the costs.

DEFENDANT: Then I have had enough of you.

The newsagent, clearly a well-known local character, was then taken out of court but discovered that he had only got a shilling in his pocket. To avoid being locked up Wells borrowed the necessary sum from the parish beadle, who happened to be in court on other business.[22]

A sensible question raised by Wells that the solicitor for the SSV noticeably left unanswered was why a summons under the Campbell Act was not attempted until 1877, given that *The Wild Boys* was first published in the mid-1860s. Either English society had become that much more repressive and puritanical in the interval or a specific complaint must have been made to the Society's officers. The implication of prosecutions cited throughout this chapter was to support campaigns attempting to ban the 'penny dreadful', tending to suggest that the above example of censorship may not be entirely isolated. The prosecutors of *The Wild Boys* claimed to have only one object in view and that was 'the stemming as much as possible the publication of all such literature which tended to the downward course of youth'. There is a remote possibility that the serial's suppression in mid-issue might have been due either to episodes in which the Wild Boys fight with the police or to their meeting three Irish Fenians come to London to proselytize their cause. This would assume a secret conspiracy between police, magistrates and the SSV, whereas there is no real evidence other than that the serial was discontinued on the, admittedly tenuous, grounds of moral obscenity.[23]

The Scapegoating of Weekly Periodicals

Boys' weekly (secular) periodicals, another category of publication also confusingly labelled 'dreadfuls', are sometimes mentioned in press reports of late-Victorian trials. For if those who promulgate and enforce laws are to classify something as a social problem, it must first be brought to their attention. The provision of precise titles, allowing one to clarify police and magisterial suppositions, was far less common. Specific periodicals were identified by name, however, during a 1870 north London trial for theft which, surprisingly for such a trivial offence, received extensive local and national press coverage. The attention the trial received perhaps testifies to its importance for newspaper editors anxious to amplify 'moral panic' over boys' papers produced by rival Fleet Street concerns. Extensive coverage of this and other juvenile court cases also acted as a stalking horse for expanding government initiatives, such as reformatory and industrial schools directed against vagrant, destitute and criminal youth, by ensuring that the institutionalization of the young working class received the support of public opinion.

Early in 1876 Alfred Saunders, a 13-year-old London errand boy of Southampton Road, Hampstead, was charged before a magistrate at petty sessions with stealing seven pounds and four shillings belonging to his widowed father, the prosecutor, a 'respectable-looking' cabman (horse-cab driver) with two sons. His youngest, Alfred, was a 'bad' boy who had been charged on a previous occasion with robbing his father, 'who then begged him off'. The seven pounds mentioned in the charge was being saved up for the oldest son and the four shillings had been deducted out of the prisoner's own earnings to buy him boots and trousers. The money was kept in a locked cupboard, the seven pounds being stowed away in a sock, but the woodwork about the lock had been cut away and the lock forced. Suspicion soon fell upon the prisoner who was found to have only two shillings in his possession when the police were eventually called.[24]

Young Alfred admitted to the police that he had taken the money and spent some of it on penny papers which 'dealt with the adventures of pirates and robbers'. Specimens of the 'exciting' periodicals produced in court by Detective Martin of 'S' Division included the Emmett brothers' periodicals *The Young Briton* (1869–77) and *Sons of Britannia* (1870–7), as well as their competitor Edwin Brett's widely circulated *Boys of England*. Significantly, the accused had also purchased a toy pistol, a lantern and a cigar-holder, items surrendered to the police. The prisoner further admitted that he had spent some of the money 'breakfasting and dining in rather an expensive way' at different coffee-shops. At his first examination, the father had volunteered that the prisoner's pockets were crammed with 'filthy books', such as George Emmett's *The Young Englishman* (1873–9), and that his son had thrown away his food at home. The boy's grandmother later testified that she had destroyed some of the periodicals brought home, as his father did not like him to read them. The prisoner, 'who appeared perfectly callous', pleaded guilty to taking only the seven pounds intended for his brother, significantly excluding the money contributed from his own wages. He was convicted and sent to Feltham Industrial School in Middlesex for 3 years. The magistrate told the boy's father that he would probably have to contribute two shillings and sixpence a week towards his son's maintenance.[25]

The periodicals cited in court, whose titles offer a patriotic combination of male youth and national identity, were all controlled by the entrepreneurs mentioned in the previous chapter with offices in and around London's Fleet Street. Thus self-publicist Edwin Brett had managed the NPC before becoming proprietor and editor of numerous, largely boys' periodicals. Brett's most profitable and long-running weekly, *Boys of England*, was first issued on 24 November 1866 and led off with three long-running serials: editor Charles Stevens' popular 'Alone in the Pirates' Lair'; followed by Vane St John's quasi-school story 'Who Shall be Leader?' and John Cecil Stagg's historical border tale 'Chevy Chase.' There were also five pages of miscellaneous items, such as 'Singular Facts' and 'Simple Gardening'; the start of a long historical series on the 'Progress of the British Boy'; a free gift of the first sheet of characters in a toy play of the Stevens story; and a chance to win 1400 prizes headed by two Shetland ponies. (Non-appearance of the latter was used against Brett by his gloating rivals.) The appellation 'dreadful' would seem an exaggerated description for such a harmless weekly pot-pourri. 'We spent our rare pennies in the uncensored reading matter of the village dame's shop, on the *Boys of England* and honest penny dreadfuls', upwardly-mobile novelist H. G. Wells confessed of his boyhood reading. 'Ripping stuff, stuff that anticipated Haggard and Stevenson, badly illustrated, and very very good for us.'[26]

The stories in the Brett-style periodicals, with their Gothic ingredients and historical trappings – Roman gladiators, Goths, Teutonic knights, Crusaders, pirates of the Spanish Main – were not far removed from the instalment-novel 'dreadfuls' which they claimed to replace, despite their alleged high principles and grand patriotic titles. The same well-worn formulas and historical themes, now incorporating heroic apprentices, schoolboys and young working-class lads, were wheeled out again and again to charm hard-earned pennies from the pockets of their loyal readers. The most popular serials were removed and sold separately in penny weekly parts, later to be reissued in sixpenny or a shilling complete novel form with chromographed wrappers (all labelled 'dreadfuls'). Brett's *Boys of England* firmly established the pattern of weekly serialized fiction which was to be followed by all of his competitors, not excepting the more up-market *Boys' Own Paper* (1879–1967). The extent of competition for the pennies of late Victorian children and adolescents can be measured by the 96 secular or commercially oriented periodicals for boys (new titles and reissues) that were published between 1866 and 1900. To succeed in this over-crowded market place, editors had to achieve just the right combination of exciting adventure serials, masculine values, imperial patriotism and jocose schoolboy humour. In America, *Frank Leslie's Boys' and Girls' Weekly* (1866–84) and Norman Munro's *The Boys of New York* (1875–94) imitated the same weekly formula, to the extent of pirating serial stories from Brett's English publications.[27]

The two rival firms of 'Hogarth House' (Emmett-Fox) and 'Boys of England' (later 'Harkaway House'), eager to supply an increasing juvenile demand for periodical literature, relied upon the economies provided by improved transport, cheaper paper and the rotary printing press, to reach the new youth market. Purchase or hire of printing plants, often using borrowed capital, led to a technology-driven necessity for a constant stream of publications, in order to keep expensive steam-driven machinery supplied with product. This involved a social shift whereby from the 1860s, if not before, juvenile readers joined a wider cultural formation, the 'mass', that was not restricted to a single age group, gender or class. For example, Brett's trend-setting *Boys of England* was read, despite its 'penny dreadful' label, by the sons of the middle, lower-middle and skilled working classes, as well as by a less discriminating and poorer, semi-literate market. The ethos of Brett's paper has been aptly characterized as that of Samuel Smiles combined with patriotism and 'sensational' adventure. Consequently, *Boys of England* made its primary appeal to the upwardly mobile: young office boys, shop assistants, apprentices and junior clerks. It also seems evident from the editorial and correspondence pages that the paper reached many older working-class adolescents. The paper had a print run at the end of its first year in 1866 of 150,000 copies per week, rising to 250,000 by the late 1870s, when Brett ran Samuel Bracebridge Hemyng's wildly popular Jack Harkaway series about an adventurous, world-travelling schoolboy. Assuming that, on average, each copy was shared by at least two or three readers every week then, at its peak, the paper would have been seen by well over half a million children and adolescents; or at least one in five of all 10–19-year-old boys at the 1881 census.[28]

Brett and the Emmett brothers were engaged in a furious cut-throat competition for the loyalty of a fickle juvenile audience throughout the late 1860s and early 1870s, both sides reputedly hurling insults at each other across Fleet Street at the height of their bitter struggle for readers. On the whole, Brett's boys' papers cultivated a spurious air of respectability, toning down the gruesome and stressing the melodramatic, whereas his rivals, the Emmetts, remained loyal to their original anarchic, blood-drenched and more horrific approach. Hence they did not shirk from a grisly engraving in *Sons of Britannia* (1870–7), depicting Christian babies being bayoneted by fez-wearing Turkish mercenaries, the Bashi-Bazouks, to illustrate a timely story of the 1875–6 Serbo-Turkish war. The Emmett periodicals appealed to a far smaller clientele than Brett's, boys from the lowest social stratum: sons of unskilled workers, errand boys, grocery assistants and young lads from the East End slums. 'High School boys read *Boys of England* [Brett] and *Young Folks* [Henderson], boys of lower social position read *Young Men of Great Britain* [Brett], lower still read *The Young Englishman* [Emmett], followed by *The Young Briton* [Emmett], while young shop assistants and errand boys read *Sons of Britannia* [Emmett]', as one collector recalled the fine social distinctions of his late-Victorian boyhood.[29] Most Emmett readers, at the far end of this spectrum of taste, could not afford annual subscriptions and bought copies sporadically, whenever they could find a penny. Bound quarterly and half-yearly volumes of Brett's boys' papers, priced at one shilling and fourpence and four shillings apiece, were evidently produced for boys from well-to-do families. Brett's policy of steering closer to acceptable late Victorian moral standards meant that he had a far wider, more sustained and therefore more profitable readership.

Since all of the boys' papers indicted in the above petty sessions trial, with the exception of *Boys of England*, were managed or edited by the Emmett brothers, an indignant response from one of the clan was not long in arriving. 'We have been attacked by the Press and in the police-courts, and why? – because a youth who had plundered his father happened to have one of our journals in his pocket', wrote George Emmett, peevishly responding to a reader's inquiry through the letters page of one of his own periodicals:

> Did it ever strike you, or any of those people who are continually crying down light literature, that the love of dress and jewellery has ruined more young men, and demoralised more women, than all the journals and 'penny dreadfuls' put together? Did you ever hear a police-officer give evidence to the effect 'We found this young man with a new suit of clothes on, made by Mr. Snip?' Certainly you have not.[30]

This laboured attempt to exonerate Hogarth House periodicals from a charge of encouraging delinquency would have possessed greater credibility had Emmett relied on press details of the actual court hearing. Motherless Alfred Saunders, much persecuted for his reading habits, spent the better part of the money he had stolen in coffee-shops and on such items as a toy pistol, rather than on clothes, jewellery or even penny periodicals.

George Emmett, a heavily bearded ex-cavalry officer, sought to counter the bad press his boys' papers were receiving by winning the support of influential weeklies through a circular letter to their editors: 'I trust, in a spirit of fair play, you will spare a few lines, giving your candid opinion as to whether these works are pernicious. By so doing you will remove the odium caused by the remarks made by the Press and the Police Courts.' Seemingly, only James Mortimer, editor of *The London Figaro* (1870–98), a gossipy political, literary and satirical weekly, rose to the challenge. A magnanimous editorial discussed serials and periodicals submitted by Emmett.

'Both the incidents and the language are free from grossness, and we may add that, unlike some novels in demand at Mudie's [circulating library], a thin veil of propriety does not disclose a mass of impropriety', claimed the tolerant *Figaro* editor. 'They are not stuffed with ghostly horrors. They do not invest vice or crime with a halo of romance.' Mortimer's analysis of their stereotypical content followed:

> In *Tom Wildrake's Schooldays* the hero dresses up as a girl, and for one or two mornings attends the classes at a ladies' school. This is not a clever joke, but the way it is told is perfectly harmless. *Shot and Shell* is a series of military stories [by George Emmett], but . . . does not contain any story of dissipation. It is, we presume, a tolerably accurate account of a soldier's early career, and parents need not fear that it will induce their sons to enlist, for there is plenty of dark shadowing in the picture. The leading story in *The Young Briton* is 'Master John Bull at the French Academy', and the two chapters before us are harmless boys' sprees. The leading story in the *Sons of Britannia* is 'Jolly Jack Johnson', and chapter xii is just the sort of fun to please boys, for Jolly Jack frightens a cellarman by concealing himself in an empty cask, and making the said cask move about.[31]

Although Mortimer was not so untypical a Victorian as to approve the absence of 'edification', he generously exonerated the Hogarth House weeklies from the charge of 'perniciousness' made against them. 'It is an absurd and altogether unjustifiable slander to say that Mr. Emmett's publications – according to sample – can tempt any boy to vice or crime.' Construction of the 'penny dreadful' label was, therefore, occasionally contested by contemporary opinion-formers.[32]

The unpredictable circulations and economic instability of the Hogarth House periodicals eventually caused the Emmett brothers to get into serious financial difficulties, with the outcome that around 1875 William Laurence Emmett went bankrupt. Brother George assumed overall control until the Hogarth's former business manager, Charles Fox, a bluff gambling man, took over the premises. George Emmett Junior attempted to revive the family's declining fortunes, under the masthead of the St George's Publishing Office in Red Lion Court, but did not prosper for long. Fox made a steady profit from reprints and reissues in succeeding decades, while also starting several new titles of his own. The Hogarth House Library, for example, regularly published serials taken from the Emmett–Fox periodicals in separate weekly parts and later in collected volume form (all labelled 'dreadfuls'). Fox's most successful venture was *The Boy's Standard* (1875–92), printed on inferior paper and with a highly emotive approach which singled it out for censure as a 'dreadful'. Profit margins for the popular *Standard* remained buoyant, but publishers such as Fox, who put out under-funded, badly edited weeklies, reprinting published material to save on production costs, over-supplied the market with a shoddy product.[33]

Prosecutions of the 1890s

With the exception of the highwayman stories discussed earlier, 'moral panics' scapegoating the 'penny dreadful' do not resurface again until the 1890s, reflecting perhaps a renewed middle-class 'cycle of anxiety' concerning deviant juvenile behaviour. Hence in November 1892 a tenuous connection was made between the reading of 'trashy novels' and, saddest of all deaths, a child's suicide. W. T. Stead's *Pall Mall Gazette* featured a brief item, bluntly headed 'A Victim of the Penny Dreadful', which reported a local inquest on George William Seymour, a 12-year-old labourer's son found hanging dead in a Georgian house in Montpellier Crescent, Brighton, where he had been employed as a page boy. The evidence purportedly showed that 'he complained of a pain in his head from over-reading, and that he was addicted to reading penny novels'. Possibly a reference to the London-based Aldine Publishing Company's 'dime novel' reprints of the 1890s, with their brightly coloured covers. According to the local Sussex press, in his summing up the deputy coroner found Seymour to have been 'a lad with an active brain, who was fond of exciting reading, and no doubt had a predisposition to suicide'. Such was the press anxiety to scapegoat 'dreadfuls' that this qualified official verdict was converted by the *Pall Mall Gazette* into an outright accusation that the deceased 'committed suicide while temporarily insane, the insanity being caused by reading trashy novels'.[34]

Three years later, a reader writing to the *Daily News* alleged that 'the recent murder by a boy of thirteen of his own mother may be traced principally to the taste he had imbibed of studying the characters that are being ominously portrayed by pictures and representations in these pernicious ["penny dreadful"] publications'. On investigation this turns out to be an allusion to the well-publicized Old Bailey murder trial, from 16 to 17 September 1895, of Robert Allen Coombes, the bright son of a ship's steward, from Plaistow in the East End of London. Robert's 12-year-old brother, Nathaniel, had complained of being beaten by their mother, Emily Harrison Coombes, while their father was away at sea. The prisoner, 13-year-old Robert, promised to kill her, buying a sixpenny knife with which he stabbed his mother while they were in bed together (the younger son slept in another room). Next day, the two boys paid the rent, told the neighbours that their mother had gone to visit relatives in Liverpool, and spent the day together at Lord's Cricket Ground. The murdered woman's sister-in-law eventually discovered the body upstairs, in an advanced state of decomposition, and Robert confessed to the stabbing. Nathaniel, giving evidence for the prosecution, claimed that his brother was going to kill their mother because he wanted to 'get away to some island'. Robert had asked him to cough twice as a signal to commit the crime. At the end of the trial, Nathaniel was found innocent of a charge of incitement. Robert Coombes, who had a history of mental illness, pleaded guilty to the murder indictment with a smile upon his lips. He was found guilty but insane and sent to Holloway Prison for an undisclosed period.[35]

A list of property found at the deceased's rooms was produced by the police, priority being given to a number of 'sensational story books'. Nathaniel gave evidence that his brother had indeed bought the paper-covered titles produced and that he had even seen Robert reading them. A doctor acting for the defence, and hence seeking a convenient scapegoat, claimed that 'pernicious literature would be worse for a boy suffering from mental affliction'. The prosecution also claimed, exaggeratedly, that the books found 'related to crimes of one kind or another'. Mr Justice Kennedy, responded: 'Some do certainly, judging from the titles.' Only one newspaper disclosed that these 'pernicious', supposedly crime-related, titles were in reality: *The Crimson Cloak; The Secret of Castle Cloney; The Witch of Fermoyle; Revenged at Last; The Mesmerist Detective; Joe Phoenix's Unknown; Cockney Bob; The Rock Rider* and *The Witch*. Recognizable among these hastily listed titles was the prolific Edwin Harcourt Burrage's topical, but otherwise innocuous, short mystery-novelette for Charles Fox, *The Mesmerist Detective: Or, Strange Doings in Littlewood* (*c*.1890). The Aldine 'O'er Land and Sea' Library contributed *Joe Phoenix's Unknown, Or Crushing the Crook Combination* (*c*.1895), part of an American detective series set this time in New York's Wall Street, as well as the inaccurately transcribed Gothic mystery *The Secret of Castle Coucy: A Legend of the Great Crusade* (*c*.1895) and *The Rock Riders* (*c*.1895). The unlocated titles appear to exhibit harmless stage-Irish, Gothic and supernatural story themes of a kind published in their hundreds by Fox, Aldine and Brett in reduced-size novelette or complete-novel 'library' form.[36]

If suicide could be attributed to the 'penny dreadful', then why not matricide? *The Times* alone was mildly equivocal about this Old Bailey murder trial. 'How far madness was the impelling cause, and how far madness was due to the vile, sensational books which seem to have been his favourite study, may perhaps be in some doubt', proclaimed its leader column sagely. 'But still it will be generally felt that the jury have returned a satisfactory verdict'. The extensive coverage afforded the proceedings by newspapers ranging from the local East End press to *The Times* is ample evidence of yet another 'transforming event' shaping the creation of a 'moral panic' over the 'penny dreadful'. A footnote to this sad affair came in a subsequent reader's letter to the *Daily News*. 'Boys, some in an unfortunate case which was lately before the public, do not hesitate at crime to gratify the extravagant taste for sport and other pastimes, which are supposed to be natural to their age, and without which no hero could deservedly be a hero.'[37] This misguided reference to the brothers' attendance at Lord's on the day after the killing may shift the blame for matricide away from the 'penny dreadful' but also shows how easily reports of a prominent trial could be transmuted in order to serve a particular fixation.

Why Blame 'Penny Dreadfuls'?

What is going on that incites magistrates and prosecutors to blame crime on the reading material a young culprit possessed rather than on his taste for fine clothes or dining out in coffee shops? Arguments rehearsed in court and in newspapers about the causes of late-Victorian juvenile crime echoed the discourse about deviancy in those and other contemporary forums that placed a heavy emphasis on family moral responsibility. Industrial and reformatory school visitors of the 1870s and 1880s, reflecting the revival of moral puritanism among the middle class, lost no opportunity to condemn irreligious parents for the delinquent habits of their children. Parental neglect, drunkenness, or irresponsibility were nominated as the primary cause of delinquency, if no corrupting 'penny dreadfuls' were found, somehow detaching a sufficient cause from the surrounding necessary economic circumstances. Hence sections of the late-Victorian middle class tended to be particularly susceptible, when a rising crime rate was invoked, to the desire to improve the morals and leisure habits of working-class youth.

Cheap fiction was a particular target because it was felt that wider literacy had led to the corruption of literature until, among street boys, reading had become an almost criminal pursuit.[38]

Male working-class adolescents were the focal point of concern here because they were perceived as potential delinquents and, therefore, in need of discipline, control, education and management. Hence the campaign against 'dreadfuls' coincided with a rise in the conscious regulation of working-class boys: encapsulated in compulsory schooling; a fixation with uncontrolled, high-earning 'boy labour'; and the rise of adult-organized youth movements. Ridiculing of authority in 'penny dreadful' highwayman and school stories has to be defined against the strict regimentation of the real late-Victorian classroom and, from 1883, of well-drilled church youth organizations such as the Boys' Brigade. Reading about the deflation of pompous masters by anarchic boarding-school pupils in 'penny dreadful' school stories provided a much-needed safety valve for the circumscribed state-school boy. The debate about the need for greater discipline and culture among the young working class also reached its height when imperialism was at its zenith. The promulgation of imperialist thinking was typified by the transition from *The Wild Boys of London* to 'penny dreadful' heroes, such as Jack Harkaway, adventuring overseas among comic or sinister foreigners. Alfred Harmsworth's campaign against 'dreadfuls' ultimately succeeded because of the more jingoistic and xenophobic tone of his halfpenny boys' papers, rather than their greater moral purity. The new recipe, 'approved by parents and children alike, was to blend much of the violence, boisterousness, and cruelty which had poured from the penny dreadfuls with the late-nineteenth century world view'.[39]

If Victorian critics and moralists had taken the trouble to examine the publications of the NPC and its rivals without prejudice, they would have discovered that, far from recommending the values of a criminal or oppositional subculture, their 'point of view' was consistently aligned with support for the established order. In common with other forms of Victorian commercial entertainment, the outward animation of 'penny dreadfuls' concealed a remarkable degree of moral and social conservatism. As a self-confessed 'penny dreadful' author queried in 1895, with some legitimacy:

Personally, I should like to know if any members of the juries who attribute youthful crime to the so-called 'penny dreadfuls', which the tender-aged criminal is supposed to have devoured, have ever read one of the books on which they pass such wholesale condemnation? I have read every book that an example of boyish depravity has brought to notice, and so far I have been unable to find any incentive to matricide, to dishonesty, or vice of any description. The villain is invariably outwitted, the hero is all honour and bravery, and the heroine chaste as the Lady in Milton's *Comus*.[40]

Examination of the texts cited in the criminal prosecutions dealt with above would endorse a similar conclusion. The delusion that there was such a thing as a 'pernicious' taste in popular fiction rapidly became self-fulfilling. The actual content of highwaymen and London low-life serials suggests that, rather than encouraging crime, 'dreadfuls' offered little challenge to the prevailing middle-class moral ethos.

Decline of the Penny Dreadful

The expansionist 1890s, which saw a more pronounced racism and imperialism in English popular culture, were also to leave many 'penny dreadful' journals looking rather old-fashioned. They appeared relics of an era of breezy and jocular adventures, embracing Jack Harkaway, Tom Wildrake, Cheerful Ching-Ching and other disreputable young heroes, unable to compete in sales with Alfred Harmsworth's cheaper, more jingoistic boys' weeklies, such as *Halfpenny Marvel* (1893–1922) and *Union Jack* (1894–1933). After Edwin Brett's death in 1895, his executors carried on the business, seemingly for the benefit of his large family. Seven halfpenny or penny weeklies, mostly reissues, and numerous sixpenny novels continued to appear under the Harkaway House imprint. Ultimately, on 11 January 1900, the business was incorporated as Edwin J. Brett Limited with £30,000 nominal capital, operating from new premises in West Harding Street, near Fleet Street. Edwin Charles Brett, the eldest son, and the family's solicitors held over half of the stock. Company returns suggest that limited liability was almost synonymous with imminent collapse. For Edwin Charles, who presided over the firm as chief shareholder, manager and company director, possessed little of his father's business or editorial aptitude and profits soon plummeted. The Amalgamated Press, as the Harmsworth firm was renamed in 1902, had made publishing cheap fiction far more competitive and capital-intensive. Consequently, a new manager, journalist and novelist T. Murray Ford, was rapidly hired to avert the Brett company's complete failure.[41]

Ford came up against a nostalgic but unhelpful refusal, on the part of the family's trustees, to kill off the firm's many out-dated publications. Why interfere, he was told, with what had sold so well for decades? A sentiment made familiar from studies of the British industrial-export sector before 1914. None the less, Ford did persuade the company's directors to reprint Brett's *English Ladies' Novelettes* (1891–2) and to put out the narrow-shaped, romantic *'My Pocket' Novels* (1900–24), which enabled the company to pay dividends for a brief period. Ford meanwhile discovered that Brett's were one of the last Fleet Street firms to print illustrations from expensive wood-engraving blocks; an impracticable memorial, perhaps, to the founder's early career as an artist-engraver. By 1906 Edwin Charles had retreated to Broadstairs, near the Brett family mansion at St Peter's, Kent, and the company was effectively without active family leadership. A generous offer for the business from Alfred Harmsworth, the future Lord Northcliffe, tempting shareholders with 38 shillings for every £1 share, was ill-advisedly turned down by the elderly and out-of-touch board of directors. As a result, Ford asked Edwin J. Brett Limited to cancel his contract and, not long after, went to work for Harmsworth.[42]

One method of assessing the performance of small metropolitan publishers such as Brett's, in the absence of sufficient data for a proper econometric survey, is to utilize the 'classic' late-Victorian entrepreneurial failure thesis. This places an emphasis on the technological backwardness of British firms, their difficulties in raising capital, poor growth rates, deficient company structures and the business inadequacies of succeeding generations. The Brett firm's wood-engraved illustrations demonstrate an attachment to old technology and their reluctance to diversify into new areas of popular fiction by paying authors competitive rates, while profits could still be wrung out of low-cost reprints, exemplifies second-generation management failure. Publishing entrepreneurs such as Edwin Brett, who made small fortunes by acting as wholesale distributors to the local metropolitan market, would be judged as business failures in the longer term by the 'classic' performance criteria. They lacked large-scale distribution networks and were slow to identify market changes, plus their businesses were under-capitalized and, by the 1890s, no longer expanding.[43]

Not unexpectedly, the Brett firm's reissued late-Victorian titles failed to find a new market in Edwardian England. Hence debentures of £5000 were secured on the firm's property assets, apparently for the benefit of the printers. In June 1907, excessive liabilities led inexorably to the company being wound up but, because the sale of its effects would not realize sufficient to pay off debentures, the appointed liquidator suggested that another company, Edwin J. Brett (1907) Limited, be formed with £5000 capital to exploit remaining business assets. This company, operating out of Long Acre, traded at a loss and was also soon heavily mortgaged. In 1909 the debenture holders stepped in to salvage what they could and Edwin J. Brett (1907) Limited went into irretrievable collapse. Perhaps because Odhams Limited, one of the largest creditors, was made joint receiver, John Allingham claimed a few years later that a powerful combination of publishers held all Brett's original blocks and moulds. A remainder-buyer put out some Harkaway House titles on his own initiative but with often mismatched covers. This was a sad end for the publications of Edwin John Brett, neglected pioneer of boys' weekly periodicals and, until Harmsworth, the most significant figure publishing juvenile fiction for a mass audience.[44]

Until too many entrants increased competitive pressures, returns from publishing a successful boys' periodical could be quite substantial. Yet long-term profits could only be guaranteed by volume sales, low unit costs and profitable reprints. The question of how lucrative or, on the contrary, how marginal a living could be made from this kind of publishing is complicated by evidence that while some proprietors became rich and prospered, others went bankrupt or ended their lives in alcoholic poverty. Thus Edward Lloyd, whose early-Victorian 'penny bloods' helped finance a cheap newspaper empire, left over half a million pounds in 1890. Five years later Edwin Brett left an estate valued at £76,500 (nearly seven times that of popular novelist Wilkie Collins) and was buried in a family vault on the west side of Highgate Cemetery. Conversely, Brett's business rival William Laurence Emmett became a bankrupt in the mid-1870s, ruined by a commercial warfare that necessiated the regular supply of new periodical titles. Equally, John Allingham was left in 1886 with a debt of over £16,000 when *The Boy's World* (1879–86), of which he was editor – proprietor, went under. Only by surrendering most of his assets and giving up the copyright to all of his stories was he discharged from liability. Fortunes were certainly made and lost by London's publishers of cheap juvenile fiction, suggesting the scale and significance of a business catering specifically to the cheap end of the juvenile market.[45]

The history of London firms producing 'penny dreadfuls' suggests that ambitious journalists, engravers, newsagents, printers and even authors, could try to make fortunes by setting up their own publishing companies; at least until Fleet Street, with the advance of new technology, became subject to a much stricter division of labour. Small 'penny dreadful' publishers and wholesalers, such as the Emmetts, Charles Fox and Edwin Brett, merit a secure place in the pantheon of Britain's economic innovators, pioneers in the mass production of standardized articles for commercial distribution. The small publishing houses surveyed here either went into liquidation or were swallowed up by the Harmsworth brothers' omnivorous Amalgamated Press in the 1900s. Relatively impersonal but highly successful large firms, presaging the rise of the twentieth-century corporate economy, henceforth dominated the publication of cheap periodical fiction and comics for the young, as well as mass-circulation adult magazines. The creative process was made subordinate to institutional management. 'In the old days, writing for boys was something of an adventure', lamented John Allingham, from the vantage point of 1913, 'now it is very much a trade.'[46]

The 'penny dreadful' label lingered on for years after the First World War as an imprecise term for highly coloured adventure fiction read by the young. Teachers and librarians used it anachronistically as a term of abuse against a new breed of popular weekly story papers for boys put out by the Amalgamated Press and D. C. Thomson of Dundee. Yet only the tiny Aldine firm in Crown Court, off Chancery Lane, former specialist in reprinting 'half-dime novels' for the British market, retained any vestigial links with the late-Victorian 'penny dreadful', before itself succumbing in the early 1930s to lack of investment, poor sales and changing markets. The modern inter-war boy wanted more up-to-date scientific ingenuity in his adventure stories from new-style Sexton Blake-type detectives. 'Highwaymen, pirates, and red indians don't excite his imagination; he wants fights with submarines, daring stunts in aeroplanes, and wonderful electric machines', explained a news-agency's head salesman in 1925. 'Tales of Dick Turpin, Claude Duval and Jack Sheppard interest him not.'[47]

4

GANGSTER FILM PANIC: CENSORING HOLLYWOOD IN THE 1930s

From the end of the nineteenth century onwards, the technological innovation that, commercially exploited, completely transformed the non-working lives of ordinary urban youth was a device for the projection of moving images, an apparatus to resynthesize motion. British electrical engineer Robert W. Paul gave the first exhibition of his Theatrograph projector (an adaptation of ideas embodied in inventor Thomas Alva Edison's coin-operated peepshow device, the Kinetoscope) to a scientific audience at Finsbury Technical College on 20 February 1896, but had considerable problems achieving any sort of adequate image on the screen. The first screening outside Paris of the Lumière brothers' more famed Ciné-matographe was given *on the same evening* to the London press (admission charges were made the following day) hosted by entertainer and magician Félicien Trewey in the Great Hall of the Regent Street Polytechnic. It transferred on 9 March, as an attraction in the variety bill of the Empire Theatre, north of Leicester Square, where it ran to full houses. The race was now on to bring moving pictures to the general public. On 19 March, Paul's Theatrograph opened at the Egyptian Hall, almost opposite the Royal Academy in Piccadilly, under the aegis of magician David Devant. Another screening of Paul's invention, renamed as the Animatographe, ran at the Alhambra Music Hall in Leicester Square from 25 March 1896 and enjoyed a long residency. By the end of this momentous year for popular media, 'movies' had become part of the regular programme of London music halls – coexistent with rather than immediately replacing popular live entertainment.[1]

The first American screening of the French cinématographe took place in New York on 29 June 1896 at Keith's Vaudeville Theatre, in front of a crowd of eager viewers, but the formidable Edison had already acquired the patent for the first American projector, and on 23 April 1896 presented it under the name of Vitascope at Koster and Bial's Music Hall in New York. The American Customs Service unknowingly assisted Edison's patent monopoly by seizing French projectors, alleging that equipment was coming into the country illegally, until the Lumiére brothers' branch director fled the country. Within a few years, Edwin S. Porter's *The Great Train Robbery* (1903), a crucial Edison film inaugurating both the western and crime genres, and a host of tawdry 5-cent urban diversions known as nickelodeons, confirmed the popular American habit of watching films. From 1909 onwards, grand picture palaces were being erected in London and New York by architects like the Scottish-born Thomas Lamb to exhibit four- or five-reel feature films and the lowly origins of cinema in British penny gaffs and American Kinetoscope parlours were soon left far behind.[2]

The immediate visual impact of moving pictures, and the international appeal of screen stars, such as Charlie Chaplin, Mary Pickford and Douglas Fairbanks, helped make the cinema popular. Even the silent cinema's prolonged lease of life for Victorian melodrama, evident in the screen output of pioneer actor-turned-director David Wark Griffith, made 'dreadfuls' appear redundant. Why spend hours poring over fine print when three halfpence could gain admission to the fantasy world of the silent cinema? The sons and daughters of the readers of the 'penny dreadful' or the 'half-dime novel' became members of a mass audience for what became known as the cinema that far outstripped any previous form of commercial entertainment in its appeal to the young. Moving pictures attracted a steadily increasing underage patronage, until it was calculated that up to 30 per cent of total British audiences were under 17. Age soon proved the statistically most significant variable in audience composition. A 1933 survey showed 63 per cent of a large sample of adolescents aged between 14 and 21 went to the cinema weekly, while in 1943 the figure for those between 14 and 17 was 80 per cent. Hence, adults who had enjoyed 'dreadfuls' when young made amends for their dissolute past by excoriating this new form of mass culture. 'It pleases me to think that these [penny dreadful] stories – notably the Jack Harkaway series, in which a robust humour was an ingredient – wrought not one per cent of the harm to their boy-readers that the Gangster films have done to the boys of the last quarter of a century', wrote the Northcliffe editor J. A. Hammerton in 1944.[3]

Censorship and the Gangster Film

The film industry's love affair with members of criminal gangs was only natural, they were colourful, violent and charismatic men and women, whose law-breaking activities were followed by millions of law-abiding Americans. Yet, when brought to the screen, gangster films more than any other Hollywood genre created problems, not only for the usual censorship lobbies but also for judges, lawyers, teachers, policemen, mayors, newspapers and local councillors. The American urban gangster can be traced in the cinema from Griffith's *The Musketeers of Pig Alley* (1912), a one-reeler with Lillian Gish, through to Tod Browning's gangster film collaborations with Lon Chaney and on to Josef von Sternberg's crime trilogy with George Bancroft – *Underworld* (1927), *The Drag Net* (1928) and *Thunderbolt* (1929) – until reaching a high point in the Warner Brothers gangster cycle of the early 1930s and not leaving our screens thereafter. Many respectable citizens believed that films such as these, based on the lives and activities of Prohibition-era criminals, led to an increase in juvenile delinquency and accused Hollywood of delivering impressionable youth into a career of crime. The harmful effects of fast-moving and exciting gangster films on young cinema patrons thus became a prominent concern of those eager to control and censor this pervasive new mass medium.[4]

After a series of sex scandals rocked the American film industry, in 1922 Hollywood's Jewish moguls hired a midwestern Presbyterian elder and influential Republican, William Harrison (Will) Hays, former Postmaster General in President Warren Harding's cabinet, as their front man to clean up the image of the movies. The industry's self-monitoring Motion Picture Producers and Distributors of America Inc. (MPPDA) or Hays Office in New York tried a variety of ways to regulate films before adopting a formal code. Written in 1930 by two midwestern Catholics, a Jesuit professor of drama in St Louis and a lay publisher of trade magazines, the new Motion Picture Production Code stipulated, partly in reaction to the increasing popularity of gangster films, that movies stress proper behaviour, respect for government and 'Christian values'. The Hays Code, made mandatory in 1934, began with an attack on what was seen as a general tone of lawlessness and on depicting specific criminal methods in recent gangster films. Criminal acts were 'never [to] be presented in such a way as to throw [*sic*] sympathy with the crime as against law and justice or to inspire others with a desire for imitation'. This was followed by eight double-column pages of detailed applications. Murder must be presented in a manner that 'will not inspire imitation' and 'revenge in modern times shall not be justified'. Methods of crime such as theft, robbery, arson, safecracking, smuggling and dynamiting of trains, should not be explicitly presented. If these strictures were not met, a film project would no longer receive the code's seal of MPPDA approval.[5]

In the years from 1930 to 1933, before President Roosevelt's New Deal, gangsters were without doubt the American cinema's most conspicuous heroes. The dominant image of the movie gangster was formed primarily by the two charismatic stars who played the gangster character so successfully – Edward G. Robinson and James Cagney. The former was best known for his strutting energy as Caesar Enrico Bandello in Mervyn LeRoy's otherwise reticent *Little Caesar* (1930), the first of the classic gangster movies, and the latter for his stunning kinetic performance as Tom Powers in William Wellman's *The Public Enemy* (1931), with its famous breakfast scene where Cagney pushes a grapefruit in the face of his wife (Mae Clarke). British cities such as Birmingham refused to show *Public Enemy*, even after the industry-appointed British Board of Film Censors (BBFC) lifted its own year-long ban; Manchester's watch committee were more indulgent, accusing the BBFC of being too strict. 'It seems to me to be probable that the new and youthful type of dangerous criminal mentioned in connection with the Dartmoor revolt is largely the product of such encouragement', according to a letter to the London *Times* of 24 February 1932, referring to a recent prison protest. In New York a police court judge declared that the case of 17-year-old Joseph Wilkinson, arrested for armed robbery, was typical of juvenile crimes caused by the movies. The teenager scoffed at the judge's comments, claiming that a picture like *Little Caesar* 'would make him want to stop before he was gunned down like Edward G. Robinson's character'. If anything, he blamed his delinquency on his mother not letting him go to the cinema until he was 12, forcing him to hang around with a street gang.[6]

Organized protest against the gangster movie reached its height with the publicity surrounding director Howard Hawks' *Scarface* (1932); in which the versatile Paul Muni overacted as Tony Camonte, yet another thinly disguised Al Capone figure. This violent and fast-paced film, produced by millionaire Howard Hughes and scripted by former Chicago newspaperman Ben Hecht, reached the screen a year after *Public Enemy* but was actually made at the same time. The delay came about because, in an effort to appease the American censors, a subtitle 'Shame of the Nation' was added to *Scarface*, along with a scene in which civic reformers preach ('You can end it. Fight!') directly to camera. In another new scene, the city's chief of detectives denounces the glorification of gangsters, echoing the very cries of the censors who ordered the changes. A different ending was also filmed using a double (Muni was acting in a Broadway play) in which Camonte is brought to trial and sentenced to be hanged by the state, rather than being shot down by the police on the sidewalk outside his hideout. New York and Chicago censorship boards rejected *Scarface* outright until Warners agreed to make these changes, but Jason Joy, who enforced the Hays Code, still had to convince them to show it cut. Each state in America had its own board of censors, so the original ending could still be seen in some theatres when the film was finally released in the spring of 1932. British local authorities such as Beckenham, Kent and Birmingham thought the BBFC policy towards gangster films too liberal and went so far as to ban *Scarface* outright. Nazi Germany followed suit.[7]

Young men in Britain and America enjoyed watching gangster films during the 1930s, in their estimation surpassed only by war films and westerns. Based on 21 schools from all areas of the city, the 1933 Edinburgh Cinema Enquiry received replies from 1310 boys and 1270 girls between the ages of nine and 18. The films the boys liked best were war films and gangster/mystery films and the ones they liked least were love stories and 'society life' films. Scottish girls, on the other hand, liked cowboy, comic and musical films but disliked war and gangster films. Romance and love stories were clearly disliked by boys but more popular with girls aged 11–14. As a general rule, based on a 1932 London enquiry, the older children grew the more their interest in cartoons, cowboy and war films declined and their interest in mystery and detective films increased. The latter were seen in Scotland as likely to produce 'unhealthy excitement in children' or as an incentive to crime. 'As we review the immense and dominating importance of the film in the lives of children, especially in the cities and large towns, the question cannot be evaded as to whether the time is not ripe for the appointment by the Government of a Commission in Film Censorship', proclaimed the Edinburgh enquiry to little effect. For the oft-argued link between cinema and juvenile crime was no longer accepted by the British Home Office and those who still believed that the cinema was responsible for a certain amount of juvenile crime were in a distinct minority by the 1930s.[8]

What children and adolescents should or should not be permitted to see on film was, none the less, a source of incessant public controversy in Britain throughout the inter-war years. From the outset the BBFC had been concerned about how crime was depicted on British screens. Their annual report for 1929 commented on screen gangsterism:

In many cases, there is in addition an admixture of the criminal or boot-legging element, with the introduction of an atmosphere of riotous luxury. One such film by itself may not be prohibitive, but the Board cannot help feeling that a continuous succession of them is subversive, tending to indicate a lower outlook and to invest a life of irregularity with a spurious glamour.

Yet there was no concentrated effort by the BBFC to outlaw American gangster films. Even *Little Caesar* ran into only minor difficulties and suffered merely nominal cuts when allowed onto British screens from February 1931. Albeit in that same year, the now-forgotten gangster dramas *The Secret Six* (1931) and *Doorway to Hell* (1931) were submitted on numerous occasions, the latter being severely cut. The British censor first viewed *The Public Enemy* on 22 June 1931, but it was almost 2 months later before the BBFC declined to award it a certificate for reasons which are far from clear. In May 1932 the BBFC allowed a modified version of *Scarface*, but the print submitted was almost certainly heavily cut and reconstructed, due to the severe American censorship problems. In the light of this BBFC decision, the ban on *Public Enemy* was lifted in the following month.[9]

No American crime or gangster film was rejected by the BBFC throughout 1932 and the whole genre was ignored in the last of the regular published annual reports for that year. 'The BBFC thus bowed to commercial pressures and accepted organised crime in films provided that the setting was the United States', writes James C. Robertson, historian of British film censorship, 'whereas scenarios covering organised crime in Britain were strongly discouraged between 1932 and 1934'. Thus a potential film of the Edgar Wallace thriller *When the Gangs came to London* was banned in 1932 by Colonel Hanna, Britain's elderly chief censor, not only because it described London in a state of terror under rival gangs of Chicago gunmen, but also because 'in this country we do not allow our police to be shown on the screen as incompetent or accepting bribes from criminals'.[10] Gangster films, with their presumed moral dangers and incentive to youthful imitation, were only acceptable if American. In any case, the BBFC's problems over gangster films were considerably reduced in the second half of the 1930s with the advent of both Cagney and Robinson as crusading lawmen and of films that showed juvenile gang members being successfully rehabilitated. Despite a shift in subject matter, moral censors failed to support the violent law and order films of the late 1930s as anti-crime propaganda.

Slum Gang and Reform School Films

Between 1926 and 1939 the number of cinemas in Britain rose from 3000 to 4800, with new cinemas opening at the average rate of 138 per year. From 1934, the first year for which reliable figures exist, admissions to British cinemas rose from 903 million to 946 million in 1937 and to a massive 990 million in 1939. The enormous popularity of American films among the majority of young British cinema-goers at this time served to encourage mounting fears among the intellectual elite of cultural annexation. Audience rapport in the late 1930s with the young stars of a cycle of slum gang and reform school films further reinforced a tendency towards 'moral panic' over the supposed effects of Hollywood crime and gangster movies. On 22 December 1938, Sir Reginald Kennedy Cox, chairman of the juvenile court in Stratford, East London, made a solemn request for the specific 'A' certificate film title referred to in a probationer's report on three 15-year-old youths charged with burglary. The probation officer, J. Coletherup, said it was called *Crime School*. 'I understand', he continued, 'it has a very bad effect on young lads like these. I have not seen it, but I know that its influence on youths in hostels has been noted, and it is not a good influence. I have no doubt it played its part in these offences.' Sir Reginald agreed, before placing the boys on 6 months probation, and added that the film should be shown only to adult audiences.[11]

Warner's B-feature *Crime School* (1938), which the BBFC allowed to pass virtually unscathed, was a reworking of the offbeat James Cagney vehicle *The Mayor of Hell* (1933) and a curious choice as a detrimental influence on the young. It featured the popular Dead End Kids (Billy Halop, Bobby Jordan, Gabriel Dell, Huntz Hall, Leo Gorcey, Bernard Punsley) as New York slum dwellers who, on being arrested for theft and assault, are sent to Gatesville Reformatory for delinquents. The dishonest warden of the reform school, superintendent Morgan (Cy Kendall), is a political grafter who unfairly places an innocent member of the Dead End gang in solitary confinement. Humphrey Bogart is cast against type as do-gooder Mark Braden, head of a New York settlement house, who is made the reform school's deputy commissioner of correction. Braden eventually suspends Morgan and institutes a cadet-style 'honour system' among the inmates. He also saves the Dead End Kids from committing a tragic error when their escape is engineered by the sadistic head keeper. Justice triumphs, the boys are rehabilitated to be released on parole and Morgan meets his comeuppance. A moralistic reform-school melodrama directed by Lewis Seiler, *Crime School* did not recommend or glamorize juvenile crime, whatever those who had not seen it might believe. Brutalizing youngsters in institutions, the film's message ran, only made their delinquent situation worse. A contemporary reviewer thought it a realistic, grim and sordid story, 'a strong indictment of any prison system which employs similar methods, and of slum conditions in general'.[12]

Like other youth-orientated crime films of the period, *Crime School* built upon the success of producer Samuel Goldwyn's *Dead End* (1937), a theatrical but grim portrait of slum life which again featured Humphrey Bogart, this time in the more familiar role of a gangster on the run. In March 1936, Goldwyn, his wife Frances, and director William Wyler, had gone to the Belasco Theatre in New York to see Sidney Kingsley's smash-hit play set before the 'dead end' of one of the city's streets that runs into the East River. A wall separates wealthy residents of the East River Terrace apartment houses from squalid tenement buildings that line the other side of the street, until the rich are forced to confront the poor when a back entry must be used because of frontage repairs. Goldwyn was impressed by the play and decided to bring it to the screen, although he had refused to make gangster films in the early 1930s because he believed they were a bad influence on children. The gruff producer hired Wyler to direct, left-winger Lillian Hellman to do a screenplay, brought over Bogart from Warners to play the villainous 'Baby Face' Martin, cast Sylvia Sydney to play Drina, a hardworking girl out on strike for a living wage, and Goldwyn contract-player Joel McCrea to play Gimpty, a rickets-disabled product of the local gangs. In the movie version McCrea becomes handsome, all-American hero Dave Connell, an unemployed architect ('six years at college and all you get is handouts') with a hopeless crush on a society girl ('I don't belong in your world'). Goldwyn also brought out the stage play's 'Dead End Kids' to Hollywood from New York to repeat their roles as a vibrant gang of young street kids preparing to become career criminals. Their leader Tommy (Billy Halop) is the much put upon Drina's younger brother.[13]

The film is set in motion when the Bogart character, a childhood gang friend of Dave turned killer now disguised by plastic surgery, returns to the tenement slums to seek out his mother ('you ain't no son of mine') and Francie (Claire Trevor), an old flame who has turned to prostitution. Dave is not intimidated by Martin, who becomes a role model to the Dead End Kids ('"Baby Face" he was the tops'), for he challenges the gangster's every move and, in a violent resolution typical of Hollywood, ultimately guns him down. Sam Goldwyn expected censorship problems in filming such a controversial play about the privileged and the oppressed. Hence he instructed Hellman to clean it up and, fearful of too much realism being injected, insisted on the film being shot on the studio lot rather than in the slums of New York. 'Do not show, or emphasize, the presence of filth or smelly garbage cans, or garbage floating in the river', the American censor, Joseph Breen, warned. Goldwyn complained that Richard Day's studio set was 'filthy' and evidently had fresh fruit trucked in daily to 'litter' it, muttering to himself: 'There won't be any dirty slums – not in my picture.' The Hays Code Office supported and encouraged Goldwyn as a result and met privately with him during pre-production to work out how far the movie could go in delivering playwright Kingsley's damning message that America's urban slums bred criminality.[14]

The increasing collaboration between Hollywood and the BBFC during the 1930s ensured that hard-hitting if histrionic pictures like *Dead End* could be passed uncut for exhibition in Britain. This was a far cry from earlier British attitudes to the American gangster film. The Hays people even pressed the British censor to approve Goldwyn's film for the important British market, illustrating the role of the MPPDA in protecting the financial investments of Hollywood producers. Hellman's screenplay was first submitted to the BBFC in June 1937, where it was received rather tepidly by Colonel Hanna. 'Though the setting is squalid and many of the characters are not attractive', the Colonel reported, 'I do not think we can say it is too sordid for exhibition, unless of course the producer concentrates on getting sordid effects.' This was exactly the kind of effect that Sam Goldwyn, in consultation with the American censors, was trying to avoid. The latter had already insisted that the vulgar language and criminal activities of the Dead End Kids be cleaned up, the play's reference to Francie's venereal disease be expunged, that the violence be tamed, and 'Baby Face' (Bogart) not be allowed to kill a policeman. Breen also strongly objected to the play's anti-capitalistic 'endorsement of government action' to replace slum tenements. In London the BBFC's fastidious Mrs N. Crouzet, not to be outdone, sought among other deletions the removal of a neighbourhood-gang character T. B. (Gabriel Dell) whose symptoms of tuberculosis ('He is always coughing') she found rather disturbing.[15]

The British censors, Hanna and Crouzet, insisted repeatedly that the poverty of *Dead End* should be glossed over, but the Hays Office were more cautious, particularly since Goldwyn had been one of those to originally appoint Hays. The producer refused to make any changes to satisfy the British censors on a script of which he had become proud and to which he pinned his hopes of remaining independent of the major Hollywood studios. Thus some surprisingly radical dialogue in Hellman's final draft remained uncut, such as Joel McCrea's diatribe about the struggle of the poor to survive in the 'rotten holes we live in'. The BBFC must have felt, in the aftermath of economic depression, such liberal sentiments would strike an uncomfortable chord in Britain's paternalistic, class-structured society. We need only recall that they did not allow *Love on the Dole* (1933), Walter Greenwood's depression-set Salford novel, to be filmed until 1941. Ultimately, for Hollywood, Britain was just one more foreign market to be exploited. Even if 'it was an important market to which concessions had to be granted, it was rapidly becoming apparent to the BBFC that only so much interference in major American films would be tolerated'.[16]

As already indicated, *Dead End* saw the first appearance in neighbourhood movie theatres of the 'Dead End Kids', whose louche presence graced so many of the slum gang and reform school films of the period. This temporary popularity soon passed but, minus Billy Halop, they became the East Side Kids then, known from 1946 as the Bowery Boys, carried on in low-budget action-comedies, their middle-aged appearance straining audience credulity until retirement in 1957. Nearly all of the films in Hollywood's juvenile gang cycle of the late 1930s garnered the same adverse reaction from those in authority as had *Crime School*, despite their ingenuous Hays-Code-approved storylines. 'B' movie specialist Monogram's *Boys of the Streets* (1937) was a pale imitation of the *Dead End* plot with former child star Jackie Cooper as Chuck Brennan, the head of a gang of youngsters involved in crime and living in a squalid tenement district. When a policeman is shot by some small-time racketeers Chuck has fallen in with, he is brought to his senses and decides to make a proper start in life by joining the US Navy. Universal soon came up with Harold Young's less than credible *Little Tough Guy* (1938) that imitates both *Dead End* and *Crime School*. Johnny Boylan (Billy Halop) is forced by the wrongful imprisonment of his father into the New York streets where he becomes the leader of a Lower East Side gang, played by the other Dead End Kids, taken over and betrayed by a rich youth (Jackie Searl) in search of excitement. The latter eventually delivers them, with guns in their hands, into an armed police cordon and they are sent to reform school.[17]

In the 'A' film category, Warner's *Angels with Dirty Faces* (1938), directed by Michael Curtiz, cast James Cagney as a charismatic gangster, Rocky Sullivan, who is hero-worshipped by the Dead End Kids, and starred Humphrey Bogart as an unscrupulous lawyer and racketeer. Rocky is persuaded by a childhood friend who is now a priest (Pat O'Brien) to destroy his heroic gangster image at the end of the film by 'dying yellow' or going to the electric chair acting convincingly like a snivelling coward. For youngsters in the cinema audience, of course, Rocky remains the heroic figure he has been throughout. Inevitably, *Angels Wash their Faces* (1939) and *Hell's Kitchen* (1939) followed, both with the now over-familiar Dead End Kids but more tritely formulaic. Based on a Borden Chase novel, Universal's *The Devil's Party* (1938), directed by Ray McCarey, featured a waterfront gang of slum kids in New York's Hell's Kitchen who grow up to follow different occupations. The death of a man who owes money to the gang's leader (Victor McLaglen), now an underworld nightclub owner, involves all five of them and resulting complications end in McLaglen's death. The latter dies nobly, one of the five now wearing a clerical collar (Paul Kelly) kneeling beside him, and has a plaque unveiled at a boys' club in his memory. Finally, MGM's *Boy's Town* (1938), directed by Norman Taurog, featured Spencer Tracey as an Irish priest, Father Edward Flanagan who, in 1917 Omaha, Nebraska, set up a famous rehabilitation campus for juvenile delinquents. Mickey Rooney is his toughest enrolee, torn between loyalty to Boy's Town and to his old life, represented by a gangster older brother. Pious sentimentality and the singing of 'Ave Maria' are prominent in this sanctimonious middle-American movie. Altogether, aside from showcasing the roster of Hollywood's young stars, these 1937–9 pictures could hardly be accused of condoning crime.[18]

American Panic over Gangster Movies

As more Hollywood gangster films were released – nine in 1930, 26 in 1931, 28 in 1932 and 15 in 1933 – the cuts relating to breaches of the law ordered by American state and municipal censorship boards also increased. Half of the censored material ordered by the Chicago censorship board in 1930–1 pertained to 'glorification of the gangster or outlaw' and 'showing disrespect for law enforcement'. In New York, state censors slashed over 2200 crime scenes during 1930–2. Yet gangster films were far too popular for the Hollywood studios to pay much attention to the Hays Code, one that, after all, the film industry itself administered. None the less, to mollify the criticism of society's moral guardians, the studios tacked on prologues, added scenes with concerned and angry citizens groups, and had the new film 'czar', Will Hays, assure everybody that gangster films projected the message that 'Crime Does Not Pay'. According to the censorship code that then prevailed, the gangster had to die as a deterrent in each crime film ('Mother of Mercy – is this the end of Rico?'), a scapegoat for the miseries and anger bred by Depression conditions. Yet to those who protested that gangster films were corrupting youth, it did not really matter whether or not these criminals came to a bad end. Moralists believed such films were a violation of the Hays Code simply because their central characters were gangsters, rather than heroic and incorruptible policemen.[19]

By mid-1931, an avalanche of protest, pressure from American church leaders, women's clubs and civic organizations, had resulted in gangster films being banned outright in Worcester, Massachusetts; Syracuse, New York; Evanston, Illinois; and West Orange, New Jersey. Mayor Cermak of Chicago, understandably sensitive about his city's public image, threatened to ban all crime films if Hollywood did not stop using the place as its favourite gangster backdrop. The director of New York's state censorship board, Dr James Wingate, was flooded with complaints about *Little Caesar* from people who were appalled when children watching the film 'applaud the gang leader as a hero'. The respected reform warden of Sing-Sing prison, Lewis E. Lawes, claimed naïvely that 'many prisoners have told me that crime pictures started them on their course'. The public safety director of Philadelphia blamed a contemporary crime wave in his city on 'the meticulous care which the moving picture people take in instructing the youth of our nation exactly how to commit crime'. The new breed of 'flashy movie gangsters' were also attacked by many leading newspapers and magazines, as cited in Gregory D. Black's well-informed study of Hollywood censorship. The conservative *Christian Science Monitor* deplored Hollywood's determination to create 'an admiration of the criminal as a dramatic figure'. The Houston *Chronicle* attacked films for infecting the public with a plague of 'bedroom, liquor, gangster and criminal themes'. The Newark, New Jersey, *Ledger* claimed gangsters were 'poisoning the minds of the youth of this country'. *Commonweal* branded the cinema as a 'social milieu that serves as a very fair kindergarten of crime'. The *Kansas City Times* observed that, although gangster films were alright for adults, 'they are misleading, contaminating and often demoralizing to children and youth'.[20]

In April 1931, Will Hays responded to these criticisms by hiring August Vollmer, one of America's most respected law enforcement officials, to examine six recent gangster films for their impact on children: *City Streets, The Finger Points, The Last Parade, The Public Enemy, Quick Millions* and *The Secret Six*. Vollmer, considered by many 'the father of modern police work', had been a reform police chief in Berkeley, California, before moving to the University of Chicago as a professor of police administration. He had recently headed a federal commission to study the effectiveness of American police departments. Hays asked Vollmer to determine whether or not the chosen films incited crime, ridiculed law, created sympathy for the criminal, or violated the Production Code. Should they, asked Hays, be banned? Vollmer eventually reported back that he had found nothing wrong with *The Public Enemy* which was 'more or less a correct depiction of events which transpired in Chicago recently'. The film would, he believed, make the potential gangster hesitate because the moral of the movie was that in the end either the police or other gangsters would get you. *The Secret Six* was a violent Wallace Beery gangster vehicle based on a vigilante committee in Chicago. Rouben Mamoulian's *City Streets* concerned nice young couple Sylvia Sydney and Gary Cooper who get in over their heads with mobster Paul Lukas and his gang. Vollmer thought *Quick Millions*, a film based on the life of gangster Bugs Moran, was 'a good picture'. Only a 'weak-minded suggestible moron' would want to enter a life of crime after watching this movie. *The Finger Points*, based on the true story of a crooked Chicago journalist, was 'not harmful' in any way and, although it highlighted unpleasant aspects of American life, 'it is just as well that the naked truth be revealed'. As a former police officer, Vollner knew full well that many of the events represented in such films had in fact taken place. Criminals were protected by corrupt politicians, policemen, or lawyers and romanticized in the press. Arguments about the harmful effects of these crime movies were, in Vollmer's view, the same as those constantly raised against the 'dime novel' and equally unverifiable. Gangster films might be 'trashy and vulgar', but there was no proof that they created criminals. If anything, Vollmer thought Hollywood movies exaggerated the effectiveness of law enforcement officers in bringing criminals to justice, thereby placing small-town morality above big-city social realism.[21]

Hays' damage-limitation exercise did little to silence criticism and there was evidence of growing state and municipal censorship, while reformers wanted to go further and persuade the federal government to institute a national motion-picture censorship office. A research time-bomb was quietly ticking away, meanwhile, that would eventually shatter the complacency of the Hollywood moguls. Rising concern about the harmful effects of the cinema on youthful American minds had in 1928 led anti-Hollywood campaigner the Revd William H. Short and his Motion Picture Research Council (MPRC) to commission a series of studies financed from the Payne Study and Experiment Fund, a philanthropic organization based in Cleveland, and headed by Professor W. W. Charters, director of educational research at Ohio State University. The celebrated Payne Fund Studies, which took 4 years to complete, were published from 1933 to 1934 in eight sober, black-bound volumes of scholarly reports which, in a qualified academic style, tended to avoid sweeping conclusions. They also showed that 30 per cent of the American cinema audience was made up of children and adolescents. One early volume to be published, *Movies, Delinquency, and Crime* (1933), offered self-reporting by delinquent youths in which they blamed gangster films for aspects of their undesirable social behaviour, but the authors went no further than arguing that movies only indirectly encouraged criminal activities by stimulating fantasies and day-dreaming. Another volume concluded that the influence of movies on children was strong but was 'specific for a given child and a given movie'. Failure to publish one of the key projected studies, announced as *Boys, Movies and City Streets*, was owing to its authors' suggestion that film, instead of being the negative influence on social behaviour predetermined by Short's MPRC, could have positive educational value if used properly in schools. None the less, when Charters himself summarized the Payne findings in *Motion Pictures and Youth* (1933), he coined the term 'emotional possession' to describe children sitting before a cinema screen, albeit concluding tentatively that movies were only 'one among many influences which mold the experience of children'.[22]

Yet the Payne Fund's ostensibly 'scientific' research, conducted by reputable sociologists, psychologists and social psychologists, had already been distorted to support the kind of statements about the effects of movies on young audiences that moral reformers had been making for years. A requirement of the original funding was that a single author abbreviate the carefully qualified results into one companion volume for general consumption. This assignment went to Henry James Forman who produced *Our Movie Made Children* (1933), the first book in the Payne series to be published and an exaggerated indictment of Hollywood which quickly became a best-seller. The cautious findings of Charters and his colleagues were quickly forgotten when, by taking phrases out of context, Forman exaggerated incidences of insomnia, rapid eye movements, excitability and other undesirable effects from exposure to the movies. Far more attention was given by the media to this deliberately sensationalized and glib condensation than to the eight volumes written by academics. Within 18 months *Our Movie Made Children* had gone through four printings and was widely reviewed and discussed as the authoritative public source, a salutary warning that something had to be done. Forman accepted at face value the claims of juveniles themselves in regard to the effects of gangster films. ' " *The Big House*", says a ten-year old, "made me feel like I was a big, tough guy. I felt just like Machine Gun Butch". An 11-year old Italian boy chortles, "When I saw Jack Oakie in *The Gang Busters* I felt like a big gangster". "I feel like the big shot that knows schemes and hiding places", confessed another, "and knows how to kill and capture cops and get a lot of money".' Anecdotal evidence such as the above was used to portray gangster films as making boys more tolerant of crime and sympathetic towards the tough criminal, hence day-dreaming fantasies could lead to the acting out of criminal behaviour. Such films were depicted as supplying the spark that led to delinquency: '"from these criminal pictures I got the idea that I wanted to participate in crime, robbing stores preferably". "I learned something from *The Doorway to Hell* gangster picture. It shows how to drown out shots from a gun by backfiring a car".' There remains a huge void, of course, between observing the techniques of crime in a film and choosing to put them into practice. It does not follow that this youthful fantasizing had any long-term effect on those juveniles cited above, probably none of whom will have gone on to become career criminals. The impulse to persistent criminality lay far deeper in domestic, environmental and psychological factors.[23]

The turning point in controlling film subject matter hence came when the carefully qualified discoveries of the Payne Fund researchers were misrepresented with evidence taken out of context and made palatable for a popular audience. Forman toured the country denouncing the movies, especially gangster films. When he addressed the New York State Governor's Conference on 'Crime and Criminal and Society' held towards the end of 1935 in Albany, one report carried the headline: 'Film – A School for Crime'. Forman reminded the assembled dignitaries of a child's alarming capacity for almost total recall of films seen. He cited a midwestern study that had examined 115 films appearing at random in a local cinema in which 449 crimes were committed or attempted, or almost four crimes per picture. That deviant acts on film might provide drama, suspense, and even therapy for the law-abiding was overlooked. Because of the large number of crimes taking place on screen, young filmgoers were supposedly given 'a supplementary system of education, in which crime is a major subject'. And the criminal, be it said, was frequently made 'very attractive, gay, care free, jaunty, courageous'. Just as girls acquired hints of how to dress, even techniques of lovemaking from screen characters, so boys supposedly learnt methods of crime from their film heroes. 'It has been found that no less than 31 different techniques of crime are learned by young lads from the movies and subsequently practised in their crime activities.' Forman concluded with an appeal that those present had to consider what could be done to 'mitigate some of the dire consequences that may ensue from socially undesirable motion pictures'.[24]

Evidently, the comatose 1930 Production Code was not being enforced and, in any case, was not legally enforceable, so from 1934 the renowned Legion of Decency, formed by the Committee of Catholic Bishops, took up Forman's challenge and went on the march. The Legion claimed it was dismayed by the then declining movie industry's sex-and-crime formula films of the early 1930s and so had organized a campaign to boycott 'vile and unwholesome' motion pictures. Catholics were asked to sign a pledge, in regard to gangster films, swearing to 'do all that I can to arouse public opinion against the portrayal of vice as a normal condition of affairs and against depicting criminals of any class as heroes and heroines, presenting their filthy philosophy of life as something acceptable to decent men and women'. A boycott campaign, utilizing other like-minded groups, was launched though the media, lists of condemned films were circulated and some movie houses were picketed. Film producers broke ranks in mid-1934, even before this anti-crime film propaganda picked up full steam. They agreed not to release or distribute a film that did not have an MPPDA certificate of approval which was to be issued according to the 1930 Code and administered by a Hays Office promising to be more serious about censorship. 'The movie industry', writes Eugene Rosow, 'finally consented to take self-regulation seriously'. A $25,000 penalty was to be charged for producing, distributing or exhibiting a picture without the certificate of approval, but there is no record of it ever having being levied. In order to force Hays and Hollywood to censor movies more vigorously, the Legion had also engineered the appointment of Joseph Breen, a rabid Catholic anti-semite, as head of the Production Code Administration. In future, gangster films would have to be made with more care for the censors' point of view. Hollywood managed, none the less, to avoid federal government regulation and even after 1934 continued to evade the Code 'whenever profitable'.[25]

As the decade wore on, Hollywood producers discovered that the best way to exploit the crime genre's immense popularity and to satisfy the censors at the same time was to turn the gangster character into a law officer. The time was right for the reincarnation of the gangster as a federal government man drafted into the war on rising crime, one of the worst effects of the Depression. By the mid-thirties Warners started to offer idealized portraits of policemen and the Federal Bureau of Investigation (FBI), rather than of gangsters or criminals, in patriotic films such as William Keighley's *G-Men* (1935) and *Special Agent* (1935), starring James Cagney and George Brent respectively. An advertisement for *G-Men* proclaimed of Cagney that 'the king of ACTION joins the crime smashers!' Edward G. Robinson was also enlisted as a crusading cop infiltrating a gang led by a vicious Humphrey Bogart in Keighley's outstanding *Bullets or Ballots* (1936). The transformation of the movie gangster into an FBI agent or G-man was in part a response to criticism from censorship lobbies such as the Legion of Decency. Warner Brothers were also making a contribution to propaganda for a strong New Deal administration by launching this new cycle of films. *G-Men*, for example, used the resources of a popular film form and one of its star names to advocate the arming of the FBI, because 'federal power depends ultimately on firepower'. After 1935, writes critic Andrew Sarris, it would be decades before Hollywood could recapture the 'lustful licence' it had accepted as a matter of course in 1929. For decades Breen, Hays and the Legion of Decency virtually controlled the content of all Hollywood films. The Hays Code itself remained in force until 1967 when it was re-placed by a system of certificated categories.[26]

Local Panic over Hollywood Movies

If the interwar era in Britain was one of falling crime and unparalleled so-cial stability, modern commentators suggest this may have had something to do with the mass public being offered a diet of 'wholesome entertain-ment'. Yet those churchmen, policemen, politicians and others who cam-paigned for stricter censorship in the 1930s were angered over what they felt were incitements to crime in the Hollywood glorification of gangsters on the screen. 'In this complex age it was race suicide to allow foreigners to impregnate falsehood into the lifeblood of this nation', expostulated Sidney Dark, editor of the English *Church Times*, in 1933 with American gangster films in mind. 'Any film that prompts a child to commit crime, teaches him to conceal stolen goods, or to evade the Police or the truth, should never be allowed to circulate', declared the Chief Constable of Wallasey, near Birkenhead, in his 1936 annual report. 'I believe that a lot of the trouble among children today would cease if only they would put a stop to these horrible gangster films', suggested Mrs L. Smythe, a Croydon mother of two, early in 1939. 'It is not to be wondered at that children come away from the cinema full of mad ideas about holding up banks and shoot-ing and killing people'.[27]

A headline in *The Kentish Express* of 16 December 1938 proclaimed 'Council to Ban "Horrific" Films Because of Great Increase in Juvenile Crime', indicating the muddled nature of this particular 'moral panic'. For the local campaign focused on below offers a striking demonstration of how both 'horror' and 'crime films' could be linked, however spuriously, to juvenile delinquency. Sittingbourne and Milton Urban District Council (UDC) had decided, under powers delegated to them, to ban the showing of 'H' certificate or 'horrific' films to all 'children' under 16, owing to the 'serious increase' in juvenile crime in their district of Kent, the garden of England. While the 1930s Universal cycle of horror movies, featuring luminaries such as Boris Karloff, Lon Chaney Jnr and Bela Lugosi, contained frightening Gothic ingredients and even gave fantasy release to hidden sexual desires, their potential for inciting delinquency is far less evident. In any case, it was only after 1939 that something like a juvenile 'crime wave' occurred in England. The number of 16–21-year-olds found guilty of serious offences recorded by the police during the 1930s fluctuated between a narrow band of 350,000 and 450,000 annually.[28]

The 'H' certificate had been introduced by the BBFC in 1932 but there was no suggestion then that British children should be banned altogether from these films. Sittingbourne UDC, imitating the London County Council, were merely seeking to make mandatory the BBFC's warning to parents that no under-16s should attend 'H' films and also to take care of films issued before their ban – *Frankenstein, King Kong, Werewolf of London, Mystery of the Wax Museum, The Walking Dead, Hands of Orlac, Dracula's Daughter*. A columnist in *The East Kent Gazette* went on to congratulate the local council on their decision, while stating that the fathers of those who now blamed the cinema for juvenile delinquency used themselves to blame the 'penny dreadful'. He approved because 'horrific' films were usually adapted from novels, 'the product of a warped mind'. The writer believed that 'if parents will not take the trouble to keep their boys and girls from seeing "horrific" pictures, then the Council is to be commended for exercising its restraining influence'.[29]

A report of the relevant mid-December 1938 UDC meeting elsewhere in *The East Kent Gazette* gave some space to Councillor F. L. Walsh, the sole objector to the 'horror film' resolution. His fellow Sittingbourne councillors were interfering with legitimate business, Walsh argued, usurping something which should really be done by parents. 'When his father was a boy the evil was put down to reading, now it was the films. It was a matter for the cinema trade and parents.' The next speaker, Councillor Baker, had no wish to be an 'old Mother Grundy' but it was 'a serious thing when juveniles were allowed to see some of these films'. He referred to the recent report of a case of shop-breaking in the local press headed: *'"Red Arrow" Gang Before Court. Boy's Shop Breaking Offences. "Due to the Pictures".'*

Five boys had been charged on 10 December 1938 with breaking and entering the Sittingbourne Bargain Centres 2 weeks earlier through a window, also with stealing swiss rolls, four dozen boxes of matches, two tins of apricots, two boxes of cheese, a dozen bath cubes and a key, valued at six shillings and twopence. In a drainpipe behind the shop, Detective Sergeant Johnson found an incriminating notebook and the boxes of matches.[30]

The oldest boy arrested, regarded as the ringleader, had been brought up by his grandmother, from whom he had stolen, and had also recently run away from home. The notebook produced in court contained entries describing the head of the gang as 'Red Arrow', plans of the shop, and the Plaza Picture Theatre, plus a letter with the incriminating message: 'Going to raid the B. C. Sunday 27 November.' The Bench dismissed the case against the two youngest boys, aged eight and 11, because they had probably been led astray. The three older boys were bound over for 3 years under a court-appointed probation officer. They were all ordered to pay five shillings costs each. The Chairman of the Bench, magistrate W. F. Wood, thought that 'this arrangement of maps, etc. found in the notebook is due to the pictures, and one of the conditions of the probation will be that you do not go to the pictures for another three months'.[31] This was indeed a punishment fitting the crime. How far a particular gangster picture may have provided a trigger for the Red Arrow gang's delinquency, or even a direct cause, cannot be ascertained because local press reports omitted to supply any relevant film title. The oldest boy's domestic circumstances would, in any case, appear more germane to the causes of the break-in.

Back in the council chamber, Councillor A. J. Bedelle said he agreed with Councillor Baker and mentioned that he was one of the magistrates who had heard the 'Red Arrow' case referred to above. 'It was absolutely apparent to the magistrates that many of the ideas these boys put into practice they got entirely from the cinema and improved upon them. By licensing these films we are going to do a lot towards nipping in the bud this juvenile crime', Bedelle claimed. 'My opinion is that parents do not exercise sufficient control as to what their children should or should not see. That is a way the Council can help considerably in doing away with this serious menace of juvenile crime.' In a subsequent interview, Councillor Bedelle opined that, as a magistrate, he believed much of the increasing juvenile crime was directly due to the influence of undesirable films. 'Several cases have come to my notice where it is perfectly obvious that boys of an impressionable age visit the cinema, and, as a result, are in the habit of forming gangs, with a leader bearing a name such as "Red Arrow". These gangs plan schemes which are often contrary to the law, and, as a result, the boys find themselves in trouble.' He added that he would like to see 'horrific' and gangster films banned to all under 16. Councillor C. F. Cloake then rose, as a teacher, to endorse Bedelle's simplistic argument, claiming he saw the influence of films on children more than any of those present. 'I am dealing with boys and girls every day', he said. 'Directly they get into the playground they go copying gangsters. It is just the influence of the films. They do not play jolly good games like we did as boys.'[32]

The *East Kent Gazette* went on to interview an anonymous cinema manager about the British licensing system with regard to 'horror' and 'crime' films. He claimed that when 'H' films were exhibited at his cinema, children under 16 were automatically barred. 'H' films were, however, mostly of the 'Frankenstein' type, rather than crime films. 'With regard to crime and gangster films', he said, 'I think that as all these films have an "A" certificate, parents must decide whether or not their children see them.' The astute manager further pointed out that invariably in these films the gangsters or criminals received their just deserts in the end, and the theme was almost without exception that 'crime doesn't pay'. He ended by making the relativistic point that a great many heroes of British history, such as Francis Drake and Robin Hood, would, by modern standards, be termed gangsters. This particular manager was clearly well briefed and quite capable of dealing with a journalist by delivering the film industry's standard position in regard to BBFC licensing.[33]

Not long after, *The Daily Herald*, a left-wing British newspaper, ran a column on 18 January 1939 in its topical debate series asking 'Do Gang Films Spoil A Boy?' or whether 'sensational films of gangsters and bandits often lead to juvenile crime?' The column began by citing the case of a boy charged at a juvenile court in Sidmouth, Devon, with stealing a bicycle who, after returning from the pictures, would 'dress up and remark he was a tough guy'. The local press reported that, according to his parents, he had also been reading a lot of books about bandits. Announcing the Bench's decision that the boy would be placed on probation for a year, the chairman, Sir Archibald Bodkin, remarked, 'whether it is the reading of these rubbishy books . . . or of going to some of these ridiculous pictures that are shown I do not know, but there are plenty of good wholesome books of adventure which should appeal to a boy like you instead of this ridiculous nonsense about gangsters and the like'. Moving the motion in *The Daily Herald*, the self-same Sir Archibald, a former director of public prosecutions, admitted he was bored stiff by gangster films, 'even if there is a good film to see one generally has to sit through this rubbish and watch gangsters shooting each other and having mad car races'. Whether or not crime films 'definitely leave an impression on a boy's mind. . . . I think it is quite definite that they leave no good effect', claimed Bodkin illogically. The irony of this kind of attack on gangster films was that, seemingly unknown to their critics, Warners and other American studios had changed direction in the mid-1930s and were now making crime-related films vigorously supporting law and order.[34]

To oppose the motion, *The Daily Herald* cited Dr Emanuel Miller, director of the East London child guidance clinic, who thought there were no grounds for believing that Hollywood films produced gangsters. 'Most boys already have it in their minds that they are "tough guys", and these films just provide a mirror of what they like to think they are. Naturally, boys like plenty of action and pugnacity in their entertainment, so these gangster films are popular.' He was supported by Otto L. Shaw, headmaster of the progressive Red Hill School, near Maidstone, who believed that 'an impressionable child who goes wrong and finds himself in a juvenile court is generally the type who would go wrong in any case, whether he saw films of gangsters or not'. The head's own schoolchildren went 'to see "horror" films and they produce no dreams or sleepless nights. Films play a very minor part in the causes of child delinquency. In fact, I would state definitely and categorically that films have no lasting effect on a child.'[35]

The British Home Office, then a liberal bastion, lent support to such views and was never seriously concerned about the cinema's role in juvenile delinquency. Home Secretary Sir Herbert Samuel told the House of Commons, when it debated juvenile crime on 15 April 1932, that 'my very expert and experienced advisors at the Home Office are of the opinion that on the whole the cinema conduces more to the prevention of crime than to its commission. . . . In general, the Home Office's opinion is that if the cinemas had never existed there would probably be more crime than there is rather than less.' During a Commons debate in 1938 the new Home Secretary, Sir Samuel Hoare, reported inquiries which showed that 'it is not so much films and shilling shockers that make juvenile crime, but broken homes, indulgent mothers, unkind stepmothers or unemployment'. Further support came from noted criminologist Karl Mannheim and his assistant Dryden Donkin who had analysed the records of 1106 boys discharged from English borstal (penal) institutions during the period 1922–36. They demonstrated that for only six of these boys was delinquency in any way related to the cinema, while 'reading crime stories' was a predisposing cause in only one case. 'It is useful to note that some factors which are frequently spoken of as being of grave moment in producing delinquency appear in very few cases in our enquiry, and it may be that opinion is in need of revision in such cases', Mannheim dryly concluded.[36]

Conclusions

In comparison to the staged or printed forms of commercial entertainment discussed in previous chapters, the immediate visual and visceral impact of moving pictures on youngsters in the first half of the twentieth century was overwhelming. There is little real evidence, on the other hand, to suggest that what was seen on the screen could somehow originate criminal behaviour, except possibly in regard to the extremely impressionable of low intelligence. An exaggerated 'hypodermic-needle theory' of media effects, that American gangster films by 'injecting' passive young filmgoers generated imitative forms of criminal behaviour, cannot be sustained, despite its constant repetition. Those who argued along these lines produced little or no concrete evidence to support their case, relying simply on unproven assumptions about the monocausal relationship between crimes portrayed in films and crimes committed by juveniles. Watching crime films could hardly be as significant a determinant of delinquent behaviour as an individual's psychology, family history, opportunities or environment. Even if we accept the possibility that seeing theft or assault acted out on the screen could operate as a trigger, only the already highly motivated in an audience of millions would go on to act out criminal behaviour first seen on film. Similarly, the use of guns in gangster movies as a preferred way to solve problems, on both sides of the law, was a cultural product of America's confrontational and violent history, reinforcing rather than initiating behaviour patterns.

If little credence can be attached to the 'behavioural effects' argument of contemporary film censors and moral guardians, can anything positive be said about such a violent and sleazy cinematic form as the gangster film? 'Morality groups might fulminate against them as primers for juvenile delinquency and draw dark comparisons between their inherent anarchic immorality and the increase in actual crime in the streets practiced by Capone, Dillinger and their ilk', writes an historian of the Legion of Decency. 'But the movie-going public found a narcotic in thrillers that banished from the mind, for a few hours at least, the cruel world of soup kitchens and Hoovervilles [shanty towns] that lay beyond the Bijou and the Ritz.' Crime and gangster films also merit greater attention than they have so far received as an important American film genre, illuminating how deviant lives are lived on the streets in each decade of the twentieth century. They represent the anti-social and criminal underside of urban America in a way that other film genres cannot. Gangster films, however violent, shoddy or formulaic, also possess an energy, pace and excitement, a driving force represented in the 1930s by outstanding actors such as Edward G. Robinson, Humphrey Bogart and James Cagney. Many of these films were, and still are, based on contemporary crime figures and events, 'wrenched from today's headlines' as Warner Brothers proclaimed. Because they are so near in time to actual events, 'crime films provide a useful means to review a major strain of American violence along a dynamic continuum'. The genre continues to thrive and must surely have earned the right to be studied by cultural historians as 'neither a producer nor a controller of crime, but rather as the expression of America's changing attitudes towards crime'.[37]

5

'HORROR COMIC' PANIC: CAMPAIGNING AGAINST COMIC BOOKS IN THE 1940s AND 1950s

This chapter focuses on a controversial period of American comic-book history, from the late 1940s to the mid-1950s, during which a wide variety of violent and explicit 'crime' and 'horror comic' titles could be purchased for only 10 cents. The term 'comic book' refers to four-colour pamphlets, 165 mm by 255 mm, with narratives in sequential illustrated form (usually in conjunction with text), slick covers and a pulp-paper interior. They represent a relatively new form of commercial culture emerging out of New Deal America, like the law-and-order cycle of crime movies, to act as an eventual replacement for declining newsstand sales of the 'pulps' or detective, sport, adventure and science-fiction short-story magazines with racy covers, printed mostly on cheap wood-pulp paper.[1]

Publishing comic books rapidly became a million-dollar business and one of the few economic success stories of the Depression years. The consequent 'moral panic' over comic-book reading and its supposed influence on juvenile delinquency during the early years of the Cold War will be placed here within the context of McCarthyism, intellectual hostility to mass culture, and the cult of domesticity in 1950s America. Campaigns against the comic book during the Truman and Eisenhower Presidencies were also fuelled by the presence of a firm sense of 'good taste' in cultural matters that in our own postmodern age, where aesthetic standards can no longer be assumed, has largely evaporated. Raising the issue of taste invites consideration of the 'social construction of value' and exploration of ways in which this critique of the judgement of taste can be applied not just to social relations but also to stratification based upon age.[2]

The Gaines Connection: EC Comic Books

A major contribution to the emergence of the comic-book publishing industry in the early 1930s was made by salesman Maxwell Charles Gaines
(1896–1947), the quick-tempered and ambitious father of the man who, 20
years later, helped launch the 'horror comic' trend. Assisted by Harry
Wildenberg, sales manager of the Eastern Color Printing Company of
Waterbury, Connecticut, Max Gaines first interested prominent advertisers in using the comic book, containing reprints of familiar Sunday newspaper comic strips, as a 'premium book' or free promotional gimmick.
Eastern's sales personnel then came up with the innovative idea of selling
their 'premium' compilations directly to children by persuading the
American News Company, distributor of 'dime novels' to a previous generation, to deliver a monthly comic book to newsstands across the country.
In May 1934, under Gaines' supervision, 35,000 copies of the first issue of
Famous Funnies hit the stands priced at 10 cents. This was the first American
comic magazine in a modern format to be placed on newsstands for sale. It
launched an entire new service industry.[3]

By 1941 there were over 30 comic-book publishers producing 150 different monthly titles, with combined sales of from 15 to 18 million copies
every month, and a projected multiple readership of nearly 60 million.
Two years later, comic book sales had almost doubled again, swollen by the
Pacific War's armed-service readers, to a new high of at least 25 million
newsstand sales a month. Gaines' and Harry Donenfield's AA Group and
the latter's Detective Comics (DC) group accounted for about one-third of
total sales. New York publishers such as Donenfield adopted assembly-line
methods to manufacture a consumable product, not unlike the late-Victorian proprietors of 'penny dreadfuls'. Comic-book editors and writers were
employed in warren-like Manhattan offices producing formula plots that
were drawn, inked and lettered by a succession of facile and sometimes
gifted artists; often not credited either because they disowned their work or
because publishers wanted the creative talent working on a series character
to be easily interchangeable.[4]

Early in 1945, Gaines was bought out of his soured partnership with
Donenfeld and his accountant, Jack Liebowitz, for half a millon dollars,
tax-free. Two weeks later Max was back in business on his own as the
founder of Educational Comics (EC), Inc. that went on to specialize
in didactic or innocuous titles such as *Picture Stories from the Bible, Animal
Fables* and *Tiny Tot Comics*. Sales were unimpressive, despite the initial mar-
ket-led demand for superhero comic books having subsided. On the other

hand, more astute publishers such as Leverett ('Lev') Gleason, who had worked in the advertising department of Eastern Color, benefited from a lucrative post-war trend towards 'crime comic' books targeted at the adult reader, such as his influential market leader *Crime Does Not Pay* (1942–55). In 1948 this pseudo-realistic comic book and its equally lurid companion title, *Crime and Punishment* (1948–55), were selling over two million monthly copies. Thus comic books were already a well-established form of American mass culture by the time they came under critical investigation.[5]

In the meantime, Max Gaines, pioneer of comic-book publishers, was drowned in 1947 while out boating on Lake Placid, in upstate New York, and his 25-year-old son William Maxwell Gaines (1922–92), training to be a teacher at New York University (NYU), reluctantly took over his father's loss-making company and changed the acronym from 'Educational' to 'Entertaining Comics' (EC). Following current fashions, EC initially put out western, romance and crime comic books, using a talented pool of freelance artists and writers, among them Wally Wood, Jack Davis, Harvey Kurtzman, Reed Crandall, Bill Elder, Johnny Craig and 'Ghastly' Graham Ingels. In April 1950, 2 months before North Korea invaded South Korea and raised the temperature of the Cold War, Bill Gaines and his creative partner, artist-editor Albert ('Al') Feldstein, decided to launch the first of the EC 'New Trend' titles. Gaines may have got the idea for the new horror tendency from artist Sheldon Moldoff who had packaged a prototype comic book. The EC firm's no longer commercial 'crime comics' were dropped and replaced with two macabre 'horror comics', *The Crypt of Terror* (1950), later retitled *Tales from the Crypt* (1950–5) and *The Vault of Horror* (1950–4), hosted by a cadaverous Crypt Keeper and Vault Keeper whose origins lay in the ghoulish hosts of American radio thrillers. Television ownership was in its infancy during the heyday of comic books, so EC's talented contributors were functioning in a primary visual medium and doing their best, interfacing with a mass audience, to raise the level of comic book literacy.[6]

If not the first 'horror comics', EC's were certainly among the best and most innovative. Gaines and Feldstein inspired a boom for graphic horror fantasy that in the next 4 years would see comic-book publishers circulate over 100 new horror titles and 2400 separate issues. Together they launched a series of comic books that changed the face of juvenile reading in America, but which their critics viewed as debauching the young. For EC's imaginative horror stories dealt not so much with the remote past as with contemporary America, portraying families consumed by murderous

hatreds, businessmen killing for profit and young slaying old for inherit-
ances. The celebrated EC horror trilogy was made complete when Gaines
axed his remaining western comic and in May 1950 started *The Haunt of
Fear* (1950–4), filled with 'illustrated suspenstories [*sic*] that we dare you to
read'. Gaines' other New Trend title for 1950 was *Crime SuspenStories*
(1950–5), a more adult version of the popular crime comics of the day.
Supported financially by the immediate popular success of his 'horror
comics', Gaines also printed some innovative science-fiction titles, *Weird
Fantasy* (1950–4) and *Weird Science* (1950–4), that famously ran stories by
author Ray Bradbury. In February 1952 Gaines added another New Trend
title, *Shock SuspenStories* (1952–5), hard-hitting in its treatment of topics
such as racism, drug addiction and anti-communist 'witch hunts'. The EC
horror titles, along with equally gory and violent imitations by their competitors, Marvel, Ace, Harvey and Story, created a massive backlash
against the entire comic-book industry that led eventually to Gaines being
called before a Senate subcommittee.[7]

Warshow, the Horror Comics and Dr Wertham

The sales peak for comic books was reached in 1953–4, at the height of the
'horror comic' craze, by which time a staggering 75 million 10-cent copies
were being bought and traded by various age groups in America each
month. Cultural and film critic Robert Warshow, a pioneer in studies of
popular culture ('The Gangster as Tragic Hero'), drew the attention of the
Eastern intellectual establishment to the significance of the new trend in
comic books when, in June 1954, he published an informative piece, 'Paul,
the Horror Comics, and Dr. Wertham', in *Commentary*, the respected New
York-Jewish intellectual review. In the spring of 1954, French colonial
forces had been defeated at Dien Bien Phu in north Indochina by the communist Vietminh, a prelude to subsequent American involvement in Viet-
nam. Warshow's article was editorialized as 'displaying one parent and one
child in their *cold war* over the question of comic books' [my emphasis].
The current international deadlock was used, that is, as a metaphor of this
particular father's stand-off with his 11-year-old son, Paul, over comic-
book reading. Warshow's article focused on the 'horror comic' titles of the
EC Group owned by Bill Gaines, of which Paul was an avid collector, particularly *The Haunt of Fear* and *Tales from the Crypt*. A prominent New York
psychiatrist, Dr Fredric Wertham (1895–1981), engaged at this time in a

highly publicized campaign against 'horror comic' books, completed the triumvirate of the essay's title.[8]

Warshow emphasized the 'mechanical' nature of the comic book medium in his article and, while admitting that the EC line, particularly the satirical titles *Mad* and *Panic*, displayed a certain imaginative flair, would have preferred Paul not to read them. Yet Dr Wertham's major proposition, in his influential *Seduction of the Innocent: The Influence of Comic Books on Today's Youth* (1954), drawing a significant correlation between reading comic books and the more serious forms of juvenile delinquency, met with considerable scepticism from Warshow. He characterized Wertham's extraordinary diatribe as morally confused, intemperate and simple-minded, 'a kind of crime comic book for parents'. Warshow's own son had not been turned into a delinquent by his comic-book reading, 'the bloodiest of ax murders does not disturb his sleep or increase the violence of his own impulses'. Even so, this otherwise liberal critic did advocate 'some kind of regulation' or censorship of the 'worst' comic books but without mentioning any titles.[9]

Dr Wertham's tendentious book tackled an emotive issue but was considered by most reviewers to be mediocre in execution. The general public, not the psychiatric community, was clearly the intended audience. He had used inadequate sampling and the book lacked a proper control group, consisting mostly of random, undocumented and unverifiable case histories about children who had supposedly been harmed by reading comic books. Wertham failed to substantiate that his case studies were in any way typical of all delinquents who read comics, or that delinquents who did not read 'horror comics' did not commit similar types of offences. His book also encouraged the habit of projecting resentment at rising juvenile crime upon some specific element in popular culture which became a convenient scapegoat for failure to control the whole range of social breakdown. 'The scientific worker in this field can place no credence in his results', claimed a Professor of Education at NYU. 'One feels admiration for the author's single-mindedness and courage, yet cannot fail to be critical of superficial documentation and his habit of jumping to conclusions', concluded an anonymous British reviewer. *Seduction of the Innocent* was given a much wider currency when condensed in the pages of the *Reader's Digest*, thereby creating an exaggerated fear among American parents of what was lurking behind the covers of the comic books read so avidly by their children. In making a reductionist causal link between comic books and crime, Wertham's book was more responsible than any other critique of the medium for forcing self-censorship upon the

American comic-book industry and thus substantially altering 'product' content.[10]

Wertham's crusade against media violence, eventually embracing television and movies, resonated with an argument prevalent among American cultural critics of the period. How could intellectuals, like Robert Warshow, influence the preferences of an audience whose culture was based on the supposedly 'passive' reception of manufactured entertainment largely defined by the commercial designs of the corporate producers of the mass media? Those in cultural authority were also preoccupied with the concept of 'good taste' in juvenile reading, given the supposedly more impressionable nature of the young audience. This related to the way in which a cultural hierarchy was constructed by taste arbiters such as Warshow who felt that '*Superman* and *The Three Musketeers* may serve the same psychological needs, but it still matters whether a child reads one or the other.' While generally sympathetic to the popular arts, Warshow despaired of 1950s youth subculture, or the large number of high-school students he imagined living, 'almost entirely in a juvenile underground largely out of touch with the demands of social responsibility, culture and personal refinement'. They would grow up into an 'unhappy isolation', Warshow prophesied darkly, 'sustained by little else but the routine of the working day, the unceasing clamor of television and the juke boxes, and still, in their adult years, the comic books'.[11]

'The Real Evil of this Class of Story'

What was it about the pictorial stories in 'horror comics' that so upset contemporary American educationalists, intellectuals, bureaucrats and politicians? In mid-1954 Richard Clendenen, on loan from the US Children's Bureau to head the investigating staff of a Senate subcommittee looking into juvenile delinquency, obligingly provided senators with summaries of stories taken from the following crime and horror titles: *Black Magic* (Prize), *Fight against Crime* (Story), *Mysterious Adventures* (Story), *Crime Must Pay the Penalty* (Ace), *Strange Tales* (Marvel), *Haunt of Fear* (EC), *Crime SuspenStories* (EC) and *Shock SuspenStories* (EC). Significantly, half the stories sampled featured horrifying violence within a contemporary marriage, typically the disposal of a rich, older wife by a young, greedy husband, closely followed by the gruesome revenge of a reinvigorated corpse. Clendenen felt one particular story taken from *Haunt of Fear* would

'greatly increase a youngster's feeling of insecurity, anxiety, and panic re-
garding placement in a foster home'. It concerned a boy placed from an or-
phanage to live with nice-appearing foster parents who provide excellent
care and insist that he eat nourishing food in abundance. A month later the
boy discovers the reason for their solicitude when they sneak into his room
at night and announce that they are vampires about to drink his rich, red
blood. 'It might be said that right triumphs in the end since the boy turns
into a werewolf and eats both his foster parents', Clendenen wryly commented.[12]

'Orphan', a story of some notoriety from EC's *Shock SuspenStories*, was
outlined by Clendenen as the story of a small, golden-haired, 10-year-old
girl named Lucy who hates both her alcoholic father and her adulterous
mother but loves her Aunt Kate, with whom she would prefer to live. The
child's chance to alter the situation comes when father enters the front gate
and meets his wife running away with another man. Through Lucy's per-
jured testimony at the subsequent trial both the mother and Steve, her boy
friend, are convicted of murdering the father and are shown being electro-
cuted. In the last frame, Lucy tells us how she shot her father from the front
bedroom window, then ran into the yard and pressed a gun into the hands
of her mother who had fainted 'and started the crying act'. All works out as
Lucy had planned and she is now free to live with her Aunt. Children were
often shown in 'horror comics' as observers of internecine strife, usually
avenging one parent murdered unjustly or cuckolded by the other but
here, unusually, as the nemesis of both father and mother. This particular
story was a prime target of campaigners against 'horror comics' who were
offended by its perversion of the romantic idea of childhood innocence. A
modern cultural critic argues, on the other hand, that 'Orphan' represents
comic work at its best and that, because of its retrospective tension, 'Lucy's
tale is a brilliant piece: subtle, effective, and significantly political.'[13]

A grisly story which Clenenden overlooked is 'The Neat Job', taken from
the first issue of the above comic book. It opens with police interviewing
Eleanor Berdeen about her 3-year marriage to obssessively neat Arthur.
EC's publisher Bill Gaines was, coincidentally, a man of compulsive neat-
ness and his old chum Arthur Dreeben was married to a woman called
Eleanor. In the story, Arthur Berdeen makes his wife's life a misery with his
perverted mania for orderliness. Everything has a specific place in his
workshop, including shelves of jars, each labelled carefully, where tiny
screws, nuts and other items are sorted and filed. Eleanor eventually cracks
up, after accidentally shattering a jar full of nails in the cellar, and chops
Arthur to death with an axe. She neatly places the various parts of his

anatomy, precisely labelled, in the rows of jars that line the shelves. The police have already discovered their contents.[14]

That marital disharmony and infidelity were commonplace in EC's output, to evident adult disapproval, is shown by 'A Trace of Murder' taken from *Crime SuspenStories* (known as *Weird SuspenStories* in Canada where 'crime' could not legally be used on a comic book cover). Felix Morley reads in the newspaper about a man who has confessed to poisoning his wife with arsenic and, consequently, serves his own rich but unloved wife with a toxic but non-traceable poison in her coffee. Felix celebrates the death by taking his mistress away on a cruise. Meanwhile, the murdered women's gravestones, conveniently alongside each other in the same cemetery, are switched by mischievous boys. On return, Felix is convicted after a postmortem, albeit for the traceable arsenic murder. Unexpected retribution, the reader learns, invariably strikes the guilty.[15]

EC's polemical *Shock SuspenStories* also took on forthright, liberal and anti-McCarthyite political themes in simple but effective comic-book form. Thus in 'The Patriots!', a Jack Davis story from the second 1952 issue, a crowd watches a military parade of Korean War veterans march past. They are aggravated by a sneering man at the curb who appears immune to the excitement ('He must be one of them lousy Reds!'), making no move to take off his hat when the American flag passes by. Accordingly, the stranger is savagely beaten to death by the hysterical crowd ('That'll teach him a lesson in Americanism he'll never forget!'). The man's wife suddenly returns ('Stop it! Please! What you're doing is wrong! Act like Americans!') and reveals to the mob that when her husband smiled it had come out as a sneer – a result of plastic surgery because of a Korean War shell wound that had also made him blind.[16]

Parent–teacher groups across America would certainly have been disturbed by the kind of present-day nightmare exemplified in the above stories, if they had ever troubled to read 'horror comics' before calling for their suppression. Published and mostly taking place during the Truman and Eisenhower Presidencies, stories in EC titles such as *Tales from the Crypt* are far removed from the origins of horror in the Gothic fantasies of Edgar Allan Poe, Mary Shelley's *Frankenstein* (1818) and Bram Stoker's *Dracula* (1897). They offer instead a domesticated version of horror centred on the modern American family, invariably featuring mutual antipathy, hidden secrets, divorce, adultery and violent impulses. Mass-produced yet well-crafted artifacts that used horror imagery to construct the hidden fears and desires of suburban America, EC's *contes cruels* also reflected twice-married Bill Gaines' own misogyny, phobias and obsessions, acting as a counterpoint to the positive image of marriage and the canonization of the housewife so evident in other media representing this outwardly conformist period.[17]

Hence the 'normal', feminine, American woman of those years, as depicted in the appropriately titled *Ladies' Home Journal*, was supposedly happy staying at home, isolated in a suburban housing tract. In reality, a third of all American women worked for wages, and total female employment grew in the 1950s from 16.5 million to 23 million, representing a third of the total workforce. As depicted in the popular media, none the less, a woman's role was to raise children and think constantly and selflessly about how best to please her husband. When a wife in an EC 'horror comic' was shown indulging her spouse's every whim, it was usually as a prelude to poisoning his favourite meal. Yet EC's egregious attempts to locate horror in the bosom of the American nuclear family went entirely unnoticed by critics like Dr Wertham. He made no attempt whatsoever to analyse the narrative trajectory of comic-book stories, merely selecting a few frames out of context to illustrate his preconceived thesis that comic books taught the techniques of crime and brutality. The frequency of marital violence and breakdown in EC 'horror comics' could be interpreted, with equal validity, as a subversive attempt to undermine the sentimental foundations of the cult of domesticity in contemporary America. EC comic books, by updating the horror formula, presented a forceful and paranoiac critique of America's most hallowed social institution, the middle-class white suburban family, to both a juvenile and an adult audience.[18]

For the readership of these stories in the early 1950s was not by any means confined to American children and adolescents. The 'horror comic' was purchased by both sexes and all ages, by an adult as well as a juvenile customer. 'Our magazines are written for adults, it isn't our fault if the kids read 'em, too', said Bill Gaines in a self-serving interview, when questioned about the harmful effects that 'horror comics' might have on children. 'We were writing for teenagers and young adults, we were writing for the guys that were reading it in the Army', according to Al Feldstein looking back in 1972. 'We were writing for ourselves at our age level, and I think perhaps that was responsible for the level we reached.' One British visitor to America in 1954 claimed to have seen 'hundreds of physically mature men reading comic books. They loved them.' An American survey of 1950 revealed that there was indeed a large adult readership for comic books, horror and otherwise. Roughly 41 per cent of adult males and 28 per cent of adult females read comic books regularly. In the same year a government-sponsored survey of an Ohio town found that 54 per cent of all comic-book readers were over 20 years of age. These percentages are placed in perspect-ive by the 95 per cent of boys and 91 per cent of girls between six and 11 who read comic books, while 80 per cent of all American 'teenagers' (a market-research term popularized by Eugene Gilbert's Youth Marketing Company of Chicago) read comic books as well, usually a dozen or more every month in the 1950s. This is not to deny the possibility, with respect to a particular genre such as horror or crime, that comic-book readership might have been age-specific.[19]

The factor of the audience in the history of cultural production has re-cently been enlarged by literary critics far beyond such manipulative exer-cises in reader participation as the EC Fan-Addict Club, with its 25-cent membership, 9000 charter members and elected chapter presidents. Pro-gressing from the simple insight that a 'horror comic' was an outlet for its reader's fertile imagination, reader-response or reception theories high-light the significance of consumer response to the comic book as an en-coded text. Plots dealing with the murder of wicked step-parents had an evident wish-fulfilment element, allowing, like fairy stories, for the cathar-tic projection of violent impulses. Graphic fantasy stories about spouse murder, as well as about werewolves, resurrected corpses and vampires, might also have been interrogated by adolescent readers as a means of coming to terms with the inevitability of their parents' and their own age-ing, death and decay. Horror represents the safe embodiment of the worst aspects of teenage fantasies, it externalizes those feelings so that the young can protect themselves against them.[20]

McCarthyism and Fear of Mass Culture

From the late 1940s, comic books came under increasing attack in America from teachers, the media, parent groups, legislators, the clergy, police de-partments and psychiatrists. In 1949, public burnings of comic books took place outside several schools in New York State. The initial 'moral panic' was directed against 'crime comic' books, the avalanche of titles inspired by Lev Gleason's *Crime Does Not Pay*, long before EC's 'horror comics' were even a remote gleam in Bill Gaines' eye. 'Crime comics' were accused of glorifying violence, crime and sex, as somehow being responsible for the decline in morals of American youth and what was perceived as a growing number of juvenile crimes. In 1946 the House of Representatives Commit-tee on Un-American Activities (HUAC), investigating alleged subversives, charged left-wing comic-book publisher Gleason with contempt of Congress, arising out of an investigation into the Joint Anti-Fascist Refugee Committee of New York City. This was an organization formed by veterans of the Spanish Civil War to aid Spanish refugees that had been labelled a 'communist front' by the California Senate's Committee on Un-American Activities and with an active Hollywood section that came under attack from HUAC and the Hollywood Right. When the Refugee Committee's New York chairman refused to turn over subpoenaed records, a contempt citation was issued. Lev Gleason, already accused of being 'communist party influenced', was indicted along with a group of 16 others that included *Spartacus*-author Howard Fast. This did not prevent Gleason from becoming the next president of the Association of Comic Magazine Publishers, given that the combined monthly circulations of his titles soon ranked tenth among all American magazines. The preoccupation of Gleason's best-selling comic books with crime and violence may even have provided a catharsis for the pent up fears and supercharged aggression generated by anti-communist hysteria.[21]

Early in 1950, one of the first televised congressional hearings, the Senate's Special Committee to Investigate Organized Crime in Interstate Commerce, under the chairmanship of rising politician Senator Estes Carey Kefauver, decided to look at the problem 'relative to the incidence of juvenile delinquency and the possible influence of so-called crime comic books during the five-year period 1945 to 1950'. A subcommitte was established, 'because of frequently heard charges that juvenile delinquency has increased considerably during the past five years and that this increase has been stimulated by the publication of the so-called crime comic books'. Evidence was solicited from interested parties, such as FBI director J. Edgar Hoover, about the relationship between juvenile crime and 'crime comic' books. Led by their association's president, Lev Gleason, comic book publishers made a convincing case with expert testimony, readership surveys, testimonials and charts of criminal activity by age groups. It appeared that American juvenile delinquency was actually declining during the years that 'crime comic' books increased in popularity. As a result, the majority of Kefauver committee members gave a relatively clean bill of health to the comic books. Newspaper headlines anounced the results of the Senate investigation as 'Comics Don't Foster Crime' and 'Study Finds Doubt Comics Spur Crime'.[22]

Dr Wertham none the less convinced a number of New York state legislators that comic books posed a serious danger to the welfare of children. As a result, in December 1950 he asked the state's joint legislative committee to study comics to support 'a public health law which would forbid the sale and display of all crime comic books to children under the age of fifteen years'. A year later he told the committee that comic books were 'the cause of a psychological mutilation of children' and again urged that his proposed law be enacted. Eventually the New York state legislature passed a bill in March 1952 making it a misdemeanour to either 'publish or sell comic books dealing with fictional crime, bloodshed, or lust that might incite minors to violence or immorality'. The following month Governor Thomas E. Dewey vetoed the bill, on the grounds that its vague wording could be interpreted as being unconstitutional. Wertham pressed forward with his national anti-comic book campaign despite this setback, in the November 1953 issue of the *Ladies' Home Journal* reaching mothers across the nation with 'What Parents Don't Know About Comic Books', a provocative article excerpted from his forthcoming book. 'The parent who shrugs and says his children read only "good" comics usually hasn't read these books himself', Wertham asserted. 'Here is the startling truth about the 90,000,000 comic books America's children read each month.' Media amplification of the comic book 'threat' to parental authority was, in at least 50 American cities, followed by the 'solution' of preventitive or regulatory laws. Nothing like Wertham's single-minded crusade had been seen in North America since the campaign against the publishers and distributors of 'half-dime novels' for boys led in the 1880s by Anthony Comstock's New York Society for the Suppression of Vice.[23]

Wertham's preoccupation with the 'horror comic' signified an extreme variant of the initial reaction by expatriate European intellectuals to American commercial entertainment. Refugee Jewish academics, abandoning lives in central Europe during Hitler's rise to power, fled to American universities and colleges but were often repelled by the ubiquity of American popular culture. They mostly depicted Hollywood and Madison Avenue as threatening and degenerate, sapping the nation's moral fibre for commercial profit. The so-called 'Frankfurt intellectuals', housed in the Institute of Social Research at Columbia University in New York during the late 1930s and early 1940s, were all preoccupied with the problem of what they labelled 'mass culture'. Theodor Adorno, Herbert Marcuse, Leo Lowenthal and Max Horkheimer, German–Jewish Marxists or neo-Marxists who sought to explain the failure of socialism in Europe, were among the most important of this school. They blamed radio, cinema, newspapers and cheap books for 'the disappearance of the inner life', the rise of the 'culture industry', and the development of 'false consciousness' in the 'masses'. The Frankfurt school's vision of an undifferentiated 'mass culture' sweeping away genuine popular or folk culture is currently unfashionable, criticized for its lack of historical specificity or empirical grounding. Fredric Wertham, although of an earlier migrant generation and not theoretically oriented, shared much of the Frankfurt school's indiscriminate hostility towards commercial forms of mass entertainment.[24]

Wertham kept company, however, with the very group of American censors and conservatives that most of the Frankfurt intellectuals abhorred. This is shown by the support he received from Gershorn Legman's *Love And Death: A Study in Censorship* (1949), an anti-mass-culture diatribe which, by adopting a crude mesmeric theory of media effects, recommended banning comic books for:

> peddling the same old violence, the same old illiteracy, the same old 'passive reception of manufactured entertainment', requiring of the reader nothing more than to hand over his ten cents and then sit there drugged while little effortless pictures flow over him, isolate him in a world of suspicion and fear, and leave him mentally helpless and still frustrated, floundering in imaginary blood.

Legman also alleged that two comic-book companies were staffed entirely by homosexuals, 'operating out of our most phalliform skyscraper'. It does not require much psychological insight to interpret such denigration of mass culture as a way for alienated intellectuals to externalize dangerous or suppressed aspects of their own personalities. Wertham's anti-comic-book articles and speeches of this period, with their recurrent corporal symbolism of 'disease', 'pollution', 'depravity' and 'seduction', adopted Legman's intemperate style. They also took on a sinister conspiratorial tone ('I think Hitler was a beginner compared to the comic-book industry') similar to the rhetoric of the McCarthyite witch-hunters.[25]

Wertham thus encouraged a lobby to censor the most horrific and violent aspects of the media that received little support from the academy, despite his unconscious popularizing of Marxist ideas. American historian James Gilbert has drawn attention, even so, to the oblique but important relationship between Wertham's crusade against the comic book and the anti-mass-culture position that was emerging during the 1950s among American intellectuals like Dwight Macdonald, coiner of 'masscult' and 'midcult', and David Riesman, author of *The Lonely Crowd* (1950). An outspoken Wertham supporter Gilbert does not mention is Geoffrey Wagner who, in his hostile but amply illustrated study of American popular iconography, *Parade of Pleasure* (1954), bitterly accused the mass media of 'cretinising public taste.' Wagner also alleged that, because so many war comics had 'reds' as their villains, criticizing comic books had laid him open to publishers' charges of communism, 'the most easily accessible and at present most potent method of vilification in the USA.'[26]

Conversely, the discourse of Wertham's campaign against comic books also developed covert metaphorical links to the paranoia of McCarthyism. 'As long as the crime comic-book industry exists in its present forms there are no secure homes', alleged Wertham. Sexy and violent comic books had invaded the sanctity of American suburbia in order to swell the profits of a greedy mass culture industry. The enemy 'nestled in the bosom of the American family', according to a 1948 *Collier's* magazine spread, 'Horror in the Nursery', popularizing Wertham's arguments. If suburban homes were not safe from the worst kind of comic book, in a post-war age of anxiety engendered by the Berlin blockade and the nuclear threat, then America itself was not safe from communism. An emphasis on domestic intrusion by vile comic books also struck a chord with those who saw in mass culture a threat to conservative values but did not share the psychiatrist's unexpectedly liberal credentials as an anti-racist. In March 1946 Wertham had opened the Lafargue Clinic in a black Episcopalian church basement in New York's Harlem, a low-cost psychiatric clinic with a particular interest in troubled black teenagers, financed primarily by voluntary contributions and operating only in the evenings. He believed that school segregation prevented the normal psychological development of black children, perhaps leading to delinquency. Wertham also felt, initially, that the best way to prevent violence was to provide psychiatric counselling for those who performed or contemplated violent acts, as elaborated in his books *Dark Legend: A Study of Murder* (1941) and *The Show of Violence* (1949). While running Lafargue in an attempt to implement this approach, Wertham discovered that for many of the teenagers counselled, reading comic books depicting crime and violence was a preferred pastime. Convinced that he had discovered a causal relationship between such reading and the commission of crimes, Wertham began to explore the issues surrounding social psychology and the power of mass culture that have been identified as his unique, if much overstated, contribution to the study of juvenile delinquency. The LaFargue Clinic survived penury, controversy and disputes with the state licensing bureau until it closed down in 1957.[27]

The 1953–5 Juvenile Delinquency Subcommittee

Wertham's media campaign carried on relentlessly until, shortly after publication of *Seduction of the Innocent* in 1954, the Senate Judiciary Committee decided to take a look at the new furore caused over 'horror comic' books, having previously made investigations into communist infiltration of various Washington agencies. The underfunded subcommittee to investigate juvenile delinquency of the Committee on the Judiciary of the United States Senate, created on 1 June 1953, became a focal point for registering complaints about the mass media. Its chairman, Senator Robert C. Hendrickson of New Jersey, received over 15,000 unsolicited letters during 1953–5 from community leaders and the general public, nearly 75 per cent of which reflected concern over the relationship between delinquency and the media. 'Juvenile delinquency is on the increase', according to Senator Kefauver. 'Children in scores of cities are committing more crimes than at any time since World War Two, a national survey shows.' In 1953 alone, American crime statistics recorded by the FBI had risen by 20 per cent, with a particularly large increase in burglary and car theft by juveniles, although expanding ownership of houses and cars were themselves a symptom of a more affluent society. According to the FBI, 53.6 per cent of those arrested for stealing vehicles in 1953 were classified as juveniles. A pervasive social anxiety about the spread of juvenile delinquency, amplified by the media and politicians, lent support to Wertham's unsubstantiated allegation that the parallel phenomenon of rising crime figures and rising sales of 'horror comic' books were somehow causally related. In the 1960s, juvenile crime rates continued to rise but the American public lacked the incentive to blame the media which the Senate investigation into juvenile delinquency had once provided, although as late as 1961 ineffectual hearings on television violence were held under that body's auspices.[28]

Senator Hendrickson acknowledged that 'thousands of American parents are greatly concerned about the possible detrimental influence certain types of crime and horror comic books have upon their children'. Confused and divided expert opinion, as well as 'vociferous' public concern, helped convince the subcommittee's chairman that public hearings were necessary to address directly the 'possible delinquency producing effect' of comic books. A British authority on comics, Roger Sabin, argues that the hearings had all the appearances of the communist witch-hunts in microcosm, and with television and other coverage demonstrated 'all the trappings of a show trial'. The subcommittee's members became Senator

Kefauver of Tennessee, Senator Thomas C. Hennings Jnr of Missouri, judiciary committee chairman Senator Bill Langer of North Dakota and Hendrickson in the chair. Kefauver, a powerful Senate liberal, was widely known for chairing the 1950–1 Senate investigations into organized crime which had first brought him into contact with Dr Wertham apropos 'crime comics'. The Tennessee Senator had also run for the Democratic presidential nomination in 1952 but, despite early victories in the primaries, his candidacy could not compete with that of Adlai Stevenson. Kefauver's ambitions for high office were not yet dead, however, and televised hearings into juvenile delinquency provided yet another valuable platform from which to launch a political campaign, although until 1955 Kefauver was the chairman's understudy.[29]

Coincidently, Dr Wertham and his arch-enemy, EC publisher Bill Gaines, were both called before this subcommittee on 21 April 1954 at the Foley Square Federal Court House in New York's Manhattan, not far from the EC offices in Lafayette Street. Kefauver himself had invited Wertham to appear. On the surface, crime as much as horror provided the impetus behind the psychiatrist's testimony to the subcommittee on the comic book medium ('I never spoke of comic books, I only spoke of crime comic books'). Yet he defined 'crime comic books' liberally as those that depicted any form of violent behaviour, not excepting western, superhero or science-fiction comic books ('if a girl is raped she is raped whether it is in a space ship or on the prairie'). Consequently, for Wertham 'crime comic books' became the overwhelming majority of all comic books and, because of their mass appeal, an important contributory factor in numerous cases of juvenile delinquency.[30]

The exceptional but indefensible 'Foul Play' horror story from EC's *Haunt of Fear* (June 1953), ending with a man's intestines being used to demarcate a baseball diamond, was then paraded before the assembled Senators, as was the 'injury to the eye' motif which Wertham claimed, obsessively, to discern in several comic book stories. Even DC's innocuous *Superman* comic books were extravagantly accused of encouraging in children 'phantasies of sadistic joy in seeing other people punished over and over again while you yourself remain immune'. In many comic books, apparently, the whole point was that evil triumphed. 'If it were my task, Mr. Chairman, to teach children delinquency', Wertham announced, 'to tell them how to rape and seduce girls, how to hurt people, how to break into stores, how to cheat, how to forge, how to do any known crime, if it were my task to teach that, I would have to enlist the crime comic-book industry'.[31]

Wertham's testimony to the hearings was characteristically rambling, obsessive, frivolous and incoherent. Yet he was treated by the subcommittee with an exaggerated respect, unlike Bill Gaines, overweight and insufficiently deferential, who followed Wertham to the stand. Gaines began by tracing the history of EC comics, proudly but inaccurately admitting responsibility for being the first to publish 'horror comics' in America. 'Some may not like them', he admitted. 'That is a matter of personal taste. It would be just as difficult to explain the harmless thrill of a horror story to Dr. Wertham as it would be to explain the sublimity of love to a frigid old maid.' Gaines argued that you could find more extreme descriptions of violence in any daily newspaper than in a comic book. His horror and crime stories, with their O. Henry surprise endings, should be treated as fantasy rather than as blueprints for imitative action by readers. Gaines also admitted to guaranteeing his advertisers sales of 1,500,000 a month for the entire EC group of titles, among the most prominently displayed on American newsstands. The subcommitte's chairman, Senator Hendrickson, later recalled accusingly, 'I shall never forget his [Gaines'] testimony nor his demeanour.'[32]

There followed a classic exchange about the boundaries of 'good taste' between Kefauver and Gaines which, because of the latter's refusal to accept immutable definitions, called into question the then predominant and hierarchic sense of cultural value. The assembled middle-aged Senators proved unable to comprehend Gaines's testing of acceptable limits:

SENATOR KEFAUVER: Here is your May 22 issue [of *Crime SuspenStories*]. This seems to be a man with a bloody ax holding a woman's head up which has been severed from her body. Do you think that is in good taste?

MR. GAINES: Yes, sir; I do, for the cover of a horror comic. A cover in bad taste, for example, might be defined as holding the head a little higher so that the neck could be seen dripping blood from it and moving the body over a little further so that the neck of the body could be seen to be bloody.

SENATOR KEFAUVER: You have blood coming out of her mouth.

MR. GAINES: A little.

SENATOR KEFAUVER: Here is blood on the ax. I think most adults are shocked by that.

THE CHAIRMAN [Hendrickson]: Here is another one I want to show him.

SENATOR KEFAUVER: This is the July one. It seems to be a man with a woman in a boat and he is choking her to death here with a crowbar. Is that in good taste?

MR. GAINES: I think so.

MR. HANNOCH [*chief counsel*]: How could it be worse?[33]

The Senators finally quizzed Gaines about Exhibit 8b, his open attack on censorship in 'Are You A Red Dupe?', a spoof scripted by Gaines, illustrated by Jack Davis, and running on the inside front cover of five of EC's then current monthly titles. Satirizing the McCarthyite smear, this damp squib set out to prove that the group most anxious to destroy comic books were the communists:

> So the NEXT time some joker gets up at the P.T.A. meeting, or starts jabbering about the 'naughty comic books' at your local candy store, give him the ONCE-OVER. We're not saying he IS a Communist! He may be innocent of the whole thing! He may be a DUPE! He may not even READ the 'Daily Worker'! It's just that he's SWALLOWED the RED BAIT . . . HOOK, LINE, and SINKER!

The humorous inversion of this spoof was entirely lost on the literal-minded Senators, meeting as they were at the time of one of the first great national television events in American history, the Army–McCarthy hearings, which ultimately discredited the Senator from Wisconsin. Gaines' concurrent testimony failed to clarify the satirical intention behind 'Are You A Red Dupe?' and so the subcommittee took offence at what was perceived as a blatant attempt to smear those who criticized comic books as card-carrying communists.[34]

It has been alleged that the American government used Wertham's book, *Seduction of the Innocent* and the controversy it created, as a convenient way to get anti-establishment comic-book publishers such as Bill Gaines into legal difficulties, bearing in mind EC's adult, as well as juvenile, audience. Gaines was a liberal Democrat hostile both towards Senator McCarthy and the politics of opportunism named after him. None the less, despite overtly political stories such as 'The Patriots!', EC comic books were not characterized as anti-McCarthyite by the subcommittee, who focused purely on their violent episodes and failed to distinguish them from more tawdry competitors. Po-faced disapproval ('utter perversion') of a blatant Mickey Spillane sex and violence parody in Gaines' *Panic* ('My Gun is the Jury! By Melvie Splane') further testified to the inability of politicians to read comic books in a figurative or satirical sense. The low level of awareness in congressional circles of EC's liberal, non-racist bias, suggests that more research needs to be done before a 'containment' theory can be properly substantiated.[35]

The preoccupation with the boundaries of 'good taste' evidenced by Senators and chief counsel on this Senate subcommitee is significant, because the process of establishing taste differentials ('most adults are shocked by that') here becomes a symbolic weapon in the struggle for ideological domination between established cultural arbiters and a new generation of commercial harbingers like Bill Gaines. The way in which 'culture' is formulated is ideological, according to cultural studies guru Pierre Bordieu, and so the consequences of discrimination in taste are that aesthetic distinctions become operations of social domination and subordination. This class-based approach might also be applied to age relations, exploring how certain denigrated forms of amusement come to be associated with a prepubescent age group, such as comic-book reading, while other tastes, values and hierarchies are established as culturally adult, 'respectable' and preferential. Cultural consumption is predisposed, consciously or not, to fulfil the function of legitimating not just social but also generational differences. Labelling thus represents a way for cultural authorities to construct taste hierarchies and to amplify anxiety or rejection over products of the mass culture, such as EC comic books, which threaten established adult taste. Hence the invention of labels like 'horror comic' or 'penny dreadful' signifies the struggle between middle-class moralism, mass culture and youthful demand.[36]

Self-regulation and the Collapse of EC

In 1955 the Senate delinquency subcommittee's interim report on the comic book industry actually disclaimed Wertham's monocausal model of juvenile delinquency and merely noted that 'pernicious' violence in comics might be one factor in the 'total problem'. The report also emphasized the potential ill-effects of 'crime comic' books on abnormal, rather than normal 'innocent', children and enthusiastically supported industry self-regulation – 'this nation cannot afford the calculated risk involved in the continuing mass dissemination of crime and horror comic books to its children'. Many of Wertham's propositions were incorporated into the report, nevertheless, such as his attack on the 'superman complex'; the poor influence of 'horror comic' publications on American cultural relations abroad; and the accusation that several expert witnesses were paid consultants of the comic-book industry.[37]

Although the subcommittee felt that neither legislation nor federal government intervention was necessary, local ordinances restricting the sale of 'crime' and 'horror comics' were passed in 18 states of the union. The outright nationwide banning of 'horror comics', as with the British act of parliament discussed below, would have been a violation of first amendment rights that went against the grain of the American constitution. Publishers were warned, however, that they could not simply clean up their comic books by merely discontinuing a few objectionable crime and horror titles. They were recommended to 'seek and support ways and means of insuring that the industry's product permanently measures up to the standards of morality and decency which American parents have the right to expect'.[38]

If industry self-regulation did not succeed, the subcommitee's report threatened that 'other ways must – and will – be found to prevent our Nation's young from being harmed by crime and horror comic books'. Senators need not have worried. In response, a majority of the intimidated comic book publishers, among them Lev Gleason, formed the self-censoring Comics Magazine Association of America in September 1954, creating a set of editorial standards for their comic books called the Comics Code Authority with its own independent review board. Dr Wertham turned down a half-serious offer to become the Code's new commissioner, so a New York juvenile court judge, Charles F. Murphy, was hired instead. The self-regulatory Code made it impossible for horror (but not crime) titles to continue, since after October those that did not abide by its over-zealous guidelines ('no comic magazine shall use the word "horror" or "terror" in its title') would not get distributed. The Code expressly forbade 'all scenes of horror, excessive bloodshed, gory or gruesome crimes, depravity, lust, sadism, and masochism', as well as the 'walking dead, torture, vampires, ghouls, cannibalism and werewolfism'. One curious side-effect of the new Code was that the first assignment of a new art assistant at wholesome Archie Comics was to remove cleavages and lift up low-cut blouses on *Katy Keene*, a comic-book about a voluptuous teenage model. Whereas in 1952 about 500 comic-book titles were available, by 1955 the number had dropped to around 300. Monthly sales of Gleason's crime titles fell from 2,700,000 full-blooded issues in 1952 to around 800,000 cleaned-up issues, before being discontinued altogether in 1955. Within a year he had ceased publishing comic books. The Comics Code was hence self-serving, as it forced many of the smaller competitors of the major comic-book publishing companies, such as DC and Marvel, out of the marketplace.[39]

The mid-1950s also saw the collapse of every one of Bill Gaines's EC horror, crime and suspense titles. He announced for public consumption that he was stopping comic-book publication 'because of a premise, that has never been proved, that they stimulate juvenile delinquency. We are not doing it so much for business reasons as because this seems to be what the parents want – and the parents should be served.' Privately, Gaines confessed, 'I'd been told that if I continued publishing my magazines, no one would handle them. I had no choice.' Wholesalers and retailers refused to take EC titles, with the exception of *Mad*, a future money-spinner, converted into a 25-cent bimonthly magazine specifically to avoid the peremptory Code. The boom times were over for the American comic book industry, at least until the Marvel-led superhero revival of the 1960s and 1970s. New titles are no longer available from newsstands but through 'direct sales' specialist comic-book shops and in book stores. While the tremendous expansion of television in the 1950s had certainly played a part in falling sales, so too had the anti-comic book crusaders and, in the McCarthy era, the middle-class public's shared, socially constructed, sense of value. After 1954, American parents also had the Comics Code seal of approval, a form of self-censorship, to guide them in distinguishing between 'good' and 'bad' comic books. The social and political neutering of the comic-book industry which the Comics Code institutionalized was effectively maintained until the emergence of the West-coast 'underground comics' movement in the late 1960s.[40]

The British Campaign against 'Horror Comics'

Late in January 1955, A. W. Peterson, a top Home Office civil servant of impeccable tastes, sitting alone in his Whitehall office, picked up the second issue of *Tales from the Crypt*, a shoddy British black and white compendium of American 'horror comic' stories. He had been told to provide his political masters with a careful précis of this comic book's contents, owing to the growing 'moral panic' about the influence of such material on young British readers. The bare plot outlines given in Peterson's eventual memorandum ('If nine stories of this kind are not enough, how many are needed?') evidently proved quite shocking to the refined sensibilities of cabinet ministers at Westminster.[41]

American 'horror comics' first reached Britain in the early 1950s as ballast in ships crossing the Atlantic, unsold copies were also imported from Canada and Australia. Few penetrated much further than the environs of the great ports of Liverpool, Manchester, Belfast and London. One member of a vociferous anti-comic-book lobby known as the Comics Campaign Council (CCC) sought out elusive copies from a London East-End trader's market stall, 'I must confess that I put on an off-white accent and an old coat before I won the vendor's confidence.' Using blocks made from imported American matrices, subsequent British versions such as *Tales from the Crypt* were printed in Leicester and London by firms such as Arnold Miller and Thorpe & Porter to be sold in small back-street newsagents.[42]

On 17 May 1952, *Picture Post*, the popular Hulton Press photo-magazine, drew widespread public attention to the British 'horror comic' trade in a provocative article 'Should U.S. "Comics" Be Banned?' by Peter Mauger, a communist teacher who later confessed his anxiety to exploit anti-American feeling. Two years later Mauger published a follow-up article, 'The Cult of Violence Persists', in the same magazine. A *Picture Post* reader from Crowborough, Sussex, responding to this latter article, felt that 'it is not only American comics that should be banned, but also many of the other false practices that have been imported into this country. The sooner we return to a sane British way of life (built on traditional lines) the better for this great nation.' The campaign against 'horror comics' brought together some strange bedfellows. If Hulton feared competition for the British juvenile market, as publishers of the irreproachable *Eagle* range of comic papers started by the Revd Marcus Morris to combat American imports, parliamentary deputations of teachers and churchmen feared American mass culture invading Britain. All gave voice to an orchestrated groundswell of opinion demanding urgent government action. Martin Barker has charted the origins and development of this extraordinary and multifarious campaign, as well as mounting a persuasive cultural and political defence of the horror stories themselves, so what follows uses Home Office records to offer some insights into the drafting and passage through the British parliament of legislation outlawing 'horror comics'.[43]

'The problem which now faces society in the trade that has sprung up of presenting sadism, crime, lust, physical mostrosity, and horror to the young is an urgent and a grave one', thundered *The Times* on 12 November 1954. 'There has been no more encouraging sign of the moral health of the country than the way in which public opinion has been roused in condemnation of the evil of "horror comics" and in determination to combat them'. Yet the relatively small sales of American 'horror comics' in comparison to home-grown British comics was openly admitted by Dr Sam Yudkin, an active British Communist Party (BCP) lobbyist and force behind the CCC. During a somewhat disingenuous address given at Westminster to the Tory Education Committee, Yudkin estimated that perhaps only 10 per cent of

British school children bought 'horror comics'; albeit because of 'swopping' their circulation was somewhat wider. This small circulation did not prevent such unlikely allies as the CCC, the BCP, the Established Church and the National Union of Teachers (NUT) from vigorously campaigning against these comics. On being made aware of the political affiliations of many of those active in the anti-comic-book campaign, the NUT eventually distanced itself from the CCC. Instead, the teachers' union organized their own exhibition of gruesome 'horror comic' illustrations which was allowed in the Palace of Westminister for 2 weeks, before touring the country attracting publicity and intensifying the demand for action. Furthermore, the Eisenhower administration in America was concerned, according to the British Foreign Office, 'about the extent to which American participation in the production of horror comics is being used to foster ill-feeling between the United States and this country'. The commander of American forces in England even tried to get American PX's to stop bringing 'horror comics' into the country, so desperate was the threat to basic British values.[44]

Ultimately, Britain's Conservative government could not afford to ignore the swelling chorus of 'moral panic' amplified through the press. 'Who can look at these comics and escape the conclusion that there is a connection between them and the increasing volume of juvenile delinquency?' queried a *Picture Post* reader's letter. One problem was that 'horror comics' could not be prosecuted under the 1857 Obscene Publications Act, despite calls for a test case to be brought, because by legal definition – their chief content was not one of sex and sadism – 'horror comics' were not indecent or 'obscene'. Amending the 1857 Act to cover brutality, cruelty and horror, was considered too risky and all-embracing by civil servants, so it was decided to proceed with government legislation, despite all the difficulties which framing a law restricted to the prohibition of 'horror comics' would present. The new Home Secretary, Major Gwilym Lloyd-George, son of the great Liberal politician and war leader, told the Tory cabinet, meeting at premier Winston Churchill's office in the House of Commons on 6 December 1954, that if the government failed to take the initiative, 'there was a risk that legislation might be brought forward in the form of a Private Member's bill, which would involve the Government in even greater embarrassment'. To forestall such a move, Major Lloyd-George received the authority to make an early statement in the House that legislation was being considered, restricted to the type of publication which had 'aroused so much public concern in recent weeks'. The Home Secretary wished to avoid a delay in announcing proposals, 'in the present state of public opinion', to remove an impression that the government had been pushed into legislation by pressure from the opposition. On 27 January 1955 the cabinet expressed general support for legislation along the lines of a draft bill which applied 'to any book, magazine or other like work which consists of stories told in pictures in such a way that the work as a whole would tend to incite or encourage to (a) the commission of crimes or (b) acts of violence and cruelty or (c) otherwise to corrupt, a child or young person into whose hands it might fall'. The wording of the bill as finally amended read 'or (c) incidents of a repulsive or horrible nature, in such a way that the work as a whole would tend to corrupt a child or young person into whose hands it might fall'. The sale or publication of 'horror comics' would be punished by up to 4 months in prison or a fine not exceeding £100 or both, with the option of trial by jury.[45]

Civil servants produced an avalanche of papers, once official authority to proceed with legislation had been received, passing on and correcting the views of their respective political chiefs as regards definition of terms, amendments, redrafting of clauses, and possible penalties. The Children's Department of the Home Office, a liberal bastion, felt that the original draft bill was misconceived because it laid too much emphasis upon 'horror comics' as an incitement to juvenile delinquency which was, in any case, statistically declining in mid-1950s Britain. 'First, there is no evidence that the kind of publication aimed at does incite to "the commission of crimes" by juveniles and, second, crimes of violence, cruelty or horror . . . are definitely infrequent among children and young persons.' A general tendency for such reading to corrupt through 'the lowering of moral standards, rather than causing particular acts on a particular occasion' was considered preferable wording. This proposal was rejected, despite receiving support from the Tory Attorney-General, Sir Reginald Manningham-Buller, who felt that the cumulative effect of 'horror comics' on the young was the real evil, leading to 'contempt for the law and an entirely wrong view of adult society'. A Home Office official also suggested that a comic book containing acts of violent crime might be corrupting because 'it encourages a wrong attitude towards society generally', glorifying the criminal and 'holding the forces of law and order up to ridicule'. Almost a century earlier, the Lord Chamberlain's office had used similar language to justify banning stage plays portraying prison-escaper Jack Sheppard (see Appendix I) as an heroic role model.[46]

The ideologically subversive content of 'horror comics', particularly those of the EC stable, made an implicit contribution to the 'moral panic' in British Establishment circles. Treasury counsel and barrister Mervyn Griffith-Jones, whose legal practice was kept busy prosecuting backstreet publishers of American-style 'Hank Janson' gangster novels for obscenity (see Appendix III), recognized that 'horror comic' stories questioned conventional values such as the sanctity of the family but opined that it would be difficult to charge them under the Obscene Publications Act. Griffith-Jones offered the following sententious advice, in a memorandum of 11 November 1954, to the Director of Public Prosecutions:

> I suspect that the real evil of this class of story and the way in which it is told in illustrated form in these publications lies in the false picture which is engendered in the minds of children and young people of the way in which the grown-up world thinks and behaves. The characters are ordinary human beings with ordinary faces and clothed in ordinary clothing. These usually normal people are represented as being selfish, violent and filled with greed and hate. Husbands and wives are continually shown as unfaithful; parents as hating their children and vice versa. Almost as a matter of course and without there being anything unusual about it, many of them are in possession of guns and all are prepared to relieve themselves of their immediate troubles by the simple expedient of murder.[47]

This striking comment on the disruption of normalcy by the comic book draws attention, however naïvely, both to the 'horror comic' representation of family life as dysfunctional and to the ubiquity of violence as a problem-solver in American popular culture. EC's horror stories of internecine strife, adulteries and murderous impulses, were pronounced unfit for the consumption of children, in British culture considered the only readers of comic books, which tended to infantilize a sizeable adult audience for 'horror comics'.

Pushed through Whitehall and the Tory cabinet in just a few months, fuelled by the 'moral panic' over 'horror comics', the Children and Young Persons (Harmful Publications) Bill was piloted through the House of Commons by Major Lloyd-George and the Attorney-General. The bill's second reading on 22 February 1955 was attended by a full House of Commons and the debate lasted for over 6 hours, with strong views being expressed both for and against. The House traditionally got excited whenever a question of the liberty of the subject was involved and this debate was no exception. Roy Jenkins and Michael Foot for Labour took up the cudgels in defence of freedom of expression, seeing no apparent contradiction in arguing that a more comprehensive measure should have been introduced to reform the 1857 Obscene Publications Act (eventually modernized by the 1959 'Jenkins Act'). Tory backbenchers who caught the Speaker's eye protested an ardent desire to protect children from being corrupted by the sort of reading matter so graphically exposed in the NUT's highly selective exhibition of 'horror comic' illustrations. Several members of parliament were worried that legislation against 'horror comics' could be given a wider application than intended by the bill's framers, making even the brothers Grimm fairy stories liable to prosecution. On the other hand, parliament's interference in liberty of publication was justified by both government spokesmen and Labour's Shadow Home Secretary, Sir Frank Soskice, as necessary to plug gaps in existing obscenity legislation.[48]

'It is true that the public outcry last autumn [1954] and the decision to introduce this bill have stopped the publication of "horror comics" in this country', confessed Major Lloyd-George. 'But I am convinced that, if the House had not been resolute in its determination to deal with this evil, we would have been faced with a much more serious problem.' The redundant bill passed its second reading by a unanimous majority and became law on 6 May 1955. Six months later, only one complaint had reached the Home Secretary and of three other comic books brought to the attention of the Attorney-General, none were proceeded against. The sledge-hammer of parliamentary legislation had been brought to bear in order to crack a very small nut indeed. The Children and Young Persons (Harmful Publications) Act was renewed without discussion in 1965 and is still on the British statute books. The only prosecution that can be found under this legislation came on 22 October 1970, when W. L. Millers and Co. of Stepney, East London, was charged at Tower Bridge Court with importing from America 25,000 copies of *Tales from the Tomb*, *Weird*, *Tales of Voodoo*, *Horror Tales* and *Witches Tales*. Part early-1950s reprints, part poorly-drawn originals, they had been allowed past customs. Despite being fined only £25 with £20 costs, the firm closed down soon after.[49]

All the symptoms of a classic 'moral panic' had been made manifest in the British 'horror comic' scare: the media definition of a 'threat'; the stereotyping of comic books as 'horror comics'; a spiralling escalation of the perceived 'threat' through the media and censorship lobbying; and, finally, the emergence of a parliamentary 'solution' in terms of tough legislation, moral isolation and symbolic court action. British reaction to this Americanized threat was more than slightly hysterical, temporarily effective, and then completely forgotten. When the EC comic books were reprinted many years later, politicians, churchmen, teachers and journalists, whose predecessors had campaigned against them so vigorously in the 1950s, were now completely indifferent.

6

MASS MEDIA PANIC: THE 1980s AND 1990s

During a 'moral panic', the suspect category is either created or, more often, argue Goode and Ben-Yehuda, relocated, dusted off and attacked with a renewed vigour. New charges may be made, old ones dredged up and reformulated. In many cases a deviant category or stereotype already exists, but is latent and only activated at times of crisis or panic because secondary targets are needed to deflect attention away from some of society's most pressing or insoluble problems. Since the reasons for scapegoating them vary according to historical circumstances, deviant categories are often refurbished over time. Violent crime or action movies reproduced on video are a case in point.[1]

Following Michael Ryan's Rambo-style Hungerford killings in the summer of 1987, the availability on British video of the Sylvester Stallone movie *Rambo: First Blood Part II* (1985) became the scapegoat for moral outrage. In the wake of Scotland's Dunblane tragedy, when in 3 minutes of carnage on 13 March 1996 Thomas Hamilton shot dead 16 small children, their teacher and then himself, David Alton MP, who had already campaigned for tougher restrictions on video certification, sought to ban the release on video in Britain of Oliver Stone's inept movie *Natural Born Killers* (1994) because of its violent content. Alton also proposed adoption in Britain of the V-chip – a device installed in televisions which will automatically scramble programmes coded as containing sex or violence. President Clinton aimed to have these chips in every new television in America by 1997. The parents of Dunblane felt that the licensing of handguns provided a more direct cause of their bereavement and, through the Snowdrop campaign, pressed for a complete ban.[2]

The brief survey of recent press-generated excitements over the supposed effects of popular culture on young audiences that follows cannot disregard the British campaign that helped to pass the Video Recordings Act of 1984. This statute ended the free circulation of films on video by requiring their separate certification under the criminal law and not simply, as was still the case with cinema films, by private agreement with the trade. The cry of children at risk who needed protection, film critic Alexander Walker notes, 'supplied the motive for a repressive measure affecting every adult in the country'.[3]

Video Nasties

The successful passage of the Video Recordings Bill through parliament also merits attention as the product of a fabricated 'moral panic' over so-called 'video nasties' that dominated British newspaper headlines for weeks on end. Towards the end of July 1993 Tory backbench MP Graham Bright sponsored a private member's bill that was debated after the summer recess in a classic atmosphere of 'moral panic' both in parliament and outside. Media-promoted hysteria was whipped up by sensation-seeking journalists drawing attention to American titles briefly available on British video like *Driller Killer*, *I Spit on your Grave* and *The Evil Dead* (now acclaimed by some as horror classics). The tabloid press and that most Thatcherite of newspapers the *Daily Mail* mounted a carefully orchestrated campaign against this new 'threat' to innocent children which, following campaigner Mary Whitehouse, they labelled 'video nasties'. The Bright bill was also supported by a coalition of powerful moral-interest groups including the police, the National Society for the Prevention of Cruelty to Children, the Order of Christian Unity and CARE Campaigns (formerly the illiberal Nationwide Festival of Light).[4]

Mrs Thatcher's Conservative government were anxious to improve their law and order image by assisting the passage of Bright's bill. 'No one has the right to be upset at a brutal sex crime or a sadistic attack on a child or mindless thuggery on a pensioner if he is not prepared to drive sadistic videos out of our high streets', cried David Mellor, Minister of State at the Home Office, in a widely quoted speech made during the second reading debate on 11 November 1983. The dramatic spread of the new technology of the video-cassette recorder in the early 1980s was ostensibly to blame for a rise in violent crime. Academic respectability was provided for the bill in March 1984 by a report, later published as *Video Violence and Children* (eds Geoffrey Barlow and Alison Hill, 1985), issued under the name of the Parliamentary Group Video Enquiry, an offshoot of the Order of Christian Unity. The Group's associate director, Dr Brian Brown, Head of the Television Research Unit at the former Oxford Polytechnic, had already disowned the report as a campaigning pamphlet assembled in haste in order to catch the committee stage of the Bright bill. Banner headlines exploiting the report none the less highlighted such dramatic but unsubstantiated National Viewers' Survey claims as that 45.5 per cent of the nation's under-16s had seen at least one 'video nasty'. Brown later claimed the report was substantially the work of the Group's director Dr Clifford Hill, a consultant sociologist to the Home Office, Police and Prison Services, credited with writing only a tenth of the book. In the panic atmosphere of the times, the Video Recordings Bill sailed through parliament in July 1984 with the Home Office's full support to become British law.[5]

The censorious terms of the Video Recordings Act were nearly extended 10 years later by a fatuous Criminal Justice Bill amendment that, in a compromise formula worked out between proposer Liberal Democrat MP David Alton and Tory Home Secretary Michael Howard, obliged the British Board of Film Classification (BBFC) by statute to consider banning from home viewing those videos that could cause 'psychological harm' to children or present them with 'inappropriate role models' and techniques. 'It signals nothing less than a return to responsible censorship by popular demand', crowed the *Daily Mail* on 13 April 1994. The act as eventually passed some months later omitted Alton's amendment but raised the penalties for shopowners who rented unsuitable films to children and also specified for the first time that the BBFC should consider how a video dealt with certain listed 'adult' themes.[6]

'Gangsta-Rap'

Popular music has long been a favoured candidate for 'moral panic', particularly since the emergence of rock 'n roll in the mid-1950s out of hillbilly music, gospel singing and black rhythm and blues. Then it was Elvis Presley's gyrations, Little Richard's suggestive lyrics, and an incessant beat that incited southern gospel belt tirades against 'nigger music'. More recently America has seen campaigns against 'gangsta-rap', which grew out of the rap music explosion of the 1980s, graphically describing life on the streets of tough black neighbourhoods in Los Angeles and New York. Protests reached a peak in the summer of 1995 after being taken up by Republican presidential hopeful Senator Bob Dole. Moral panic was aroused by the messages of black gangsta rappers such as Snoop Doggy Dogg, Biggie Smalls, Dr Dre or Tupac Shakur portraying women as 'bitches' and 'hos' (whores), and their extolling of guns, violence and hatred of the police. When Ice-T's release 'Cop Killer' gained notoriety, the $16 billion entertainment giant Time-Warner said it supported artistic expression, then dropped their recording star at the first opportunity. They also unloaded their half of Interscope Records, distributors of the hard-core Death Row label featuring gangsta rappers on compact disc.[7]

Time-Warner were responding to pressures brought to bear upon shareholders by C. Delores Tucker of the National Congress of Black Women, William Bennett, Republican codirector of the conservative Empower America advocacy group and Senator Dole, united in seeking to ban sexually explicit, sometimes violent, gangsta lyrics. 'You can't listen to all that language and filth without it affecting you', Tucker exclaimed. Hip-hop culture with its in-your-face realism was intended as a calculated offence against a complacent black bourgeoisie. Of course, lyrics extolling gratuitous violence and virulent misogny should be condemned, but neither Dole, Bennett nor Tucker made reference in their speeches to gangsta rap's homophobia. Many of the same conservative politicians who campaigned against gangsta rap also attacked poor black mothers, affirmative action and the redrawing of voting districts to achieve parity for black voters.[8]

In February 1996 gangsta rapper Snoop Doggy Dogg (Calvin Broadus) was acquitted of murder for driving the jeep from which his bodyguard shot Philip Woldemariam, allegedly in self-defence, in Woodbine Park, West Los Angeles. On 7 September 1996 rapper Tupac Shakur was mortally wounded after the BMW of Marion 'Suge' Knight, chairman of Death Row Records, ground to a halt in traffic and two gunmen jumped out of a white Cadillac alongside and sprayed the car with bullets. He clung to life for 6 days. Shakur's shooting was widely considered to be the bloody culmination of a feud between Death Row (West Coast) and the East Coast Bad Boy label. The murdered man's depiction of violent street life was evidently not imaginary but his rise and fall says as much about the millions of white American kids who brought his music as the black brothers he rapped about. For Shakur was one of the few gangsta-rap artists who achieved mainstream success, selling to affluent white mall youth who would never set foot in the ghettoes, as well as to angry black teenagers. In life he was marketed as one of the most prominent and reckless exponents of a sexist and violent musical genre that horrified both white conservatives and black middle-class leaders. In death he was portrayed as a symbol of that style's moral bankruptcy, underscoring the dispiriting contrast between the unfocused, self-destructive anger of his generation of black youths and the disciplined politicization of the generation of black activists before them. Shakur's mother, for example, had been prominent in the Black Panthers.[9]

Scapegoating gangsta-rappers such as Shakur, or the companies that record and distribute them, provides an easy target. If a Republican politician like Bob Dole had really wanted to do something about urban violence, points out black professor Michael Eric Dyson, he would have done better to change his mind about repealing the White House ban on assault weapons. If not as attention-grabbing or self-serving as attacking popular culture, President Clinton's limited measure might help to save lives. Censorship of gangsta-rap could not begin to solve the problems of poor black youth but diverted attention away from the more substantive threats posed to women and blacks by a Republican-dominated Congress. After Time-Warner decided to give up its gangsta-rap business, critics of popular music styles turned to other targets. When politicians take on the entertainment business, their attention soon wanders.[10]

Television Violence

The use of the term 'violence' in recent censorship campaigns as if it were an easily defined homogeneous group of actions is clearly inadequate. When the Director General of the British Broadcasting Corporation (BBC) in 1985 invited the public to write in with any complaints about objectionable scenes on television, some 4000 people responded – 90 per cent of whom complained about television violence. Even so, despite the request to identify particular programmes or series that they objected to, only 3 per cent cited specific incidents. Bad language topped the list of viewer complaints 10 years later and, according to one university survey, the level of violence on British television across the equivalent of four complete weeks in 1995–6 was astonishingly low, amounting to roughly 1.4 per cent of all broadcast output, including cable and satellite channels. 'Violence' on television can cover an enormous diversity of acts taking place in different contexts for different reasons and with quite different messages for different viewers. How successful a film or television director is in conveying that violence is something to be condoned or condemned, to be appalled by or laughed at, is an empirical question ultimately only

answered by interrogating the audience. Viewers ideally respond differ-
ently according to the different contexts in which violence is presented. Yet
there may be some kind of residual effect in familiarizing the young with
violent criminal behaviour. Performances of John Gay's *The Beggar's Opera*
(1728) were accused in late-eighteenth-century England of being responsible for an increase in highway robbery. Samuel Johnson wrote sceptically
in his diary on 18 April 1775: 'I do not believe any man was ever made a
rogue by being present at its representation.' Johnson's next sentence lends
partial support, however, to those who believe that glamorization of criminals in the media can affect audiences. 'At the same time I do not deny that
it may have some influence, by making the character of a rogue familiar,
and in some degree pleasing.'[11]

Moving away from the simplified 'effects' debate about violent or other
imitative behaviour, David Buckingham and a fellow researcher, funded
by the Broadcasting Standards Council, carried out interviews during
1993–4 with 124 children to examine their emotional 'responses' to British
television. Among their qualitative findings was that the centralized regulation of children's viewing, in the form of video ratings and the television
watershed, was widely ignored. Children were found to have 'negative' but
rarely lasting emotional responses not only to more predictable genres,
such as horror films and weepies, but also to a wide range of other material,
including children's programmes, news and documentaries, advertisements, cartoons and many other apparently 'innocuous' programmes.
There were common themes, none the less, such as the death of animals,
which seemed to cut across generic distinctions and, in the case of fiction,
'negative' responses were often inextricably connected with 'positive'
ones, such as excitement and enjoyment.[12]

In children's accounts of horror films and videos, there was little sense of
vicarious 'identification' with the monster or killer, their responses appeared to derive primarily from a fear of vicitimization. To avoid or deal
with 'negative' responses, children developed a variety of 'coping strategies' to protect themselves from possible distress, among them questioning
the 'reality status' (or modality) of the text, although the effects of this strat-
egy were not guaranteed. Broadly speaking, children found it easier to distance themselves from fictional material, while films or programmes that
crossed the boundaries between fact and fiction, such as crime reconstruc-
tion in *Crimewatch* or the Halloween 1992 spoof paranormal documentary
Ghostwatch, were likely to generate a complex mixture of responses, being
seen as entertaining but also as potentially 'sick' and disturbing. There was
no evidence that children were 'desensitized' or any less upset by real-life

violence as a result of watching fictional violence and, while there were often conflicts between parents and children over what was seen as 'appropriate' viewing, parents could play a positive role in helping children to cope with upsetting experiences and in learning about television in general. For most children under most conditions, concludes Buckingham, most television is probably neither harmful nor particularly beneficial.[13]

Computer and Video Games

For centuries, assertions about the negative influences of popular cultural forms have served as a focus for much broader anxieties about moral decline and disorder from below. The student of computer-driven innovations in mass culture directed at the young in recent years will be all too familiar with the kind of 'moral panic' once generated by Victorian 'dreadfuls' such as *The Wild Boys of London*, demonstrably out of all proportion to their minimal effects on juvenile crime. In America, where computer and video games are now a six billion dollar a year mass culture industry, tentative steps have been made since the early 1990s to police standards of content. This followed adverse publicity about Mortal Kombat[TM], distributed by Sega, in which characters apparently won points at the highest level by ripping out the spinal columns and severing the limbs of opponents. The chairman of a body representing 62 software publishers, including Nintendo Entertainment UK and Sega Europe Ltd, claimed to 'accept the need to provide an easy way to show parents for whom the game is suitable. Computer games have not lodged themselves in the affections of the older generation . . . and the games are viewed with suspicion.' The European age ratings were designed to give parents more information so they could feel better informed when buying computer and video games for their children. From March 1994 Monitor Man stickers clearly displayed on the packaging of games have advised parents of their suitability for different age groups. Characters such as Sonic the Hedgehog and the Mario Brothers were considered universally appropriate, but warriors in the Mortal Kombat game are now restricted to the over-15s.[14]

The above ratings move came as part of a computer games industry drive to show it could regulate itself and to deflect criticism about children's easy access to violent games. Self-regulation, as with comic books and movies, was considered preferable to statutory regulation. Only consumer power could genuinely control violent content, argued the

Guardian, these 'profit-driven merchants of death' could not be trusted to regulate themselves. An industry-formed Video Standards Council, along with teacher and family groups, had drawn up the criteria for the ratings system, depending on the amount of swearing, vandalism, alcohol abuse and graphic violence depicted in any video game. Ratings may also, of course, serve to attract certain kinds of consumer. 'I like beat-em-ups. As nasty as you can get and with lots of blood and guts', claimed 16-year-old Mark Nolan, dismissing as 'rubbish' suggestions that violent games induce violence. Adolescent boys were ever thus. A reader's letter in *Picture Post* of 1954 claimed 'the growing boy of yesterday, today and tomorrow was, and is, and ever will be, the most bloodthirsty young animal walking the earth. . . . All young boys like lurid comics. And they all know the difference between right and wrong.' In 1994 Garry Tue, aged 19, browsing at a games shop in Urmston, Greater Manchester, would have agreed. 'All this talk of regulation is a load of rubbish', he said. 'I've been playing these games since I was seven, all the violent ones involving chopping off heads and that sort of thing. But they've not made me take an axe to anyone. At the end of the day, it's only a game. You don't take it seriously.' The majority of young people soon learn to distinguish between the real and the imaginary in the modern mass media. If they do not believe something to be true, they are not as scared. Children are more frightened of the television news than of horror films, according to one survey.[15]

Violence in the Media

In the 1980s Dr Thomas Radecki, a psychiatrist, research director of the American-based International Coalition Against Violent Entertainment, constantly reiterated that the average Western child saw many thousands of hours of violent entertainment by the age of 21. 'There is no way that a person can enjoy that much violence and not be harmfully affected.' In reality, violence-prone children and the mentally unbalanced are most at risk of emulating media violence. The more heavily a weak-minded consumer relies on the media for information about the world and the greater his or her predisposition to criminal behaviour, the greater the effect. Radecki believed that heavy television use 'leads to an increased desensitization towards violence and a small, but important, increased tendency to lose our tempers'. Most Western countries, he alleged, had seen increases in violence rates of 200–500 per cent over the previous 20 years. To put such claims in perspective, violent crimes (rape, murder, assault) make up only 6–7 per cent of all reported crimes annually recorded by the British police. The trouble with studies on the effect of violent videos on children, such as those Radecki cited, is that such studies presuppose that 'violence' is something within films, television programmes, video games or comics, that can be separated from the narrative context, genre and overall construction of the particular form which contains it. Research into both media forms, and audience responses to these forms, makes clear that this separation cannot be made. The behavioural assumption of the 'effects' of media violence can also be exaggerated. Actor-director Clint Eastwood, star of several violent genre films, 'never bought into that notion that movies incite violence, because we all grew up with [James Cagney] movies like *Public Enemy* and *White Heat*, but it never made us criminals; we didn't start blowing people away just because we saw it on the screen. You always realise it's only a movie; only an idiot isn't aware of that.'[16]

Western youth in the final decade of the twentieth century requires protection from the much greater harm caused by the abuse of alcohol, drugs or the motor car, rather more than from violent or criminal imagery in the mass media. The debate over the social harm caused by violent forms of entertainment fails to consider that moral damage is also caused by trying to protect the young from such works. Restrictions on access tend to sharpen an appetite for the forbidden. Rather than violent films inciting violence, it could be argued that, by watching them, paying customers are able to purge base instincts such as fear, hatred, and anger – the therapeutic benefits of popular culture remain unexplored. In 1949 Professor Frederic M. Thrasher responded to Dr Fredric Wertham's claims that comic books were a significant factor behind American juvenile delinquency. He pointed out that an exaggerated view of the influence of comics illustrated 'a dangerous habit of projecting our social frustrations upon some specific trait of our culture, which becomes a sort of "whipping boy" for our failure to control the whole gamut of social breakdown'. In the present day it would not be difficult to find parallels in press articles about the dangerous influence of horror videos, teenage magazines or violent computer games on 'amoral' young people.[17]

CONCLUSIONS

Continuities over many generations in the 'moral panics' induced by fears of new technology interacting with revised forms of popular culture should have become apparent by now. Whatever amuses the young for a price but does not appear to elevate public taste will invite criticism. The language directed against present-day forms of mass entertainment with an in-built youth appeal has much in common with the exaggerated rhetoric once generated by the allegedly mimetic 'effects' of the 'penny dreadful', the gangster film, or the 'horror comic' on juvenile delinquency. Intellectual rigour and honesty are in short supply on all sides of the on-going debate about the behavioural effects of certain forms of entertainment on a young audience. Academics engaged in a radical re-examination of the whole 'media effects' debate have recently questioned not only whether the media is capable of directly influencing young people's views and actions, but also whether the simplistic idea of 'effects' is the most useful way of conceptualizing the relationship between the media and audiences.[1]

This account of 'moral panics' demonizing commercial forms of entertainment since the early Victorian years serves to undermine a belief that each new medium poses a unique threat to uncover criminal tendencies in susceptible children or adolescents. It also charts a shift in panic discourse over time, from pessimist elitism and censorship, as represented by the Society for the Suppression of Vice, towards a more optimistic pluralism based on tacit paternalistic measures. Thus until the 1960s intellectuals promoted 'quality' culture as a means of social and moral elevation, hence Robert Warshow's advocacy of Alexandre Dumas' *The Three Musketeers* rather than a comic book such as *Superman* (see Chapter 5). This kind of preference has been challenged more recently by a trend towards an ideal of democratic choice: in an age of media studies the young know cultural quality when they encounter it. Encouraging this kind of youthful discrimination has greatly undermined cultural elitism. The historical development of panics from elitism to pluralism is paralleled within cultural politics by what has been aptly characterized as 'a move

156

away from democratising Culture towards increased cultural democrati-sation'.[2]

Equally, the assumption that cultural influences start only from high up on the social scale and are diffused downwards to the unenlightened is con-tradicted by evidence from the 1860s that popular fiction read by the work-ing classes could overlap with, or even directly influence, more respectable middle-class reading material. 'Penny dreadfuls' 'have spread as an epi-demic spreads from the hovel to the mansion. The current demand [in 1865] for "sensation novels", to be provided for the circulating libraries at half a guinea a volume, had been absolutely generated by the weekly sheets', wrote Charles Knight, earnest provider of self-improving litera-ture for the masses. For the much-condemned 'sensation novels' of authors such as Wilkie Collins, Mary Elizabeth Braddon, Mrs Henry Wood, James Payn and Charles Reade were fashionable among middle-class readers at this time.[3]

Critical interrogation in Chapter 3 of the legal evidence brought forward in late-Victorian police courts reveals the tenuous basis of a supposition that the reading of penny fiction by the 'lower orders' would inexorably lead on to subsequent criminal convictions. It was the popularity of such reading with working-class youth, as much as its content, that so disturbed the authorities. 'Thus the seeds sown by the penny dreadful were considered all the more dangerous because they fell on the fertile imaginations of a class of youths who were, apparently, already inclined to criminal activities', points out Patrick Dunae. Among them, perhaps, the ringleader of three teenage housebreak-ers interviewed in 1841 by the Revd John Clay, prison chaplain in Preston gaol for over 30 years – except that the penny theatre takes the blame here. '"H. often compared us to Jack Sheppard and his comrades; he said we had gone through as much as Jack Sheppard very near"', confessed a 17-year-old accom-plice. '"H. seemed always to have Jack Sheppard in his head; he printed his name on the shop beam with a piece of chalk, the same as Jack Sheppard does when the first scene [of the play] opens"' (see Appendix 1). Yet the actual robberies these three committed have a modern-sounding ring to them, owing little to what they had seen on stage. 'They would, after entering houses, sit and drink and enjoy themselves, and destroy property when not able to find anything removable. On one occasion they destroyed machin-ery to the amount of 15s., on another they eased themselves [defecated] upon a quantity of cotton.' Even if a few abnormal minds, like that of 'H' and the 19-year-old Berkshire house painter who thought himself 'Captain Hawk', were affected by fantasies concocted around what they had seen on stage or read of in weekly highwaymen serials, to argue from such exceptional behaviour that drama and literature about crime and criminals should be banned is not entirely rational. Theodore Kaczynski, the Polish–American recluse and former college teacher charged in 1996 with the 18-year Unibomber killing spree, supposedly modelled himself on the Professor in *The Secret Agent*, Polish-born Joseph Conrad's 1907 novel. No one has consequently proposed outlawing such a revered work, presumably because it is not pulp fiction.[4]

Placing exceptional weight on the malevolent influence of popular entertainment upon its youthful audience generates attempts to apply an over-simplified monocausal model to individual human acts of choice taking place within an historical context of extremely diffuse and complex social phenomena. A 'penny dreadful' or a 'half-dime novel' might conceivably suggest a criminal *modus operandi* but this does not explain why only one in thousands of readers ever chose to put it into practice. Young men already disposed towards crime in the 1930s might well have taken cues for their behaviour from watching gangster films, among many other sources, yet evidence that the cinema did more than provide suggestions for the *form* of their criminal or violent behaviour is very limited indeed. Moralists tend to exaggerate the ability of the media to influence the behaviour of people less educated than themselves. Environmental, domestic and psychological factors in nearly all cases outweigh popular or mass culture as predeterminants of juvenile delinquency.

Trial reports cited in Chapter 3 may have been grist to the critical mill of those hostile to mass literacy but, rather than establishing any genuine causal link between juvenile crime and popular fiction, most press accounts made their real contribution through a 'deviance amplification system', or smear campaign, which assembled the received image of cheap juvenile reading for generations to come.[5] The 'penny dreadful' and its characterization as a provocation to crime was a work of construction with little basis in actuality. The formula melodrama of so-called 'dreadfuls' only rarely sustained the moral polemic directed against this admittedly commercial form of juvenile literature. 'Dreadfuls', like modern horror films, may even have performed a valuable socio-therapeutic function for young Victorian audiences, acting as some kind of adolescent 'rite of passage', as well as offering a fantasy escape from law-abiding everyday lives in the school, the office, the warehouse and the workshop. Yet when public opinion sought a scapegoat for supposedly rising rates of juvenile crime, convenient cultural artefacts, such as penny serials, were highlighted by the news media of the time.

The evidence presented in previous chapters suggests that scapegoating then censoring the media offers little solution to juvenile delinquency, primarily a complex structural and pathological problem. Generalized factors such as constant exposure to high television levels of materialistic consumption are, perhaps, more to blame for increases in rates of larceny than watching theft enacted in a particular televison drama. There can be no easy answers based on inconclusive psychological data and so it comes down to a battle of prejudices on either side about who or what is to blame. The trouble is that in 'moral panics', the mass media can be both the agency of public reaction and also the accused source. Those who debunk the idea that we live in an age of unprecedented media violence and rising crime tend, on the other hand, to dismiss what has been called 'the historical lineage of cultural pessimism'. Sociologists assigning each successive cultural fear to the inclusive category of 'moral panic' risk disregarding particular features of historical context, social anxiety or new technology. The very fact of a recurring cycle might suggest not so much a persistent irrationality or media-induced 'panic', but rather the expression of fundamental contradictions in relations between classes and generations. We should give more emphasis to the *continuity* of the apprehension and loathing of 'modernity' which such fears represent and the specificity of the various constituencies, populist, conservative and fundamentalist, from which they emerge. Broad social trends help define problematic issues, but a particular 'moral panic' can often be determined by a relatively small number of activists. Violent or horrific forms of popular culture can be offered in any historical age, but the public reaction to them is that age's alone.[6]

What makes the 'moral panics' over the influence of popular culture on the young discussed in previous chapters so persistent across national and historical boundaries? One theory is that the development of mass media and reactions towards them must be understood in relation to the wider parameters of 'modernity' or the economic and social upheavals of industrialization, urbanization and secularization. Modernity is presented as a dynamic of changing historical processes founded upon competitive capitalism that has also led to a profound transformation of cultural experiences. Unfortunately, because of modernity theory's emphasis on dramatic change, its proponents tend to underestimate continuities between pre-industrial and urban-industrial popular culture. Britain, as the world's first modern industrial economy, none the less saw an unprecedented growth in commercial entertainments, for example cheap serials and periodicals directed at children and adolescents with time and money on their hands. Panics in Germany and Sweden from the 1880s onwards focused less on banning such literature, argues Kirsten Drotner, than on promoting 'quality' books and journals as a means of social and moral elevation. The same case was made much earlier in Britain through self-improving weeklies such as Charles Knight's educational miscellany *The Penny Magazine* (1832–45), while *The Bookseller* believed in 1868 that 'the real remedy for the mischievous in literature seems likely to be found . . . in the spread of cheap, wholesome, good, and attractive books, rather than in any attempt to suppress the bad by legislative enactment'.[7]

A much greater threat to the twentieth-century's 'enlightened' cultural elite, such as maverick Cambridge English don F. R. Leavis, was posed by the advent of the mass media of radio, cinema and television, all with a highly visible social and cultural role. The literary elect were particularly incensed with Hollywood's ascendancy over popular cinema after 1914, accounting for much of the British middle-class animus against gangster films. Media panics also proved enduring because of the pioneering cultural position of the young in modernity: from the 1860s as dominant consumers of mass-produced penny serials; from the 1900s as major cinema patrons; from the late 1930s unrivalled as comic-book readers; obsessive television viewers from the 1950s; and from the 1980s accomplished as operators of video recorders and computer games. This cultural power of the young in the world of commercial leisure poses a potential threat to existing power relations. More recent youth leisure (discos, concerts, raves) occupies visible public space, is seen as hedonistic and presents problems within the dominant discourse of 'enlightenment'(see Introduction). Socially, media panics attempt to re-establish the generational *status quo*, culturally they act to prevent the undermining of the cultural elite as a critical force, hence their advocacy by librarians, teachers and literary critics. Media panics have been called 'cultural seismographs' that reveal the broader problems of modernity, acting as tacit or explicit social regulation through cultural enlightenment of the young, who are panic targets because they represent experiences and emotions irrevocably lost to adults.[8]

At least since the 1830s, if not before, each time British or American society has found itself in confusion or crisis, often because of perceived rises in juvenile crime, there have been attempts to shift blame for social breakdown onto the entertainment forms of the age: penny theatres, 'penny dreadfuls', dime novels, gangster films, 'horror comics', television, 'video nasties', and now video games have each in turn played the role of 'folk devils' which *must* be causing delinquency. A belief that the young can somehow be weaned away from the newest media craze on offer suffers from a profound historical amnesia. Media or moral panics often tell us a great deal more about adult anxieties – fear of the future, of technological change, and the erosion of moral absolutes – than about the nature of juvenile misbehaviour. Attacks on the influence of the media thereby act to conceal social uncertainties, such as a fear of the new technology that amuses the young but is beyond our adult capacity to comprehend ('computer games have not lodged themselves in the affections of the older generation').[9]

Hence the most popular forms of entertainment among the young at any given historical moment tend also to provide the focus of the most intense social concern. A new medium with mass appeal, and with a technology best understood by the young, such as CD-ROM games which use interactive technology, almost invariably attracts a desire for adult or government control. Film director Paul Schrader, brought up in a strict Dutch Calvinist environment in Grand Rapids, Michigan, recalls that the arrival of television in the mid-1950s was seen as a threat to this ideologically pure community which initially tried to keep TV-sets out. So children like the young Schrader would go to their Polish Catholic neighbours' houses, sitting 'surrounded by statues of the Virgin Mary and watching *Howdy Doody*. At which point they [Calvinists] sort of gave up and said "Well, if we have TV in our own homes at least we can control what they see".' [10]

The historian tempted to conclude that *plus ça change, plus c'est la même chose* should be aware that anxious parents of today's young children in the affluent Western world, surrounded by the bewildering new technology of home computers with CD-ROM players plus cable, satellite and digital television, are likely to be far less sanguine. They may be frightened of technological innovation simply because the ability of the state and of adults in general to censor or control access to forms of communication, such as the Internet with its overstated potential for delivering violent or sexual imagery, is much less evident than in the past. Each new technological breakthrough in mass communications, from the rotary printing press to the cinematograph, to the full-colour book of comics to the home computer, provides a focus for social anxiety, particularly if exploited commercially to market a new form of amusement for the young beyond the supervision of 'responsible' adults. From this perspective, the fear of 'video nasties' or of violent interactive computer games and the fear of mass consumer society often go hand in hand. The frightened would like to disinvent the new technology that has created the domestic video-cassette recorder or the home computer and return society to an imaginary, non-violent popular culture, a mythical golden age of tranquil juvenile pastimes.

Yet the history of youth, popular culture and 'moral panics' reminds us that crime, horror, sex and violence have been staple ingredients of self-selected juvenile entertainment for some considerable time. Sixty years ago a British teacher regretted that boys no longer played 'jolly good games' but, because of 'the influence of the films', had started copying murderous gangsters in the school playground (see Chapter 4). Only a few years ago Teenage Mutant Ninja Turtles were similarly being imitated and also condemned. These comic-book characters were marketed as 'Teenage Mutant *Hero* Turtles' in the UK as 'Ninja' was apparently thought to connote violence. Commentators who believe that recent Hollywood movies espouse a 'culture of violence', but that popular culture once 'sought to lift our spirits and encourage what was good, honourable and just in our society' have conveniently forgotten the violent gangster films of the 1930s, not to mention the 'horror comics' of the early 1950s. Previous chapters have also shown how, in the nineteenth century, popular entertainment for the young was steeped in 'sensation', ribaldry and melodrama. Blaming popular culture or the media for causing violence and juvenile crime, argue Martin Barker and others, 'is our society's equivalent of blaming illness and the death of pigs on witchcraft'. Western societies which refuse self-knowledge by succumbing to more or less continuous 'moral panics' over mass entertainment are hardly well-equipped to withstand the upheavals of the end of the century.[11]

APPENDIX I
JACK SHEPPARD IN VICTORIAN POPULAR CULTURE

The canonization of Jack Sheppard among the Victorian young only began after middlebrow novelist William Harrison Ainsworth (1805–84), whose early sales outrivalled the young Dickens, resuscitated this boyish criminal from the preceding century. Manchester-born Ainsworth's romantic historical novel, *Jack Sheppard* (1839), was a follow-up to his best-selling Dick Turpin novel *Rookwood* (1834). This new, highly melodramatic version of Sheppard's short but notorious life, serialized from January 1839 to February 1840 in *Bentley's Miscellany*, was swiftly gutted for even more popular consumption by the authors of cheap Edward-Lloyd-style serials, as well as by almost every provincial and metropolitan theatre from the 'legitimate' stage down to the humblest penny gaff. Hence the mechanics of the cultural translation of 'Jack Sheppard' from the realms of the polite, novel-reading, middle-class public to that of the unruly, juvenile, working-class audience at the penny theatres, or the semi-literate consumers of cheap serialized fiction, are crucial for any proper investigation of the way in which commercial forms of entertainment operated in the second quarter of the nineteenth century. The representation of thief–escaper Jack Sheppard versus evil Thieftaker-General Jonathan Wild in multiple forms of Victorian popular culture illuminates the mass appetite for criminal anti-heroes, whilst middle- and upper-class reactions to Sheppard plays and penny novels identify the fears and prejudices of those in authority, concerned about cultural encouragement being lent to deviant forms of youthful behaviour. Henry Mayhew censured Ainsworth's novel because it allegedly encouraged those who could 'read merely' to become thieves. Popularization of so-called 'Newgate fiction' by authors such as Dickens, Ainsworth and Bulwer Lytton, through the imitative agencies of the theatre and the cheap serial, was hence considered a serious threat to the social order of early Victorian England.[1]

Dick Turpin is still current as an iconic hero in the popular imagination, perpetuated through television, comics and boys' magazines, but his near-contemporary Jack Sheppard, a little Cockney guttersnipe, who boasted no Black Bess, ornate pistols or other romantic trappings, is no longer a household name. Sheppard was not, in fact, a highwayman but a young London housebreaker and footpad, with scarcely any criminal talents, whose well-publicized prison escapes briefly turned him into a hero with the ordinary people of early eighteenth-century London. Apparently Jack committed no crimes until the last year of his life when he was either 20 or 21. He was hanged several months after his first petty theft of a couple of silver spoons but within that short period escaped from various prisons at least four times. Radical historian Peter Linebaugh has reinterpreted the popularity of Sheppard and his story of freedom as one sharing in the central experiences of his class and generation. Within the 'crisis of apprenticeship' of the time, Sheppard is claimed as 'part of a deeper, structural recomposition of the London proletariat'. He had been apprenticed to a carpenter at age 15 but by breaking his indentures in 1723 Sheppard became an 'idle apprentice', a social figure as threatening to the established order as the 'sturdy rogue' of the sixteenth century, or the 'sectary' of the seventeenth century, or the 'factory proletarian' of the nineteenth century.[2]

Sheppard's first escape, after being imprisoned early in 1724 for breaking and entering, was from St Giles's Round House, a small lock-up. He was recaptured and, together with his doxy Edgeworth Bess, made an even more dramatic escape from the New Prison, Clerkenwell, despite being loaded down with heavy chains. Next, together with Joseph Blake, or Blueskin, Jack stole from a man who had earlier befriended him, a Mr Kneebone, since knowing the premises made it easier. The angry house-owner employed Jonathan Wild, the notorious Thieftaker-General, to locate the suspect for recapture; it was for this burglary that Sheppard was sentenced to death. In broad daylight, at the end of August 1724, he miraculously escaped from the condemned hold of the infamous Newgate, while Bess and another woman, Poll Maggot, talked with him through the visitors' hatch; he was so thin and agile that the filing and removal of a single bar enabled him to squeeze through. A few days later, he was caught and restored once more to his cell, becoming a great attraction for famous visitors. On 15 October 1724, Sheppard made his famous second escape from Newgate, slipping his small hands out of the heavy irons, working his way out through an impressive series of locked doors and masonry walls; winning his way to immortality with just a file, a rusty nail, and an iron bar wrenched from a chimney. Instead of leaving the country, as his mother begged, he went on a round of tavern drinking with one Moll Frisky and was recaptured yet again, after only 16 days of freedom. Under a much stronger guard, Jack Sheppard was hanged at Tyburn, aged only 21, on 16 November 1724. Friends had hoped to rescue him on the way to the gallows, or to resuscitate him after the hanging, but these plans came to nought.[3]

Harrison Ainsworth's single-handed revival of the Jack Sheppard legend was to find its widest circulation among the people, more than half a century before the advent of the cinematograph, through the medium of the London and provincial stage. Keith Hollingsworth suggests that the Sheppard story became an extra-literary popular phenomenon with the magnitude of something like a popular Broadway or West End musical, different chiefly because in the nineteenth century there were not so many media into which it might be transferred. In retrospect, the whole amazing flood of highwaymen dramas, pamphlets, serials and novels was at least the equal of anything similar in modern popular entertainment. The translation into popular form of Ainsworth's Newgate novel proved of enduring concern to the English authorities, who feared the potential effect which such 'glamorization' of criminal rogues might have upon the impressionable young. Jack Sheppard's popularity achieved its first peak in October 1839, while the original serial was still running in *Bentley's Miscellany*, when eight stage versions were produced almost simultaneously in London. 'Jack Sheppard is the attraction at the Adelphi; Jack Sheppard is the bill of fare at the Surrey; Jack Sheppard is the choice example of morals and conduct held forth to the young citizens at the City of London', declaimed John Forster, friend and biographer of Dickens. 'Jack Sheppard reigns over the Victoria; Jack Sheppard rejoices crowds in the Pavilion; Jack Sheppard is the favourite at the Queen's; and at Sadler's Wells there is no profit but of Jack Sheppard.'[4]

Even Forster's list overlooks another version at the Garrick theatre, like the Pavilion situated in Whitechapel. *Harlequin Jack Sheppard, or the Blossom of Tyburn* – a reference to Sheppard's execution – was also a popular Drury Lane burlesque pantomime in Christmas 1839, the original playscript of which can be found in the Lord Chamberlain's Day Books in the British Library. Other versions of 'Jack Sheppard' performed in the ubiquitous minor theatres were, until the Theatres Act of 1843, outside the Lord Chamberlain's jurisdiction as licenser of plays. In 1839 Sheppard plays were also put on in Hull and Edinburgh, later proving equally popular elsewhere with provincial audiences who appear to have attended performances long after the Lord Chamberlain had forbidden all variants of the 'dangerous' subject matter.[5]

Plays based upon Harrison Ainsworth's *Jack Sheppard* and Dickens' *Oliver Twist* (1839) were attacked more fiercely, both by the licensers and middle-class public opinion, than perhaps any other dramas of the nineteenth century. Their popularity with young audiences was seen as symptomatic of rising juvenile crime and as an index of the danger to society in general from the new urban working classes. The ban on Sheppard plays from the 1840s onwards, albeit erratic and often self-imposed, indicates the clear determination of the authorities to censor, regulate or prohibit drama 'turning on the subjects of Burglary, Highway Robbery, stealing from the person, etc., [which] were as a class generally objectionable for representation'. William Bodham Donne, the long-term Examiner of Plays, explained that during the 1840s the Lord Chamberlain 'had a great many letters from parents and masters requesting that such pieces should not be exhibited, because they had an ill effect on their sons and apprentices'. Successive Lord Chamberlains and their examiners or censors drew a direct parallel between the staging of Newgate dramas and a corresponding increase in, or susceptibility towards, juvenile crime. Popular drama, in this sense, was considered dangerous in its effects on those members of the audience, the working-class young, who made up what were perceived as the most vulnerable sections of the population. In doubtful cases of prohibition, the social or age composition of a theatre's clientele could ultimately prove the decisive factor. 'It is highly desirable to elevate the tone of the drama and it is specially necessary in the case of the saloons [cheap theatres], who have a tendency to lower the morals and excite the passions of the classes who frequent these places of resort', wrote a member of the Lord Chamberlain's staff to William Bodham Donne on 13 October 1853.[6]

Sheppard the famous prison-escaper was given a new lease of life with the working-class reading public through the various penny-issue novels based on his life and mostly derivative from the original Harrison Ainsworth novel. A hundred such crime and highwaymen 'penny bloods' were said to have been circulating in London in 1850, many of them taken round the provinces by hawkers. J. J. Tobias confidently states that, 'the impact on the popular imagination made by Jack Sheppard, Dick Turpin and other heroes of crime was such that they had become almost legendary by the nineteenth century, and they played an important part in the lives of [the] juvenile criminals'. Tobias correctly draws attention to the heroic status of long-dead criminals among the Victorian poor, but is too credulous of the contemporary view that this could somehow influence behaviour.[7]

More than a dozen separate versions of the Sheppard story have survived which first appeared in cheap, often serialized, form in the 10 years
following the publication of Ainsworth's novel. They were made available
in what John Forster dismissively called 'the low smoking-rooms, the common barbers' shops, the cheap reading places, [and] the private booksell-
ers'. Popular and highly imaginative versions of Jack Sheppard's brief life
were addressed to this new urban audience, with plots derived as much
from the conventions of stage melodrama as from Ainsworth's original
novel. On Sunday evenings, according to John Binny's account of the
thieves and street boys in a low lodgings house in mid-century London,
'the only books read were such as *Jack Sheppard*, *Dick Turpin*, and the
Newgate Calendar, [which] they got out of the neighbouring libraries by
depositing a shilling. These were read with much interest; the lodgers
would sooner have these than any other books.' At the peak of the juvenile
penny-part serial in the 1860s, Jack made by far his lengthiest appearance
in Edward Viles' *Blueskin: A Romance of the Last Century* (1866–7). Here he
shares heroic status with fellow criminal Joseph Blake, the 'Blueskin' of the
title. The career of Jack Sheppard continued in its fictional form well into
the next century, but lacking in the charismatic appeal which it had exerted
over the youth of the 1840s and 1850s. Thus the Aldine Publishing Company, which had earlier specialized in American dime-novel reprints, put
out 24 numbers of the adventures of *Jack Sheppard*, edited by Walter Light
from 1904 to 1906, with attractive coloured covers by Robert Prowse and
others.[8]

Even Alfred Harmsworth's *The Boys' Friend* (1895–1927), pledged
to eradicate the 'penny dreadful', published a Jack Sheppard serial, 'The
Idle Apprentice' of 1905, which revelled from week to week in his 'strange
yet wonderful, misspent career'. In the last chapter Jack was escorted to
Tyburn, but the execution was not described and it was also made clear
that before his death Jack had undergone a spiritual transformation, 'he
might die a felon's death but it would be the new Jack not the old one that
would die'. In 1911 the Aldine Boys' Library printed *The Rogues of Old London* which featured the famous jail-breaker elevated as Captain Sheppard,
along with Jack Rann or Sixteen-String Jack and Half-Hanged Smith,
noble-hearted highwaymen all. When Sheppard is finally executed at
Tyburn, Jack Rann is there to leap from the crowd and cut him down but,
before he can carry off the body, Jonathan Wild fires a bullet into
Sheppard's spine, leaving Rann to see to a decent burial at Willesden.
In 1947 author E. S. Turner listened to a BBC radio play on the life of
Jack Sheppard, called *The Bowl of St Giles* after the bowl of liquor which,

traditionally, every condemned man en route to Tyburn was entitled to claim at St Giles. In this version Sheppard was arrested at his mother's funeral before he had time to protest his grief and the last-minute attempt to cut him down from the gallows was made by Blueskin, both men being shot by Wild. The climax lacked drama, Turner protests, because a near riot by thousands sounded more like half-a-dozen men brawling in a cellar. Boisterous crowd scenes were a more convincing ingredient of the British film *Where's Jack?* (1969), novelist-director James Clavell's costly screen version of Jack Sheppard's imaginary rivalry with Jonathan Wild, featuring pop star Tommy Steele as the irrepressible Cockney hero and the late Stanley Baker as a vindictive Wild. The relative commercial failure of this film would suggest that, by the 1960s, Sheppard had ceased to be a popular culture icon.[9]

APPENDIX II

AMERICAN DIME AND HALF-DIME NOVELS

The true 'dime novel', or paper-covered, complete novel in a continuous series, at a cheap fixed price of 10 cents, did not begin to appear regularly until New York City based periodical publishers Irwin Beadle (1826–82), his older brother Erastus (1821–94), and their Ulster-born partner, Robert Adams (1837–66), inaugurated the famous series of *Beadle's Dime Novels*. This was not the first of their series publications, but it became by far the most significant. The generic American term 'dime novel' was subsequently applied to any inexpensive paper-covered 'sensation' novel. Beadle's productive authors set out to mythologize the Wild West of America, putting out 13 titles by the end of 1860, the first of which was *Malaeska, the Indian Wife of the White Hunter* by Mrs Ann S. Stephens. Their first big success came in October with 19-year-old, Ohio-born schoolteacher Edward S. Ellis' declamatory Western, *Seth Jones: or, The Captives of the Frontier* (1860). This 'dime novel' descendant of James Fenimore Cooper's 'Leatherstocking' novels eventually sold more than 400,000 copies. It was followed at monthly or 2-week intervals by 320 other titles in the original series, and by thousands of similar titles in more than 30 distinct series distributed by the American News Company (ANC) over a period of 38 years. The usual print-run for a 'dime novel' was 60,000 and, with reprints, Beadle's total sales between 1860 and 1865 approached the then immense figure of five million.[1]

The Beadle firm, known eventually as Beadle & Adams ('Books for the Million!'), were not the first to publish cheap paper-covered or 'dime novels' in America, but were the first to publish them regularly and continually at a fixed price. They dominated the field for at least 25 years with a roster of formula Western authors such as Edward S. Ellis, Prentiss Ingraham, Edward L. Wheeler and Edward Zane Carroll Judson. A content analysis of the Beadle and Adams' series of *Dime Song Books*, their first successful publishing venture, suggests that the firm identified with the more radical Unionist wing of the Republican party. In 1863 Irwin Beadle broke away from the firm, taking with him its foreman George Munro as partner. Irwin soon dropped out to start his own publishing company and left George Munro as Erastus Beadle's only real competitor. In 1870, brother Norman Munro entered the field, using the reversed name Ornum, subsequently publishing under his own name after the Munro brothers became bitter enemies. Another artisan–entrepreneur newcomer, Frank Tousey, started publishing 'dimes' in the New York district from 1878, probably financed by his uncle Sinclair Tousey, who managed the ANC set up by Beadle and Adams. In 1889 the famous combination of Street & Smith entered the cheap fiction field, becoming the ANC's biggest client and, although late in arrival, the most successful of all the 'dime novel' publishers. They achieved this by streamlining production until they had created a virtual fiction factory, and by becoming progressively orientated, like English serial-fiction publishers, towards a younger audience.[2]

Most Beadle & Adams novels were of about a 100 pages or seldom more than 30,000 words and had plain or coloured wrappers, usually with a lively front-page illustration. There were also quarto and octavo broadsheets, such as *The Boy's Library of Sport, Story and Adventure*, of 16 or 32 pages. *The Beadle's Half-Dime Library* sold at 5 cents and contained about half the number of words found in the 'dimes', many issues featuring Edward L. Wheeler's popular Free Soil and Indian-fighter hero Deadwood Dick. The famous 'outlaw of the Black Hills' made his first appearance in 1877 and in the decade following, stories featuring the Western outlaw as detective, or pioneer folk-heroes such as Kit Carson and Davy Crockett, became favourite subject matter for 'dime novels.' The creation of 'Buffalo Bill', based on the apotheosized career of plainsman William F. Cody, by prolific romancer Edward Z. C. Judson, alias 'Ned Buntline', provided readers with their own present-day Wild West epic hero. Then in 1872 Harlan Page Halsey introduced 'Old Sleuth', the first real 'dime novel' detective, to the pages of George Munro's *Fireside Companion*, and 'dimes' gradually shifted from celebrating the Wild West to a more urban crime locale. Detective fiction began to win readers until in 1883 Norman Munro put out the *Old Cap. Collier Library*, the earliest 'dime novel' publication devoted entirely to this kind of writing and a particular target of Anthony Comstock's puritanical crusade against 'evil reading'. Frank Tousey's dime *New York Detective Library* came up with 'Old King Brady' in 1885, followed a year later by Street & Smith with popular and long-lasting detective hero Nick Carter. Translations of

Carter's ingenious adventures became the subject of a Swedish campaign against '*Smutslitteraturen*' or gutter literature from 1908 to 1909 which led to their being banned from sale. Only Beadle & Adams failed to develop a famous detective, their prolific writers lacking a proper feel for the new city crime fighter formula. New 'libraries' of boys' stories were started during the 1890s, featuring innovative heroes such as college athlete Frank Merriwell.[3]

As mentioned above, Western stories were among the most popular in both 'dimes' and 'half-dimes', particularly those featuring the legendary James brothers. As members of William Clarke Quantrill's bloodthirsty Missouri–Kansas border guerrillas, the actual Jesse and Frank James were forced into outlawry on reputedly being excluded from the pardon extended at the Civil War's end. While the brothers were still active, Frank Tousey published stories about them in *The Five Cent Wide Awake Library* credited to 'D. W. Stevens' (J. R. Musick), well qualified as a Missouri-born writer. Tousey's earliest outlaw title, 'The James Boys as Guerillas', of 10 October 1881, introduced a 'persecution and revenge' motif characteristic of fictional outlaws in 'half-dime' Westerns, justifying the use of violence against established social and legal codes. When ruthless Federal militia lynch the brothers' stepfather, Jesse reacts as theatrical convention dictates: 'Now, I swear, by all I hold sacred, to be avenged! This indignity shall be wiped out with blood!' The boys become separated with the appearance of Stevens's 'The James Boys and the Vigilantes' and the story switches between their respective adventures. Jesse tries to accustom himself to farm-life in Missouri, but with a vigilante committee in hot pursuit, 'it was now next to impossible to settle down to a life of drudgery and toil on a farm'. Following a shootout with his rival for local beauty Clara Morris, the outlaw commences a bank-robbing career with the Youngers, 'the prosy life of a farmer being too quiet for his restless spirit'. Departing further from historical events, 'The James Boys as Train Wreckers' opens as the brothers prepare to rob an approaching train by taking a sledge hammer to the rails. They intercept a stranger, Tom Hatton, who also wishes to stop the train to prevent his fiancée, Lillie, from eloping with a 'sickening swell' and 'model of genteel nonsense' from Chicago who has turned her head. A familiar melodramatic plot of imminent seduction takes over with only peripheral appearances by Jesse and Frank in the story of star-crossed lovers Tom and Lillie. The authenticity of some of Stevens's earlier contributions to the James brothers' *oeuvre* is clearly absent here, albeit the chivalrous behaviour of the fictitious James boys hardly represents a dangerous role model.[4]

At the turn of the century, Street & Smith introduced 'color cover' nickel weeklies, luridly illustrated stories that replaced the old 'black and white' novels. The 'Big Five' began to face tough competition. Eventually Beadle's began to lose their hold on the market, selling out to another firm in 1898, though the imprint continued to appear for a few more years. The Munros also stopped publishing until only Frank Tousey and Street & Smith remained. Rising costs made 'half-dime novels' far too costly to produce and in 1915 Street & Smith turned all their 'nickel weeklies' into mass-circulation, 10-cent sports and adventure magazines, pioneered by Frank Munsey's *Argosy*, printed on cheap wood-pulp paper and known as 'pulp magazines.' Street & Smith continued to produce 'pulps' successfully until after World War Two, adding detective, romance and science-fiction titles. Tousey, meanwhile, carried on producing 'dimes' by cutting costs which meant dropping writers, reprinting earlier stories and increasing prices. Finally, Harry Wolff, who took over the Tousey firm, sold it to Street & Smith and joined the latter. He continued the reprints of the Tousey novels until 1929, after which 'dime novels' became rare and costly collector's items. Circulations of up to a million copies weekly for the most popular pre-1914 stories, featuring Buffalo Bill, Nick Carter, Frank Merriwell and Diamond Dick, would not seem excessive, albeit 'dime novel' publishers never revealed their sales figures. Dime and half-dime novels came to be almost universally condemned by parents, clergy and teachers, but nothing could keep them out of the hands of young Americans, and of many older readers too.[5]

APPENDIX III

HANK JANSON PAPERBACKS
OF THE 1950s

A classic 'moral panic' out of all proportion to any threat offered was that directed against a variety of cheap British paperbacks widely purchased by young adult males in the decade after the Second World War. Paper rationing was deregulated only in 1951 and because of import restrictions British publishers did not have to compete with American paperback fiction for another 6 years, so small newsagents were full of competing, somewhat shoddy, home-grown paperbacks. Matters came to a head when Winston Churchill's appointment of right-winger Sir David Maxwell-Fyfe as Tory Home Secretary in October 1951, supported by the Director of Public Prosecutions, Sir Theobald Mathew, led to the witch-hunting of homosexuals, the harrying of prostitutes and a crusade against supposedly pornographic fiction. Government persecution of England's small back-street publishers culminated in 1953 when 197 separate prosecutions were made under the 1857 Obscene Publications Act against literature judged as 'tending to deprave or corrupt'. The most widely reported trials were directed against the authors and publishers of British thrillers or gangster stories with mildly suggestive titles issued in cheap mass-produced paperbacks. Some of the most successful imitation American-style 'hard-boiled' thrillers, with titles such as *The Filly Wore A Rod* and *Frails can be so Tough*, were credited to 'Hank Janson', a pseudonym originated by South London-born writer Stephen Frances (1917–89), former communist, conscientious objector and author of a neglected Spanish Civil War saga. Barrister Mervyn Griffith-Jones specialized from 1953–4 in prosecuting this new breed of gangster stories signed with American-sounding names and also slightly risqué romances appearing under French-sounding pseudonyms. In 1960 he became notorious as the unworldly prosecuting counsel who asked, in a famous test case of the new (1959) British obscenity law, whether Englishmen wanted their wives and servants to read the Penguin paperback edition of D. H. Lawrence's *Lady Chatterley's Lover*.[1]

With large print runs of between 90,000 and 100,000 copies per title, and with earler titles being constantly reprinted, the sales figures of the 50-odd Janson titles issued between 1948 and 1953 were estimated in excess of four million copies. They were widely read in the armed services and, selling for only two shillings (20p), by young working-class males in general. Richard Hoggart's famous jeremiad against the erosion of 'authentic' British working-class culture by mass-produced Americanized entertainment, *The Uses of Literacy* (1957), contains pastiches of these gangster novels, emphasizing the general mediocrity of their treadmill prose style and sex-and-violence formula. Yet Hoggart also alludes to the raw sensual power of the sadistic scenes in some of these gangster novels. The seven books named as obscene in the original trial against the Janson publishers that opened at the Old Bailey on 14 January 1954 were *Accused, Killer, Pursuit, Vengeance, Amok, Auctioned* and *Persian Pride*. The first five were part of the fourth series of Janson gangster novels, the other two were 'specials', in this case exotic romances of female slavery set in a fantasized Middle East of deserts, nomadic arabs and caliphs.[2]

Modern readers would have considerable difficulty in detecting the faintest hint of what is nowadays thought of as 'obscene', or even any precise sexual details, in any of the seven books. This did not deter Gerald Dodson, the Recorder (judge), from observing that after 'glancing though' the books himself, he had concluded that they were obscene 'with no difficulty at all'. Portraits of leggy lovelies by post-war paperback artist 'Heade' (Reginald Cyril Webb) that adorned the front covers, wearing little but lingerie, were apparently enough to condemn these Janson titles. Dodson thought it tiresome that the jury actually wanted to read the novels before passing judgement: 'I am loath to inflict the task upon them; it seems a ghastly way of spending their time.' After receiving strong hints from the Recorder, the jury found all five defendants guilty. They received draconian sentences of 6 months' imprisonment and a fine of £2000 on each of their publishing companies.[3]

On 15 March 1954, the Appeal Court judges, headed by the Lord Chief Justice, Lord Goddard, decided that Mr Dodson's conduct of the trial had been beyond reproach and that his remarks could not possibly be deemed prejudicial. Goddard added that having had the 'misfortune' to read the books involved, he could not see that anyone could have come to any conclusion but that the books were 'grossly and bestially obscene' and 'filthy'. The Lord Chief Justice opined that if they were to 'fall into the hands of young adolescents, I do not wonder that there is juvenile crime today'. This appeal was therefore dismissed as was one to reduce the excessive sentences handed out to the publishers. Stephen Frances returned from his home in Spain to England to face trial himself in February 1955, but the case against him was dismissed on the, probably spurious, grounds that the seven books in question were actually the work of his successor. In the wake of the Janson trials, a number of Britain's other post-war 'mushroom publishers' were successfully prosecuted. Public indignation was also aroused by a simultaneous press campaign that put pressure on parliament for legislation to ban the import of American 'horror comics' (see Chapter 5).[4]

NOTES

Introduction

1. 'Keep Violence off our Screens, Says Major', *The Independent on Sunday*, 7 Mar. 1993, p. 1; 'Unparalleled Evil...', *Today*, 25 Nov. 1993, pp. 2–3. For serial killer, child abuse, paedophilia, ritual abuse and other constructed media panics see: Les Levidow, 'Witches and Seducers: Moral Panics for our Time', in Barry Richards (ed.), *Crises of the Self: Further Essays on Psychoanalysis and Politics* (London, 1989) pp. 181–215; Philip Jenkins, *Intimate Enemies: Moral Panics in Contemporary Great Britain* (New York, 1992).

2. 'Bulger Case Judge Urges Debate on Parenting and Violent Videos', *Guardian*, 27 Nov. 1993, p. 1; Martin Barker, 'Sex, Violence and Videotape', *Sight and Sound*, III (1993) pp. 10–12. For acquittal of the *Child's Play 3* video in Manchester's Suzanne Capper case see: Beatrix Campbell, 'Moral Panic', *Index on Censorship*, 24 (1995) pp. 57–61.

3. Question, 'Immoral Publications and Plays', *Hansard Parliamentary Debates*, CXCII, 15 June 1868, cols 1558–9.

4. James B. Twitchell, *Preposterous Violence: Fables of Aggression in Modern Culture* (New York, 1989) pp. 48–89; John Springhall, ' "Corrupting the Young"? Popular Entertainment and "Moral Panics" in Britain and America since 1830', *Aspects of Education: Journal of the Institute of Education: The University of Hull*, 50 (1994) pp. 95–110.

5. James Gilbert, *A Cycle of Outrage: America's Reaction to the Juvenile Delinquent in the 1950s* (New York, 1986) p. 4; Graham Murdock, 'Disorderly Images: Television's Presentation of Crime and Policing', in C. Sumner (ed.), *Crime, Justice and the Mass Media* (Cambridge, 1982) p. 104; J. J. Tobias, *Crime and Industrial Society in the Nineteenth Century* (Harmondsworth, 1972 edn) p. 53.

6. Jenkins, *Intimate Enemies*, pp. 9–10; Steven Starker, *Evil Influences: Crusades against the Mass Media* (New Brunswick, NJ, 1991 edn); Linda Martin and Kerry Segrave, *Anti-Rock: The Opposition to Rock 'n' Roll* (Hamden, CT, 1988).

7. Mark. I. West, *Children, Culture, and Controversy* (Hamden, CT, 1988) p. 7; Fredric Wertham, *Seduction of the Innocent: The Influence of Comic Books on Today's Youth* (New York, 1954); John Fulce, *Seduction of the Innocent Revisited* (Lafayette, 1990) p. 76; Michael Medved, *Hollywood vs. America: Popular Culture and the War on Traditional Values* (London, 1993 edn) pp. xviii–xix. See *The Sunday Times Film Forum*, 11 Mar. 1993, for a panel discussion of Medved's polemical book.

8. Jock Young, *The Drugtakers: The Social Meaning of Drug Use* (London, 1971); Stan Cohen, *Folk Devils and Moral Panics: The Creation of the Mods and Rockers* (Oxford, 1972) pp. 9–10; Stuart Hall, with Chas Critcher, Tony Jefferson, John

Clarke and Brian Roberts, *Policing the Crisis: 'Mugging', the State and Law and Order* (London, 1978).

9. Erich Goode and Nachman Ben-Yehuda, *Moral Panics: The Social Construction of Deviance* (Oxford, 1994) pp. 138–41; Rob Sindall, *Street Violence in the Nineteenth Century: Media Panic or Real Danger?* (Leicester, 1990) pp. 29–36.

10. Victor Neuburg, *Popular Literature: A History and Guide: From the Beginning of Printing to the Year 1897* (Harmondsworth, 1977) pp. 254–6; Kirsten Drotner, *English Children andtheir Magazines, 1751–1945* (New Haven, CT, 1988) pp. 17–27.

11. Margaret Spufford, *Small Books and Pleasant Histories: Popular Fiction and its Readership in Seventeenth-Century England* (London, 1981) pp. 72–5; Mary V. Jackson, *Engines of Instruction, Mischief and Magic: Children's Literature in England from its Beginnings to 1839* (Aldershot, 1990); Susan Easton *et al., Disorder and Discipline: Popular Culture from 1550 to the Present* (Aldershot, 1988) pp. 62–5.

12. Kirsten Drotner, 'Modernity and Media Panics', in Michael Skovmand and Kim Christian Schrøder (eds), *Media Cultures: Reappraising Transnational Media* (London, 1992) pp. 42–62; Marshall Berman, *All that is Solid Melts into Air: The Experience of Modernity* (Harmondsworth, 1982) pp. 44–5.

13. Stanley Cohen, *Visions of Social Control: Crime, Punishment and Classification* (Cambridge, 1985) p. 156; Angela McRobbie and Sarah L. Thornton, 'Rethinking "Moral Panic" for Multi-mediated Social Worlds', *The British Journal of Sociology*, XLVI (1995), pp. 559–74; 'The Hammer Blow to our Conscience', *The Independent on Sunday*, 21 Feb. 1993, p. 21; Richard Sparks, *Television and the Drama of Crime* (London, 1992) pp. 65–6.

14. Pierre Bordieu, *Distinction: A Social Critique of the Judgement of Taste* (London, trans. 1984); Lawrence W. Levine, *Highbrow/Lowbrow: The Emergence of Cultural Hierarchy in America* (Cambridge, MA, 1988).

15. W. H. Groser, *The Opening Life: Studies of Childhood and Youth for Sunday School Teachers* (London, 1911) p. 30; James Grant, *Sketches in London* (London, 1838) p. 163.

1 Penny Theatre Panic: Anxiety over Juvenile Working-class Leisure

1. 'The Penny Theatre Nuisance' [1838] in collection of unattrib. press cuttings and playbills: Frederick Burgess (ed.), *Penny Theatres: Illustrated with Views, Bills, Advertisements, etc.* ([1882]; Harvard Theatre Collection, Cambridge, MA); Edward Jacobs, 'Bloods in the Street: London Street Culture, "Industrial Literacy", and the Emergence of Mass Culture in Victorian England', *Nineteenth-Century Contexts*, XVIII (1995) p. 323.

2. 'Asmodeus', 'Shoreditch Localities: No. 3 – Gaffs', *The Shoreditch Observer*, 10 Sept. 1859, p. 3. Asmodeus was an evil spirit of Jewish mythology.

3. Eric Partridge, *A Dictionary of the Underworld*, 3rd edn (London, 1968) p. 273.

4. Michelle Cale, *Law and Society: An Introduction to Sources for Criminal and Legal History from 1800* (Kew, 1996) p. 112; V. A. C. Gatrell, 'Crime, Authority and the Policeman State', in F. M. L. Thompson (ed.), *The Cambridge Social History of Britain*, vol. 3 (Cambridge, 1990) pp. 243–310.

5. 'The Death Blow, or the Fatal Police Act', *The Examiner*, 8 Dec. 1839, p. 778. The 1839 Police Act also prevented the sale of alcohol on Sunday mornings; 'furious

driving' of carts and carriages; and shaking doormats in the street after eight in the morning.

6. *Report of the 1852 Select Committee on Criminal and Destitute Juveniles*, P.P. 1852, VII (515), App. 2; John Russell Stephens: 'Thespis's Poorest Children: Penny Theatres and the Law in the 1830s', *Theatre Notebook*, 40 (1986) pp. 123–30, and his *The Censorship of English Drama, 1824–1901* (Cambridge, 1980) p. 77; Martin Meisel, *Representations: Narrative, Pictorial, and Theatrical Arts in Nineteenth Century England* (Princeton, New Jersey, 1983) pp. 265–79.

7. Anon., 'A Candidate for the Glory of Jack Sheppard', *The Examiner*, 17 Nov. 1839, p. 6.

8. Clive Barker, 'A Theatre for the People', in Kenneth Richards and Peter Thomson (eds), *Nineteenth-Century British Theatre* (London, 1971) pp. 16–17; Michael R. Booth, 'East End and West End: Class and Audience in Victorian London', *Theatre Research International*, II (1977) p. 103; John Springhall, 'Leisure and Victorian Youth: The Penny Theatre in London, 1830–1890', in John Hurt (ed.), *Childhood, Youth and Education in the Late Nineteenth Century* (Leicester, 1981) pp. 101–24.

9. Mark Judd, ' "The Oddest Combination of Town and Country": Popular Culture and the London Fairs, 1800–1860', in John K. Walton and James Walvin (eds), *Leisure in Britain, 1780–1939* (Manchester, 1983) p. 14.

10. Henry Mayhew, *London Labour and the London Poor*, vol. 1 (London, 1861) p. 41; James Grant, *Sketches in London* (London, 1838) pp. 164–5.

11. Anon. [E. H. Burrage], *Rags and Riches: A Story of Three Poor Boys* (London [Hogarth House], *c.* 1875) p. 10.

12. Elspeth King, 'Popular Culture in Glasgow', in R. A. Cage (ed.), *The Working Class in Glasgow, 1750–1914* (London, 1987) pp. 153–7; Hugh Cunningham, 'The Metropolitan Fairs: A Case Study in the Social Control of Leisure', in A. P. Donajgrodzki (ed.), *Social Control in Nineteenth-Century Britain* (London, 1977) pp. 163–84.

13. Grant, *Sketches in London*, pp. 161–3; James Greenwood, *The Seven Curses of London* (London, 1869) p. 68; Winifred Loraine, *Robert Loraine: Actor, Soldier, Airman* (London, 1938) pp. 44–50.

14. For PLC quote, Gareth Stedman Jones, *Outcast London: A Study in the Relationship between Classes in Victorian Society* (London, 1976 edn) pp. 71–2; Michael J. Childs, *Labour's Apprentices: Working-Class Lads in Late Victorian and Edwardian England* (Montreal, 1992) pp. 51–72; Lionel Rose, *'Rogues and Vagabonds': Vagrant Underworld in Britain, 1815–1985* (London, 1988) pp. 130–7.

15. John Binny, 'Juvenile Thieves', in Henry Mayhew (ed.), *London Labour and the London Poor*, vol. 4 (London, 1862) p. 277; anon., 'The Evils of Penny Gaffs', *The Era*, 10 Apr. 1859, p. 6; Mins. of Evidence, *Select Comm. on Theatrical Licenses and Regs.*, P.P. 1866, XVI (373), 7879–82; George Godwin, 'The Struggling Classes', *The Builder*, XVI, 5 June 1858, p. 386.

16. Greenwood, *The Seven Curses*, p. 68; George Godwin, *Town Swamps and Social Bridges* (London, 1859) p. 95; Mayhew, *London Labour*, vol. 1 (1861) p. 41.

17. Mayhew, ibid., pp. 40–1; Gustave Doré and Blanchard Jerrold, *London: A Pilgrimage* (London, 1872) p. 166; Matthew Browne [W. Brighty Rands], *Views and Opinions* (London, 1866) p. 275.

18. Godwin, 'The Struggling Classes', p. 386.

19. Burgess, *Penny Theatres, passim*; Grant, *Sketches in London*, pp. 169–73; Mayhew, *London Labour*, vol. 3 (1861) pp. 131–6.

20. Mayhew, ibid., p. 144; Burgess, *Penny Theatres, passim*; Grant, *Sketches in London*, p. 173.

21. Grant, *Sketches in London*, pp. 179–80; Mayhew, ibid., pp. 143–4; Greenwood, *Seven Curses*, p. 69.

22. Tom Hopperton, 'Two-way Blood Transfusion', *The Story Paper Collector*, 4 (1962) pp. 23–7; Mayhew, ibid., p. 143; Greenwood, *Seven Curses*, p. 69; James Greenwood, *The Wilds of London* (London, 1874) pp. 12–20.

23. 'Bos' [T. P. Prest] (ed.), *Oliver Twiss* (London, 1838–9) pp. 190–4. Available on microfilm in the British Library.

24. Ibid.

25. Max Schlesinger, *Saunterings In and About London* (London, 1853) pp. 274–5; Jacobs, 'Bloods in the Street', p. 336.

26. Schlesinger, *Saunterings*, pp. 275–6; D. C. Browning (ed.), *Everyman's Dictionary of Literary Biography: English and American* (London, 1972 edn) p. 655.

27. Samuel Phillips Day, *Juvenile Crime: Its Causes, Character and Cure* (London, 1858) pp. 169–76.

28. Godwin, 'The Struggling Classes', p. 386. On the complex issue of theatrical licensing in Victorian London: Clifford Leach and T. W. Craik (eds), *The Revels History of Drama in English*, vol. 3 (London, 1975) pp. 40–4; Springhall, 'Leisure and Victorian Youth', pp. 110–12.

29. Anon. [J. C. Byrne], *Undercurrents Overlooked*, vol. 1 (London, 1860) pp. 232–4. I am grateful to Prof. Peter Bailey for this reference.

30. Ibid.

31. Mayhew, *London Labour*, vol. 3, pp. 142–3.

32. Mins of Evidence, *Select Comm. on Theatrical Licenses*, Min. 1039; 'Police Report re Garrick Theatre, Whitechapel', 4 April 1868, Lord Chamberlain's Papers, LC1/200/84, PRO; Doré and Jerrold, *London*, p. 165.

33. 'Scene at a "Penny Gaff" ', *The Era*, 30 Aug. 1868, p. 15.

34. Douglas A. Reid, 'Popular Theatre in Victorian Birmingham', in David Bratby, Louis James and Bernard Sharratt (eds), *Performance and Politics in Popular Drama: Aspects of Popular Entertainment in Theatre, Film and Television, 1800–1975* (Cambridge, 1980) pp. 78–9; Stuart Hall, 'Notes on Deconstructing "The Popular" ', in Raphael Samuel (ed.), *People's History and Socialist Theory* (London, 1981) pp. 227–39; Tony Bennett, 'Introduction: Popular Culture and "The Turn to Gramsci" ', in Tony Bennett, Colin Mercer and Janet Woolacott (eds), *Popular Culture and Social Relations* (Milton Keynes, 1986) pp. xiv–xv.

35. Christine Gledhill, 'The Melodramatic Field: An Investigation', in Christine Gledhill (ed.), *Home is Where the Heart is: Studies in Melodrama and the Woman's Film* (London, 1987) pp. 5–39; Philip Rawlings (ed.), *Drunks, Whores and Idle Apprentices: Criminal Biographies of the Eighteenth Century* (London, 1992) pp. 14–15.

36. Richard D. Altick, *Victorian Studies in Scarlet* (London, 1972 edn) p. 93; Greenwood, *Seven Curses*, p. 73; Doré and Jerrold, *London*, p. 166.

37. Godwin, 'The Struggling Classes', p. 386.

38. 'The "Penny Gaff" Recalled: A Victorian Street Scene', *The Times*, 2 Jan. 1953, p. 6; Hugh Cunningham, *Leisure in the Industrial Revolution* (London, 1980) p. 10.

39. George Pearson, *Flashback: The Autobiography of a British Film-Maker* (London, 1957) p. 14, for a 'penny gaff' cinema in Lambeth Walk of the 1900s.

2   Penny Dreadful Panic (I): Their Readers, Publishing and Content

1.   George Speaight, *Juvenile Drama: The History of the English Toy Theatre* (London, 1946) p. 159; E. S. Turner, *Boys Will Be Boys: The Story of Sweeney Todd, Deadwood Dick, Sexton Blake, Billy Bunter, Dick Barton, et al.* (London, 1948) p. 17.

2.   Michael Anglo, *Penny Dreadfuls and Other Victorian Horrors* (London, 1977); Peter Haining (ed.), *The Penny Dreadful Or, Strange, Horrid & Sensational Tales!* (London, 1975), and his *A Pictorial History of Horror Stories: 200 Years of Spine-Chilling Illustrations from the Pulp Magazines,* 2nd edn (London, 1985) pp. 16–31.

3.   [Anthony Trollope], 'An Editor's Tales: "The Spotted Dog" ', *Saint Paul's Magazine,* V (1870) p. 688.

4.   Biancamaria Fontana, 'Thrilling Plots Suspended over Centuries', *The Times Higher Education Supplement,* no. 956, 1 Mar. 1991, p. 18; anon., 'The Literature of Vice', *The Bookseller,* CX, 28 Feb. 1867, pp. 121–3; anon. [T. B. Reed], 'Penny Dreadfuls', *Leeds Mercury,* 16 Aug. 1884, p. 1.

5.   Ronald A. Fullerton, 'Creating a Mass Book Market in Germany: The Story of the "Colporteur Novel", 1870–1890', *Journal of Social History,* XI (1977), pp. 265–83. See also the Dutch 'Stuiverroman'.

6.   Henry Nash Smith, *Virgin Land: The American West as Symbol and Myth* (Cambridge, MA, 1970 edn) pp. 90–120; Alexander Saxton, *The Rise and Fall of the White Republic: Class Politics and Mass Culture in Nineteenth-century America* (London, 1990) pp. 322–32.

7.   John Camden Hotten, *The Slang Dictionary* (London, 1874 edn) p. 281; Thomas Boyle, *Black Swine in the Sewers of Hampstead: Beneath the Surface of Victorian Sensationalism* (London, 1990) pp. 64–73; anon. [P. M. Handover], 'Enough of Blood', *The Times Literary Supplement,* 4 Dec. 1959, pp. i–ii, suggests the repetition of 'dreadful' as an adjective in *The Terrific Record* (1849) may have supplied the generic name.

8.   Anglo, *Penny Dreadfuls,* pp. 11–12; Haining, *The Penny Dreadful,* pp. 16–17; Kevin Carpenter (comp.), *Penny Dreadfuls and Comics: English Periodicals for Children from Victorian Times to the Present Day* (London, 1983) pp. 11–25; Laura Quinn, *Victorian Popular Fiction: Penny Dreadfuls, Boys' Weeklies, and Halfpenny Parts* (Minneapolis, 1974).

9.   Peter Haining, *The Legend and Bizarre Crimes of Spring-Heeled Jack* (London, 1977), and his *The Mystery and Horrible Murders of Sweeney Todd, The Demon Barber of Fleet Street* (London, 1979); Turner, *Boys Will Be Boys,* 3rd edn (Harmondsworth, 1976) pp. 38–50; Henry Mayhew, *London Labour and the London Poor,* vol. I (London, 1861) p. 28.

10. Louis James, *Fiction for the Working Man, 1830–50: A Study of the Literature Produced for the Working Classes in Early Victorian Urban England* (Oxford, 1963) pp. 159–60; Richard D. Altick, *The English Common Reader: A Social History of the Mass Reading Public, 1800–1900* (Chicago, IL, 1957) pp. 202–3.

11. Sheila Egoff, *Children's Periodicals of the Nineteenth Century* (London, 1951) pp. 18–19; Kevin Carpenter, *Desert Isles and Pirate Islands: The Island Theme in Nineteenth-Century English Juvenile Fiction: A Survey and Bibliography* (Frankfurt, 1984) pp. 63–71; Louis James, 'Tom Brown's Imperialist Sons', *Victorian Studies*, XVII (1973) pp. 89–99; John Springhall, ' "Boys of Bircham School": The Penny Dreadful Origins of the Popular English School Story, 1867–1900', *History of Education*, XX (1991) pp. 77–94.

12. Patricia Anderson, *The Printed Image and the Transformation of Popular Culture, 1790–1860* (Oxford, 1991) p.193; anon., *The Newgate Calendar, or, Malefactors' Bloody Register*, 5 vols (London, 1773, revised 1814).

13. Scott Bennett, 'Revolutions in Thought: Serial Publication and the Mass Market for Reading', in Joanna Shattock and Michael Wolff (eds), *The Victorian Periodical Press: Samplings and Soundings* (Leicester, 1982) pp. 225–6.

14. B. R. Mitchell and P. Deane, *Abstract of British Historical Statistics* (Cambridge, 1962) p. 12; *Second Abstract of British Historical Statistics* (Cambridge, 1971) p. 5.

15. W. B. Stephens, *Education, Literacy and Society, 1830–70* (Manchester, 1987) p. 16; R. L. Webb, 'Working-class Readers in Early-Victorian England', *English Historical Review*, LXV (1950) pp. 333–51; David Vincent, *Bread, Knowledge and Freedom: A Study of Nineteenth-Century Working-Class Autobiography* (London, 1982 edn) p. 104, and his *Literacy and Popular Culture: England, 1750–1914* (Cambridge, 1989) p. 226.

16. Stedman-Jones, *Outcast London*, pp. 71–2; Springhall, *Coming of Age*, pp. 98–100; Springhall, ' "A Life Story for the People"? Edwin J. Brett and the London "Low-Life" Penny Dreadfuls of the 1860s', *Victorian Studies*, XXXIII (1990) pp. 223–46.

17. Patricia Mary Barnett, 'English Boys' Weeklies, 1866–1899', DPhil thesis, 1974, University of Minnesota, p. 35; Patrick Dunae, 'Penny Dreadfuls: Late Nineteenth-century Boys' Literature and Crime', *Victorian Studies*, XXII (1979) pp. 133–50.

18. Anon., *The Wild Boys of London; or, The Children of Night. A Story of the Present Day* (London, 1864–6) pp. 6–7.

19. J. P. Harrison, 'Cheap Literature – Past and Present', *Companion to the [British] Almanac of the Society for the Diffusion of Useful Knowledge or Year Book of General Information for 1873* (London, 1872) p. 70; anon., 'Mischievous Literature', *The Bookseller*, CXXVI, 1 July 1868, p. 446.

20. Anon., 'The Literature of Vice', *The Bookseller*, CX, 28 Feb. 1867, p. 121; James, *Fiction for the Working Man*, p. 38.

21. Edwin Hodder, *The Life and Work of the Seventh Earl of Shaftesbury*, vol. 3 (London, 1886) p. 469; Alexander Strahan, 'Our Very Cheap Literature', *Contemporary Review*, XIV (1870) pp. 439–60; James Greenwood, 'Penny Packets of Poison' [1874] in: Haining (ed.), *The Penny Dreadful*, pp. 357–71.

22. George Sampson, *Seven Essays* (London, 1947) p. 39; J. A. Hammerton, *Books and Myself: Memoirs of An Editor* (London, 1944) p. 21.

23. 'Mischievous Literature', p. 447.

24. Ibid.

25. [B. G. Johns], 'The Literature of the Streets', *The Edinburgh Review*, CLXV (1887) p. 43; Springhall, ' "Boys of Bircham School" ', pp. 77–94.

26. P. G. Hall, *The Industries of London since 1861* (London, 1962) pp. 96–112; R. C. Mitchie, *The City of London: Continuity and Change, 1850–1900* (London, 1992);

Frederick Sheppard, *London, 1808–1870: The Infernal Wen* (London, 1971) pp. 180–3; Thomas Catling, *My Life's Pilgrimage* (London, 1911) pp. 52–3.

27. J. J. Barnes, *Free Trade in Books: A Study of the London Book Trade since 1800* (Oxford, 1964) p. 99; Patrick Dunae, 'New Grub Street for Boys', in Jeffrey Richards (ed.), *Imperialism and Juvenile Literature* (Manchester, 1989) pp. 15–17; Steve Holland, *The Mushroom Jungle: A History of Postwar Paperback Publishing* (Westbury, 1993).

28. P. R. Hoggart, 'Edward Lloyd, "The Father of the Cheap Press"', *The Dickensian*, LXXX (1984) pp. 33–8; Francis Hitchman, 'The Penny Press', *Macmillan's Magazine*, XLIII (1881) p. 398.

29. B. Winskill, 'The Penny Dreadful Offices', *Vanity Fair*, no. 2 (1925) pp. 47–8, and his 'Publishing Offices of the Old Boys' Papers that are Gone', *Collector's Miscellany*, 4th ser., no. 4 (1942) p. 46.

30. 'Ralph Rollington' [J. J. Allingham], *A Brief History of Boys' Journals, with Interesting Facts about the Writers of Boys' stories* (Leicester, 1913) p. 17.

31. 'Mischievous Literature', p. 446; 'The Literature of Vice', p. 122; 'Rollington', *Brief History*, p. 17.

32. Sheila Egoff, 'Precepts and Pleasures: Changing Emphases in the Writing and Criticism of Children's Literature', in S. Egoff, G. T. Stubbs and L. F. Ashley (eds), *Only Connect: Readings in Children's Literature* (Toronto, 1969) p. 427; David Vincent, *Literacy and Popular Culture: England, 1750–1914* (Cambridge, 1989) p. 197; [E. J. Brett], 'The Proprietor's Farewell', *Boy's Companion and British Traveller*, I (1865) p. 527.

33. James Greenwood, *The Wilds of London* (London, 1874) p. 160; A. E. Waite, 'By-ways of Periodical Literature', *Walford's Antiquarian*, XII (1887) p. 66; J. Medcraft, 'Newsagents' Publishing Company', *Collector's Miscellany*, 5th ser., no. 2 (1945) pp. 23–6; Returns of Allotments, News Agents' Newspaper and Pub. Co., Companies House, BT31/631/2644, Public Record Office (PRO); 'Mischievous Literature', p. 446. The NPC offices, according to the street directory, were occupied in 1870 by *Judy*, the satirical magazine.

34. 'Mischievous Literature', pp. 446–7; Waite, 'By-ways', p. 66; anon., 'Recent remarks of Mr. Greenwood', *Publisher's Circular*, CCVII (1866) pp. 954–5, 988; Springhall, ' "Boys of Bircham School" ', pp. 85–90.

35. Frank Jay, 'Peeps into the past', suppl. to *Spare Moments*, 15 Feb. 1919, p. 49; 'W. M.', 'Town notes', *Kent Coast Times*, 19 Dec. 1895, p. 8; M. Plant, *The English Book Trade: An Economic History of the Making and Sale of Books* (London, 1974 edn) pp. 339–40; D. C. Coleman, *The British Paper Industry, 1496–1860: A Study in Industrial Growth* (Oxford, 1958) p. 203.

36. Tom Hopperton, 'Victorian King-pin', *Story Paper Collector*, IV (1962) p. 32; Greenwood, *Wilds of London*, pp. 159–60; 'Mischievous Literature', p. 446.

37. With a dozen different and successful titles in print, fetching £37,440 per annum before deducting £26,520 costs, gross profits of £10,920 per annum were possible. The NPC would not sell its maximum print run simultaneously on 12 titles, so James Greenwood's estimate of over £8000 per annum for the rewards of penny dreadful publishing is feasible: Greenwood, *Wilds of London*, p. 160.

38. Springhall, ' "Boys of Bircham School" ', pp. 77–94; Pierce Egan, *Life in London: or, The Day and Night Scenes of Jerry Hawthorn Esq., and his Elegant Friend Corinthian Tom, Accompanied by Bob Logic, the Oxonian, in their Rambles and Sprees through the*

Metropolis (London, 1820–1); J. C. Reid, *Bucks and Bruisers: Pierce Egan and Regency England* (London, 1971) pp. 52–69.

39. James Greenwood, 'Penny Awfuls', *St Paul's Magazine*, XII (1873) p. 162; 'Special Notice!', *Boys of England*, IV, 7 Aug. 1868, p. 192 and IV, 14 Aug. 1868, p. 205.

40. Anne Humpherys, 'Generic Strands and Urban Twists: The Victorian Mysteries Novel', *Victorian Studies*, XXXIV (1991) p. 463; J. M. Ludlow and L. Jones, *The Progress of the Working Class, 1832–1867* (London, 1867) p. 181, cited: Vincent, *Literacy and Popular Culture*, p. 206.

41. Rohan McWilliam, 'The Mysteries of G. W. M. Reynolds: Radicalism and Melodrama in Victorian Britain', in Malcolm Chase and Ian Dyck (eds), *Living and Learning: Essays in Honour of J. F. C. Harrison* (Aldershot, 1996) pp. 182–98; E. F. Bleiler, 'Introduction to the Dover Edition', *G. W. M. Reynolds's Wagner the Wehr-wolf* (New York, 1975) pp. xv–xvi; Louis James, 'The Trouble with Betsy: Periodicals and the Common Reader in Mid-Nineteenth Century England', in Joanne Shattock and Michael Wolff (eds), *The Victorian Periodical Press: Samplings and Soundings* (Leicester, 1982) p. 358.

42. Anon., *The Wild Boys of London, or the Children of Night: A Story of the Present Day* (London, 1877 edn) pp. 1, 18.

43. Ibid., pp. 2, 5, 13, 15.

44. Ibid., pp. 156, 39; Turner, *Boys Will Be Boys*, p. 66; anon., *The Wild Boys of Paris or, The Mysteries of the Vaults of Death* (London, 1866) p. 13.

45. Marjory Lang, 'Childhood's Champions: Mid-Victorian Children's Periodicals and the Critics', *Victorian Periodicals Review*, XIII (1980) p. 22; anon. [Harry Hazleton], *Charley Wag, The New Jack Sheppard* (London, 1860–1) p. 238.

46. Anon. [Harry Hazleton], *Charley Wag*, pp. 3, 20, 577.

47. Anon., *The Poor Boys of London, or Driven to Crime. A Life Story for the People* (London, c.1866) pp. 6, 42–3; Lionel Rose, *'Rogues and Vagabonds': Vagrant Underworld in Britain, 1815–1985* (London, 1988) pp. 37–44, 130–7.

48. Anon., *The Poor Boys*, pp. 18, 41; [Francis Hitchman], 'Penny Fiction', *The Quarterly Review*, CLXXI (1890) pp. 153–4.

49. Michael R. Booth, 'The Metropolis on Stage', in H. J. Dyos and Michael Wolff (eds), *The Victorian City: Images and Realities*, vol. 1 (London, 1973) pp. 211–24; Frank Rahill, *The World of Melodrama* (Pennsylvania, 1967) pp. 85–92.

50. Anon., *The Jolly Dogs of London or, The Two Roads of Life* (London, c. 1866) pp. 2, 11.

51. Anon., *Poor Jack, the London Street Boy* (London, c. 1866) p. 14.

52. George Emmett, *Charity Joe: or, From Street Boy to Lord Mayor* (London, c. 1875); [John Bennett], *The Life and Career of a London Errand Boy* (London, c. 1865); Michael Denning, *Mechanic Accents: Dime Novels and Working-Class Culture in America* (London, 1987).

53. 'Mischievous Literature', *The Bookseller*, CXXVI, 1 July 1868, p. 446; Anon., *Rose Mortimer; or, The Ballet-Girl's Revenge* (London, c. 1865) pp. 12, 15.

54. Anon., *The Work Girls of London: Their Trials and Temptations, A Novel* (London, 1865) p. 38; Lieut. Parker, S.U.S. [pseud.], *The Young Ladies of London; or, The Mysteries of Midnight* (London, 1867–8) pp. 3, 6–7, 10; Gareth Steadman Jones, *Outcast London: A Study in the Relationship Between Classes in Victorian Society* (Harmondsworth, 1984) pp. 67–126.

55. Anon., *The Outsiders of Society; or, The Wild Beauties of London* (London, *c.* 1863) p. 6; anon. [Harry Hazleton], *Fanny White and her Friend Jack Rawlings: A Romance of a Young Lady Thief and a Boy Burglar* (London, *c.* 1865) pp. 54–5.

56. McWilliam, 'The Mysteries of G. W. M. Reynolds', p. 192; 'The Literature of Vice', *The Bookseller*, CX, 28 Feb. 1867, p. 122; Anna Clark, 'The Politics of Seduction in English Popular Culture, 1748–1848', in Jean Radford (ed.), *The Progress of Romance: The Politics of Popular Fiction* (London, 1986) pp. 47–70.

57. John M. MacKenzie, *Propaganda and Empire: The Manipulation of British Public Opinion, 1880–1960* (Manchester, 1984) p. 201; Martin Barker, review of Kirsten Drotner, *English Children and their Magazines* (1988) in *Media, Culture and Society*, XI (1989) p. 508.

58. Wilkie Collins, 'The Unknown Public', *My Miscellanies*, vol. I (London, 1863) p. 186; Edward Viles [J. F. Smith], *Black Bess: or, The Knight of the Road: A Tale of the Good Old Times* (London, 1863–8) preface.

3   Penny Dreadful Panic (II): Their Scapegoating for Late-Victorian Juvenile Crime

1. Anon. [Harriet Martineau], 'Life in the Criminal Class', *The Edinburgh Review*, CXXII (1865) p. 347; Joseph Bristow, *Empire Boys: Adventures in a Man's World* (London, 1991) p. 25.

2. J. J. Tobias, *Crime and Industrial Society in the Nineteenth Century* (Harmondsworth, 1972 edn) p. 53; Mins of Evidence, *Report from Select Committe on Criminal and Destitute Juveniles*, 1852, P.P. VIII (515) 800, 1563, 1826, 2118.

3. Clive Emsley, *Crime and Society in England, 1750–1900* (London, 1987) pp. 27, 35, 71; V. A. C. Gatrell, B. Lenman, G. Parker (eds), *Crime and the Law: The Social History of Crime in Western Europe since 1500* (London, 1980) pp. 305–6.

4. Michael Denning, *Mechanic Accents: Dime Novels and Working-class Culture in America* (London, 1987) pp. 27–46.

5. Antony Comstock, *Traps for the Young* (Cambridge, MA, 1967 edn) pp. 28–9; *Annual Reports of the New York Society for the Suppression of Vice* (New York, 1883–6); John Springhall, 'The Dime Novel as Scapegoat for Juvenile Crime', *Dime Novel Round-Up*, LXIII (1994) pp. 63–72; Michael Denning, *Mechanic Accents: Dime Novels and Working-class Culture in America* (London, 1987) pp. 51, 159–60, 233, fn. 9.

6. Pierre Bordieu, *Distinction: A Social Critique of the Judgement of Taste* (London, trans. 1984); Michael Denning, 'The End of Mass Culture', *International Labour and Working-Class History*, no. 37 (1990) pp. 4–18.

7. [Francis Hitchman], 'Penny Fiction', *The Quarterly Review*, CLXXI (1890) p. 152; 'Pure Literature Society', *The Finsbury Free Press and General Advertiser*, 30 May 1868, p. 3. For further critical reaction: Patrick Dunae, 'Penny Dreadfuls: Late Nineteenth-century Boys' Literature and Crime', *Victorian Studies*, XXII (1979) pp. 133–50.

8. J. B. Twitchell, *Preposterous Violence: Fables of Aggression in Modern Culture* (New York, 1989) pp. 32–6; Kai T. Erikson, 'Notes on the Sociology of Deviance', in

H. S. Becker, (ed.), *The Other Side: Perspectives on Deviance* (New York, 1964) p. 14; Wright cited: Bristow, *Empire Boys*, p. 16.

9. 'The Editor Speaks', *The 'Halfpenny Marvel' Library*, 11 Nov. 1893, p. 16.

10. Sidney Colvin (ed.), *The Works of R. L. Stevenson: Miscellanies*, vol. I (Edinburgh, 1894) p. 249; James Greenwood, *The Wilds of London* (London, 1874) p. 246.

11. 'A Grand Treat for the Boys of Great Britain: *Tyburn Dick*', anon., *Young Will Watch: The Smuggler King* (London, *c.*1865) endpaper; Frank McLynn, *Crime and Punishment in Eighteenth-century England* (Oxford, 1991) pp. 59–60.

12. 'From a London newspaper of 22 May 1868': J. H. Friswell, *Modern Men of Letters Honestly Criticised* (London, 1870) p. 268. I have been unable to locate this reference.

13. Anon., *Tales of Highwaymen or, Life on the Road* (London, 1865); anon. [J. F. Smith], *Black Bess; or, The Knight of the Road: A Tale of the Good Old Times*, 3 vols (London, 1863–8); [Kevin Carpenter], *Penny Dreadfuls and Comics: English Periodicals for Children from Victorian Times to the Present Day* (London, 1983) p. 27.

14. Anon., 'Captain Macheath, the Daring Highwayman and the Black Rider of Hounslow', *Tales of Highwaymen*, p. 3.

15. Cited: Jno. P. Harrison, 'Cheap Literature – Past and Present', in *Companion to the [British] Almanac of the Society for the Diffusion of Useful Knowledge or Year Book of General Information for 1873* (London, 1872) pp. 75–6.

16. [Hitchman], 'Penny Fiction', pp. 154–5; anon., *Black Bess*, preface.

17. Harrison, 'Cheap Literature', p. 76.

18. Anon., *Black Bess*, p. 12.

19. M. J. D. Roberts, 'The Society for the Suppression of Vice and Its Early Critics, 1802–1812', *The Historical Journal*, XXVI (1983) pp. 159–76; 'Pernicious Boys' Literature', *Reynolds's Newspaper*, 9 Dec. 1877, p. 5; 'Police Reports', *The Times*, 13 Dec. 1877, p. 11; Janet Oppenheim, 'The Odyssey of Annie Besant', *History Today*, XXXIX (Sept. 1989) p. 14.

20. 'Police Reports', *The Times*, 13 Dec. 1877, p. 11.

21. Ibid; 'Boys' Literature', *Daily Telegraph*, 24 Dec. 1877, p. 6.

22. 'Boys' Literature', *Daily Telegraph*, 13 Dec. 1877, p. 2; 24 Dec. 1877, p. 6.

23. 'Literature for Boys', *Daily Telegraph*, 28 Dec. 1877, p. 6.

24. 'Police Courts', *Daily News*, 6 Jan. 1876, p. 6; 'Police Intelligence: Pernicious Literature', *The Daily Telegraph*, 1 and 6 Jan. 1876, p. 6.

25. 'Petty Sessions', *Hampstead and Highgate Express*, 1 and 8 Jan. 1876, p. 8.

26. H. H. Ellis, *My Life* (London, 1940) p. 60; *Boys of England: A Magazine of Sport, Sensation, Fun, and Amusement*, vol. I, no. 1, 24 Nov. 1866, pp. 1–16; Edith Nesbit, *The Story of the Treasure Seekers* (London, 1899) p. 128; H. G. Wells, *Tono-Bungay* (London, 1909) p. 30.

27. Michael Anglo, *Penny Dreadfuls and Other Horrors* (London, 1977) p. 86; Patricia Mary Barnett, 'English Boys' Weeklies, 1866–1899', unpublished PhD thesis, 1974, University of Minnesota, p. 36; Patrick Dunae, 'New Grub Street for Boys', in Jeffrey Richards (ed.), *Imperialism and Juvenile Literature* (Manchester, 1989) p. 16.

28. Patricia Anderson, *The Printed Image and the Transformation of Popular Culture* (Oxford, 1991) pp. 9–10; Louis James, 'Tom Brown's Imperialist Sons', *Victorian Studies*, XVII (1993) pp. 90–1; [Carpenter], *Penny Dreadfuls and Comics*, p. 12.

29. John Medcraft, 'The Rivalry of Brett and Emmett', *Collector's Miscellany*, 5th ser., 7 (1947) pp. 103–5; 'For Home and Freedom! A Tale of the Servian War', *Sons of*

Britannia, XIV (1876) p. 657; J. J. Wilson, 'Some of the Old "Penny Dreadful" Newsvendors', *Collector's Miscellany*, I (1928) pp. 15–16.

30. 'Our Letter Box', *Sons of Britannia*, XIII, 16 Feb. 1876, p. 64; XIV, 2 Dec. 1876, p. 720.

31. [James Mortimer], 'Pernicious Literature', *London Figaro*, no. 681, 5 Feb. 1876, p. 8.

32. Ibid.

33. [Carpenter], *Penny Dreadfuls*, p. 21; B. Winskill, 'Old Boys' Periodicals: Some of their Fleet Street Associations', *Bootle Times*, 30 June 1916, p. 6.

34. John R. Gillis, 'The Evolution of Juvenile Delinquency in England, 1890–1914', *Past and Present*, 67 (1975) pp. 96–126; 'A Victim of the Penny Dreadful', *Pall Mall Gazette*, LV, 17 Nov. 1892, p. 7; 'The Suicide of a Boy', *The [Brighton] Argus*, 17 Nov. 1892, p. 4.

35. 'Letters to the Editor', *The Daily News*, 20 Sept. 1895, p. 6; 'Central Criminal Court', *The Times*, 17 Sept. 1895, p. 13; 18 Sept. 1895, p. 5.

36. 'The Plaistow Matricide', *The Daily News*, 18 Sept. 1895, p. 7.

37. 'Leader', *The Times*, 18 Sept. 1895, p. 7; 'Leading Article', *The Publisher's Circular*, 5 Oct. 1895, p. 383; 'Letters to the Editor', *Daily News*, 1 Oct. 1895, p. 2.

38. *Annual Reports, Committee of Visitors to Feltham, 1859–89,* Feltham Industrial School Records, Greater London Record Office; Bristow, *Empire Boys*, p. 32.

39. Harry Hendrick, *Images of Youth: Age, Class, and the Male Youth Problem, 1880–1920* (Oxford, 1990); Martin Barker, 'Sex, Violence and Videotape', *Sight and Sound*, III (1993) pp. 10–12; John M. MacKenzie, *Propaganda and Empire: The Manipulation of British Public Opinion, 1880–1960* (Manchester, 1984) p. 204.

40. 'The Penny Dreadful', *The Daily News*, 28 Sept. 1895, p. 7.

41. John Springhall, ' "Healthy Papers for Manly Boys": Imperialism and Race in the Harmsworths' Halfpenny Boys' Papers of the 1890s and 1900s', in Jeffrey Richards (ed.), *Imperialism and Juvenile Literature* (Manchester, 1989) pp. 107–25; Return of Allotments, Edwin J. Brett and Co. Ltd, Companies House, BT31/8824/64753, PRO; D. J. Jeremy, 'Anatomy of the British Business Elite, 1860–1980', *Business History*, XXVI (1984) p. 5.

42. T. M. Ford, *Memoirs of a Poor Devil* (London, 1936) pp. 97–101. I am grateful to Kevin Carpenter for this reference.

43. D. H. Aldcroft, 'The Entrepreneur and the British Economy, 1870–1914', *Economic History Review*, 2nd ser., XXVII (1964) pp. 113–34; David Landes, *The Unbound Prometheus* (Cambridge, 1969), pp. 234–6; A. Levine, *Industrial Retardation in Britain, 1880–1914* (London, 1967).

44. Return of Allotments, Edwin J. Brett (1907) Ltd, Companies House, BT31/18215/94947, PRO; 'Rollington', *Brief History*, p. 21.

45. 'Wills and Bequests', *Illustrated London News*, 8 Feb. 1896, p. 186; W. M. Clarke, *The Secret Life of Wilkie Collins* (London, 1988) p. 7; 'Rollington', *Brief History*, pp. 37–8.

46. 'Rollington', *Brief History*, p. 89.

47. Thomson story paper *The Wizard* (1922–63) is labelled a 'penny dreadful' in: C. M. Stern, 'Bloods', *The Library Assistant*, 34 (1941) pp. 160–5; Return of Allotments, Aldine Pub. Co. Ltd, Companies House, BT31/31391/44339, PRO; J. J. Wilson, 'Past and Present. The Penny Dreadful. A Comparison', *Vanity Fair* (Saltburn-by-Sea), 2 (1925) p. 46.

4 Gangster Film Panic: Censoring Hollywood in the 1930s

1. Luke McKernan, 'The Arrival of British Movies', in Colin Sorensen (ed.), *London on Film: 100 Years of Filmmaking in London* (London, 1996) pp. 17–25; Roy Armes, *A Critical History of British Cinema* (London, 1978) pp. 19–22; Roger Manvell and Rachael Low, *History of the British Film*, vol. I (London, 1949) p. 36.

2. Emmanuelle Toulet, *Cinema is 100 Years Old* (London, 1995) pp. 19–22, 90; Joel W. Finler, *The Hollywood Story* (London, 1988) pp. 14, 18–19.

3. Jeffrey Richards, *The Age of the Dream Palace: Cinema and Society in Britain, 1930–1939* (London, 1984) pp. 13–14; J. A. Hammerton, *Books and Myself: Memoirs of An Editor* (London, 1944) p. 21.

4. Andrew Sarris, 'Big Funerals: The Hollywood Gangster, 1927–1933', *Film Comment*, XIII (1977) pp. 6–9. Recent epic gangster films include Brian de Palma's *Carlito's Way* (1994), Michael Mann's *Heat* (1995) and Martin Scorsese's *Casino* (1995).

5. Eugene Rosow, *Born to Lose: The Gangster Film in America* (Oxford, 1978) pp. 215–16.

6. John McCarty, *Hollywood Gangland: The Movies' Love Affair with the Mob* (New York, 1993) pp. 83–111; Audrey Field, *Picture Palace* (London 1974) pp. 109, 114; Jeffrey Richards, 'The Cinema and Cinema-Going in Birmingham in the 1930s', in John K. Walton and James Walvin (eds), *Leisure in Britain, 1780–1939* (Manchester, 1983) p. 87; Frank Walsh, *Sin and Censorship: The Catholic Church and the Motion Picture Industry* (New Haven, CT, 1996) p. 71.

7. Carlos Clarens, *Crime Movies: An Illustrated History* (New York, 1980) pp. 83–100; Gregory D. Black, *Hollywood Censored: Morality Codes, Catholics, and the Movies* (Cambridge, 1994) pp. 124–32; McCarty, *Hollywood Gangland*, pp. 66–8.

8. Comp. John Mackie, *The Edinburgh Cinema Enquiry* (Edinburgh, 1933) pp. 3, 20–30; Richards, *Age of the Dream Palace*, p. 69; David Fowler, *The First Teenagers: The Lifestyle of Young Wage-Earners in Interwar Britain* (London, 1995) pp. 116–37.

9. James C. Robertson, *The British Board of Film Censors: Film Censorship in Britain, 1896–1950* (London, 1985) pp. 76–80.

10. Ibid., pp. 80–2; Jeffrey Richards, 'The British Board of Film Censors and Content Control in the 1930s: Images of Britain', *Historical Journal of Film, Radio and Television*, I (1981) pp. 105–7.

11. Stephen Ridgwell, 'The People's Amusement: Cinema and Cinema-going in 1930s Britain', *The Historian*, 52 (1996) pp. 18–21; ' "Crime School" Film Given a Bad Name by Probation Officer', *The Morning Advertiser*, 23 Dec. 1938, p. 6.

12. Review of 'Crime School', *Monthly Film Bulletin* (MFB), 30 June 1938, p. 157; Clive Hirschhorn, *The Warner Bros. Story* (London, 1979) p. 193.

13. Black, *Hollywood Censored*, pp. 274–81.

14. Ibid; Tom Dewe Mathews, *Censored* (London, 1994) p. 82.

15. Black, *Hollywood Censored*, pp. 278–80; Mathews, *Censored*, pp. 81–3.

16. James C. Robertson, *The Hidden Camera: British Film Censorship in Action, 1913–1976* (London, 1989) pp. 67–71.

17. Films outlines from *Monthly Film Bulletin (MFB)* and other sources at BFI Library; Colin Shindler, *Hollywood in Crisis: Cinema and Modern Society, 1929–1939* (London, 1996) p. 218.

18. Nick Roddick, *A New Deal in Entertainment: Warner Brothers in the 1930s* (London, 1983) pp. 133–43; *MFB*; John Russell Taylor (ed.), *The Pleasure Dome: Collected Film Criticism of Graham Greene* (Oxford, 1980) pp.180–1, 195, 198–9. Barry Levinson's *Sleepers* (1996) is a curious revival of the Hell's Kitchen gang/reform-school/priest movie.

19. Black, *Hollywood Censored*, p. 110.

20. Ibid., pp. 109, 115, 121.

21. Ibid., pp. 123–4.

22. Herbert Blumer and Philip M. Hauser, *Movies, Delinquency, and Crime* (Chicago, 1933); W. W. Charters, *Motion Pictures and Youth: A Summary* (New York, 1933) pp. 38–9; Garth S. Jowett, Ian C. Jarvie and Kathryn H. Fuller (eds), *Children and the Movies: Media Influence and the Payne Fund Controversy* (Cambridge, 1996) pp. 9–10; Black, *Hollywood Censored*, pp. 151–3.

23. Henry James Forman, *Our Movie Made Children* (Chicago, IL, 1933) pp. 189–203; Black, *Hollywood Censored*, p. 152; Arthur R. Jarvis Jr, 'The Payne Fund Reports: A Discussion of their Content, Public Reaction, and Affect on the Motion Picture Industry, 1930–1940', *Journal of Popular Culture*, XIX (1991) pp. 127–40.

24. 'Film – A School for Crime', *Today's Cinema*, 4 Dec., 1935, p. 37.

25. James M. Skinner, *The Cross and the Cinema: The Legion of Decency and the National Catholic Office for Motion Pictures, 1933–1970* (Westport, CT, 1993) pp. 18–20; Rosow, *Born to Lose*, pp. 220–1.

26. Carlos Clarens, 'Hooverville West: The Hollywood G-Man, 1934–1945', *Film Comment*, XIII (1977) pp. 10–16; Rosow, *Born to Lose*, pp. 212–27; Roddick, *A New Deal*, pp. 107–12; Sarris, 'Big Funerals', p. 9.

27. Richards, 'The Cinema and Cinema-Going', p. 47; *Police Review*, 21 Feb. 1936, p. 3; 'Do Gang Films Spoil A Boy?' *The Daily Herald*, 18 Jan. 1939, p. 9.

28. 'Council to Ban "Horrific" Films', *The Kentish Express*, 16 Dec. 1938, p. 6; Victor Bailey, *Delinquency and Citizenship: Reclaiming the Young Offender, 1914–1948* (Oxford, 1987) App., Fig. 2.

29. 'Council to Ban "Horrific" Films', p. 6; 'Notes and News', *The East Kent Gazette*, 17 Dec., 1938, p. 9.

30. ' "Horrific" Films Ban Imposed', *The East Kent Gazette*, 17 Dec. 1938, p. 15; ' "Red Arrow" Gang Before Court', *The East Kent Gazette,* 10 Dec. 1938, p. 9.

31. Ibid.

32. ' "Horrific" Films Ban Imposed', p. 15; 'Council to Ban "Horrific" Films', p. 6.

33. ' "Horrific" Films Ban Imposed', p. 15.

34. 'Do Gang Films Spoil a Boy?', p. 9; Richard Ford, *Children in the Cinema* (London, 1939) p. 73.

35. 'Do Gang Films Spoil a Boy?', p. 9.

36. *Hansard (Parl. Debs.)*, 5th. ser., CCLXIV, 1931–32, col. 1141; CCCXLII, 1938–39, col. 272; Fowler, *The First Teenagers*, pp. 129–30; *Report of Commissioners of Prisons and Directors of Convict Prisons for 1937*, Cmnd. 5868, HMSO, 1938, App., pp. 38–42.

37. Skinner, *The Cross and the Cinema*, p. 17; Clarens, *Crime Movies*, p. 14; Douglas Brode, *Money, Women, and Guns: Crime Movies from Bonnie and Clyde to the Present* (New York, 1995). Clarens offers the best contextual account of the crime genre to 1980.

5 'Horror Comic' Panic: Campaigning against Comic Books in the 1940s and 1950s

1. William W. Savage, Jr, *Comic Books and America, 1945–1954* (Norman, 1990); Lee Server, *Danger is my Business: An Illustrated History of the Fabulous Pulp Magazines, 1896–1953* (San Francisco, CA, 1993).

2. Pierre Bordieu, *Distinction: A Social Critique of the Judgement of Taste* (London, trans. 1984).

3. Mike Benton, *The Comic Book in America: An Illustrated History* (Dallas, 1989) pp. 15–20; Ron Goulart, *Over 50 Years of American Comic Books* (Lincolnwood, 1991) pp. 18–20.

4. Coulton Waugh, *The Comics* (Jackson, 1991 edn), pp. 338–43; Mike Benton, *The Illustrated History: Crime Comics* (Dallas, 1993).

5. Goulart, *Over 50 Years*, pp. 191–217; Ray Zone, '4-Color Frenzy: The Rise and Fall of the Crime Comic Book', *Blab*, 5 (1990), pp. 46–65. I am grateful to Stephen Milligen for the last reference.

6. Frank Jacobs, *The Mad World of William M. Gaines* (Secaucus, 1972) p. 73; Digby Diehl, *Tales from the Crypt: The Official Archives* (New York, 1996) pp. 53–71; S. C. Ringgenberg, 'Oh . . . the HORROR! A Capsule History of American Horror Comics', *Comic Book Marketplace*, no. 41 (1996), p. 23; Maria Reidelbach, *Completely Mad: A History of the Comic Book and Magazine* (Boston, 1991) pp. 10–12.

7. Denis Gifford, 'William Gaines', *The Independent*, 5 June 1992, p. 6; Mike Benton, *The Illustrated History: Horror Comics* (Dallas, 1991) pp. 13–23; Goulart, *Over 50 Years*, pp. 174–82.

8. Robert Warshow, 'Paul, the Horror Comics, and Dr. Wertham: Communiqué on an Unequal Battle', *Commentary*, XVII (1954) pp. 596–604.

9. Fredric Wertham, *Seduction of the Innocent: The Influence of Comic Books on Today's Youth* (New York, 1954); James B. Twitchell, *Preposterous Violence: Fables of Aggression in Modern Culture* (New York, 1989) pp. 147–54; Warshow, 'Paul, the Horror Comics', pp. 599, 604.

10. Wertham, *Seduction of the Innocent*, pp. 148–71; Frederic M. Thrasher, 'The Comics and Delinquency: Cause or Scapegoat?', *The Journal of Educational Sociology*, XXIII (1949) p. 205; Anon., 'Marihuana of the Nursery', *The Times Literary Supplement*, 25 Feb. 1955, pp. 113–14; Fredric Wertham, 'Children's Comic Books: Blueprints for Delinquency', *The Reader's Digest*, LXIV (1954) pp. 52–6.

11. Warshow, 'Paul, the Horror Comics', pp. 603–4.

12. Testimony of Richard Clendenen, 21 April 1954, *Hearings before the (Senate) Subcommittee to Investigate Juvenile Delinquency of the Committee on the Judiciary* (Washington, 1954) pp. 8–9.

13. Clenenden, *Hearings*, p. 8; Martin Barker, *A Haunt of Fears: The Strange History of the British Horror Comics Campaign* (London, 1984) p. 106.

14. Jack Kamen, 'The Neat Job', *Shock SuspenStories*, 1 (1952), republished (1992) Russ Cochran Publishing.

15. Jack Kamen, 'A Trace of Murder', *Crime SuspenStories*, 8 (1951), republished in *Tales from the Crypt* (1990) Gladstone Publishing Ltd.

16. Wally Wood, 'The Patriots', *Shock SuspenStories*, 2 (1952), new edn (1992) Russ Cochran Publishing.

17. James B. Twitchell, *Dreadful Pleasures: An Anatomy of Modern Horror* (New York, 1985); Christopher Frayling, *Nightmare: The Birth of Horror* (London, 1996); Jacobs, *The Mad World*, p. 78.

18. Glenna Matthews, *'Just A Housewife': The Rise and Fall of Domesticity in America* (New York, 1987) pp. 210–12; Michael Schaller, Virginia Scharff and Robert D. Schulzinger, *Present Tense: The United States since 1945* (Boston, MA, 1996 edn) p. 113.

19. Benton, *Horror Comics*, pp. 36–37; 'The Transcripts: 1972 EC Convention', *Squa Tront*, 8 (New York, 1978) p. 23; Roger Sabin, *Adult Comics: An Introduction* (London 1993) p. 147; Geoffrey Wagner, *Parade of Pleasure: A Study of Popular Iconography in the USA* (London, 1954) p. 71.

20. Robert C. Holub, *Reception Theory: A Critical Introduction* (New York, 1984); Susan Suleiman, 'Varieties of Audience-oriented Criticism', in Susan Suleiman and Inge Crossman (eds), *The Reader in the Text: Essays on Audience and Interpretation* (Princeton, NJ, 1980) pp. 3–45.

21. Goulart, *Over 50 Years*, pp. 204–5; Joseph McBride, *Frank Capra: The Catastrophe of Success* (London, 1992) pp. 518, 595, 599.

22. *Special Committee to Investigate Organised Crime in Interstate Commerce. Juvenile Delinquency* (Washington, DC, 1950); Benton, *Crime Comics*, pp. 77–8.

23. Benton, *Horror Comics*, p. 41; Mark I. West, *Children, Culture and Controversy* (Hamden, CT, 1988) p. 48; Fredric Wertham, 'What Parents Don't Know about Comic Books', *The Ladies' Home Journal*, LXX (1953) pp. 50–3; Sara Selwood and Diana Irving, *Harmful Publications: Comics, Education and Disenfranchised Young People* (London, 1993).

24. Andrew Arato and Eike Gebhardt (eds), *The Essential Frankfurt School Reader* (New York, 1982); Martin Jay, *The Dialectical Imagination: A History of the Frankfurt School and the Institute of Social Research, 1923–1950* (London, 1973); Bernard Rosenberg and David Manning (eds), *Mass Culture: The Popular Arts in America* (New York, 1957).

25. Gershorn Legman, *Love and Death: A Study in Censorship* (New York, 1949) pp. 43–4; Wertham, *Hearings*, p. 95.

26. James Gilbert, *A Cycle of Outrage: America's Reaction to the Juvenile Delinquent* (New York, 1986) pp. 9–26; Dwight Macdonald, *Against the American Grain* (New York, 1962); David Riesman, *The Lonely Crowd: A Study of the Changing American Character* (New Haven, 1950); Wagner, *Parade of Pleasure*, pp. 72, 107.

27. David Caute, *The Great Fear: The Anti-Communist Purge under Truman and Eisenhower* (London, 1978); Judith Crist, 'Horror in the Nursery', *Collier's*, CXXI, 27 March 1948, pp. 22–3; Benton, *Horror Comics*, p. 39; Gilbert, *Cycle of Outrage*, pp. 92–6; James E. Reibman, 'The Life of Fredric Wertham', in Evelyn Rosenthal (ed.), *The Fredric Wertham Collection* (Harvard, 1990), pp. 11–22.

28. *Hearings*, p. 3; Gilbert, *Cycle of Outrage*, pp. 148, 150.

29. *Hearings*, p. 1; Sabin, *Adult Comics*, p. 160; James Gilbert, *Another Chance: Postwar America, 1945–1968* (New York, 1981) pp. 96–100.

30. *Hearings*, pp. 82, 84.

31. Ibid., pp. 83, 84–5, 86, 87.

32. Ibid., 98, 99, 104, 205; Joe Simon with Jim Simon, *The Comic Book Makers* (New York, 1990) pp. 135–8.

33. *Hearings*, p. 103.

34. Ibid. pp. 58–60, 62–3. The Army–McCarthy hearings, like the 1953 Coronation in Britain, helped persuade millions of Americans to buy their first TV sets.

35. Ibid., pp. 108, 205–6; Sabin, *Adult Comics*, p. 159.

36. Lawrence Levine, *Highbrow/Lowbrow: The Emergence of Cultural Hierarchy in America* (Cambridge, MA, 1988) p. 9; Michael Denning, 'The End of Mass Culture', *International Labour and Working-class History*, no. 37 (1990), pp. 4–18; Pierre Bordieu, *Distinction, passim.*

37. *Senate Subcommittee to Investigate Juvenile Delinquency: Comic Books and Juvenile Delinquency, Interim Report to the Committee on the Judiciary* (Washington, DC, 1955).

38. John Springhall, 'Horror Comics: The Nasties of the 1950s', *History Today*, XLIV (1994) pp. 10–13.

39. Benton, *Horror Comics*, pp. 47–51; Victor Gorelick, 'Introduction', in *Archie Americana Series: Best of the Fifties* (New York, 1992) p. 5; Goulart, *Over 50 Years*, p. 217. See code for 'crime' comic books: Benton, *Crime Comics*, p. 87.

40. Reidelbach, *Completely Mad*, pp. 10–12; Jacobs, *The Mad World*, pp. 112–13; Nicholas Tucker, 'What Was All the Fuss About?', *The Times Educational Supplement*, 22 Aug. 1980, p. 15.

41. A. W. Peterson, HO memo, 29 Jan. 1955, HO 302/16, Public Record Office (PRO).

42. P. M. Pickard, *I Could a Tale Unfold: Violence, Horror and Sensationalism in Stories for Children* (London, 1961) p. 118.

43. Peter Mauger, 'Should U.S. "Comics" Be Banned?', *Picture Post*, 17 May 1952, pp. 33–5; 'The Cult of Violence Persists', *Picture Post*, 20 Nov., 1954, p. 16; 'Readers' Letters', *Picture Post*, 31 May 1952, p. 12; Marcus Morris (ed.), *The Best of Eagle* (London, 1977) p. 3; Barker, *A Haunt of Fears, passim.*

44. 'A Horrible Trade', *The Times*, 12 Nov. 1954, p. 6; Barker, *A Haunt of Fears*, pp. 18–55; PPS to Home Secretary, 'Horror Comics', report of meeting on 22 Nov. 1954; (?) FO to Mr Pittam, 8 Dec. 1954, HO 302 (15), PRO.

45. 'Readers' Letters', *Picture Post*, 7 June 1952, 12; Cabinet Concs, 6 Dec. 1954, 27 Jan. 1955, CAB 128/27/28; Maj. Lloyd-George to Visct Kilmuir, 2 Feb. 1955, LCO 2/5638, PRO.

46. C. P. H. to A. W. Peterson, Home Office, 14 Jan. 1955; A. W. Peterson to Hutchison, Scottish Office, 15 Jan. 1955; A. W. Peterson to Sir A. Strutt, 20 Jan. 1955; Alistair Macdonald, Law Officer's Dept, to Chorley, Parl. Counsel's Office, 26 Jan. 1955; A. W. Peterson to Chorley, 26 Jan. 1955, HO 302 (15), PRO.

47. Mervyn Griffith-Jones, Treasury Counsel, to Director of Public Prosecutions, 11 Nov. 1954, HO 302/15, PRO.

48. Children and Young Persons (Harmful Publications) Bill, 1954–5, 2nd Reading, *Parl. Deb.*, DXXVIII, pp. 1072–186.

49. 'Notes for Third Reading', A. W. Peterson to Home Sec., HO 302 (16), PRO; 'Comics that can "Lead to Murder"', *Daily Mail*, 23 Oct. 1970, p. 9.

6 Mass Media Panic: The 1980s and 1990s

1. Erich Goode and Nachman Ben-Yehuda, *Moral Panics: The Social Construction of Deviance* (Oxford, 1994) pp. 74–5.

2. Robert Potts, 'Why Censors can't Save Us', *Guardian [Friday Review]*, 22 Mar. 1996, pp. 2–3; 'Is Oliver Stone Responsible for the Consequences of this film?', *Guardian*, 19 June 1996, p. 12; 'Dustin Hoffman blames Hollywood over Dunblane', *The Independent*, 11 May 1996, p. 1; 'Dunblane Parents see Gun Battle Lost', *Daily Mail*, 19 Nov. 1996, p. 2.

3. Alexander Walker, 'Suffer the Little Children', in Karl French (ed.), *Screen Violence* (London, 1996) p. 95; Annette Hill, *Shocking Entertainment: Viewer Response to Violent Movies* (London, 1997).

4. John Martin, *The Seduction of the Gullible: The Curious History of the British 'Video Nasty' Phenomenon* (Nottingham, 1993), supplies plot summaries of 'nasties' and little else.

5. Brian Brown, 'Exactly What We Wanted', in Martin Barker (ed.), *The Video Nasties: Freedom and Censorship in the Media* (London, 1984) pp. 68–87; Geoffrey Barlow and Alison Hill (eds), *Video Violence and Children* (London, 1985).

6. 'Video Victory for Parliament', *Daily Mail*, 13 April 1994, p. 8.

7. Patrick Rogers, 'Gunning for Gangstas', *People*, 26 June 1995, pp. 105–6; Bernard Weinraub, 'Violent Movies and Records Undercut Nation, Dole Says', *The New York Times*, 1 June 1995, pp. A1, 10; David Bennun, 'The Dogg Done Good', *Guardian*, 6 Dec. 1996, pp. 14–15.

8. Dave Marsh, 'Cops 'n' Gangstas', *The Nation*, 26 June 1995, pp. 908–9; Paul Delaney, 'Gangsta Rappers vs. The Mainstream Black Community', *USA Today*, Jan. 1995, pp. 68–9.

9. Michael E. Dyson, 'Dole's Bad Rap', *The Nation*, 26 June 1995, pp. 909–10; Ian Katz, 'Death Wish', *Guardian [Friday Review]*, 20 Sept. 1996, pp. 2–3, 19; 'Gangsta Rap', *The New York Times*, 19 Feb. 1996, p. 6. On 9 March 1997, 23-year-old rapper Notorious B.I.G. (Christopher Wallace), Shakur's arch-rival who recorded on the East Coast Bad Boy label, was shot down and killed on leaving a Los Angeles party.

10. Michael Eric Dyson, *Between God and Gangsta Rap: Bearing Witness to Black Culture* (New York, 1996) pp. 176–86; Armand White, *Rebel for the Hell of It: The Life of Tupac Shakur* (London, 1997).

11. R. McGregor, 'Television Violence: Corresponding Claims', *The Listener*, 26 June 1986, pp. 26–7; Stephen Armstrong, ' 'Ello, 'ello: Where did all those Bodies go?' *The Sunday Times, Culture Section*, 19 Jan. 1997, pp. 4–5; Barrie Gunter and Adrian Furnham, 'Perceptions of Television Violence: Effects of Programme Genre and Type of Violence on Viewers' Judgements of Violent Portrayals', *British Journal of Social Psychology*, XXIII (1984) pp. 155–64; Guy Cumberbatch with Dennis Howitt, *A Measure of Uncertainty: The Effects of the Mass Media* (London, 1989) pp. 48–50; ed. George Birbeck Hill, *Boswell's Life of Johnson*, vol. 2 (Oxford, 1934) p. 367.

12. David Buckingham, *Moving Images: Understanding Children's Emotional Responses to Television* (Manchester, 1996) pp. 303–9.

13. Ibid.; David Kidd-Hewitt and Richard Osborne (eds), *Crime and the Media: The Post-modern Spectacle* (London, 1995) pp. 8–9.

14. Paul Myers, 'Computer Games Come of Age with Monitor Man', *Guardian*, 10 Feb. 1994, p. 3.

15. David Ward, 'Small Screen Warriors take New Ratings Challenge in their Stride'; 'Readers' Letters', *Picture Post*, 7 June 1952, p. 12. At age 12, the dif-

ference between TV fabrication and reality was understood by 65 per cent of English children: *Guardian*, 26 Aug. 1992, p. 4.

16. Neville Hodgkinson, 'Videos Inspire Violent Urge for Nasty Side of Life', *The Sunday Times*, 3 May 1987, p. 6; Ray Surette, *Media, Crime, and Criminal Justice: Images and Realities* (Pacific Grove, CA, 1992) p. 140; Geoff Andrew, 'A History of Western Philosophy', *Time Out*, 19–26 August 1992, p. 30.

17. For the causal link argument see: Frank Brady (ed.), *Violence in the Media: Prospects for Change* (London, 1996); Frederic M. Thrasher, 'The Comics and Delinquency: Cause or Scapegoat?', *Journal of Educational Sociology*, XXV (1949) p. 205.

Conclusions

1. Martin Barker and Julian Petley (eds), *Ill Effects: The Media/Violence Debate* (London, 1997); David Miller and Greg Philo, 'Against Orthodoxy: The Media do Influence Us', *Sight and Sound*, VI (1996) pp. 18–20.

2. Kirsten Drotner, 'Modernity and Media Panics', in Michael Skovmand and Kim Christian Schrøder (eds), *Media Cultures: Reappraising Transnational Media* (London, 1992) pp. 52–3; Robert Warshow, 'Paul, the Horror Comics, and Dr. Wertham: Communiqué on an Unequal Battle', *Commentary*, XVII (1954) p. 604.

3. Charles Knight, *Passages of a Working Life during Half a Century*, vol. 3 (London, 1863) p. 180; Winifred Hughes, *The Maniac in the Cellar: Sensation Novels of the 1860s* (Princeton, NJ, 1980).

4. Patrick A. Dunae, 'Penny Dreadfuls: Late Nineteenth Century Boys' Literature and Crime', *Victorian Studies*, XXII (1979) pp. 135–6; Revd John Clay, *Mins. of Evidence, Select Comm. on Criminal and Destitute Juveniles*, PP, 1852, VII (515), App. 12, 422–23; 'FBI try Novel Theory on Bomber', *Guardian*, 10 July 1996, p. 11.

5. Paul Rock and Stanley Cohen, 'The Teddy Boy', in Vernon Bogdanor and Robert Skidelsky (eds), *The Age of Affluence, 1951–1964* (London, 1970) p. 311.

6. Ray Surette, *Media, Crime, and Criminal Justice: Images and Realities* (Pacific Grove, CA, 1992) pp. 121–3; Geoffrey Pearson, 'Falling Standards: A Short, Sharp History of Moral Decline', in Martin Barker (ed.), *The Video Nasties: Freedom and Censorship in the Media* (London, 1984) pp. 88–103; Richard Sparks, *Television and the Drama of Crime* (London, 1992) pp. 65–6.

7. Drotner, 'Modernity and Media Panics', pp. 42–62; Alain Touraine, trans. David Macey, *A Critique of Modernity* (Oxford, 1995); 'Mischievous Literature', *The Bookseller*, CXXVI, 1 July 1868, p. 448.

8. F. R. Leavis and Denys Thompson, *Culture and Environment: The Training of Critical Awareness* (London, 1933); Drotner, 'Modernity and Media Panics', pp. 57–61.

9. Paul Myers, 'Computer Games Come of Age with Monitor Man', *Guardian*, 10 Feb. 1994, p. 3.

10. Kevin Jackson (ed.), *Schrader on Schrader & Other Writings* (London, 1992 edn) p. 3.

11. 'Council to Ban "Horrific" Films', *The Kentish Express*, 16 Dec. 1938, p. 6; Andrew Neil, 'Shots Straight to the Heart of our Sick Society', *The Sunday Times*, 17 Mar. 1996, p. 12; Martin Barker, *et al.*, 'The "Video Violence" Debate: Media Researchers Respond', press handout (1994).

Appendix I   Jack Sheppard in Victorian Popular Culture

1. W. Harrison Ainsworth, *Jack Sheppard: A Romance* (London, 1839); Keith Hollingsworth, *The Newgate Novel, 1830–1847: Bulwer, Ainsworth, Dickens, & Thackeray* (Detroit, 1963); Henry Mayhew, *London Labour and the London Poor*, vol. 3 (London, 1861) pp. 370, 378; Frank Rahill, *The World of Melodrama* (Pennsylvania, 1967) pp. 148–50.
2. Peter Linebaugh, *The London Hanged: Crime and Civil Society in the Eighteenth Century* (Harmondsworth, 1993 edn) pp. 7–41.
3. Christopher Hibbert, *The Road to Tyburn: The Story of Jack Sheppard and the Eighteenth-century Underworld* (London, 1957); Horace W. Bleackley (ed.), *Jack Sheppard: Notable British Trials Series* (London, 1933).
4. Hollingsworth, *The Newgate Novel*, p. 140; S. M. Ellis, 'Jack Sheppard in Literature and Drama', in Bleackley (ed.), *Jack Sheppard*, pp. 64–126; anon. [John Forster], 'The Literary Examiner', *The Examiner*, 3 Nov. 1839, p. 691.
5. John Russell Stephens, '*Jack Sheppard* and the Licensers: The Case against Newgate Plays', *Nineteenth-century Theatre Research*, I (1973) pp. 1–13.
6. Bodham Donne to Earl of Bradford, 1 Apr. 1868, *Lord Chamberlain's Papers*, I/200/71, PRO, London; Mins. of Evidence, *Report from the Select Committee on Theatrical Licenses*, PP, 1866, XVI, q. 2416; *Lord Chamberlain's Day Books*, 13 Oct. 1853, fol. 314/53703, British Library Add. Mss.
7. J. J. Tobias, *Crime and Industrial Society in the Nineteenth Century* (Harmondsworth, 1972 edn) p. 99.
8. Anon. [John Forster], 'The Literary Examiner', p. 691; 'Penny Dreadfuls', Opie Collection, Bodleian Library, Oxford.
9. E. S. Turner, *Boys Will Be Boys* (London, 1948) pp. 60–1.

Appendix II   American Dime and Half-Dime Novels

1. J. Randolph Cox, 'Our Popular Publishers, No. 5: Beadle & Adams', *Dime Novel Round Up*, LXV (1996) pp. 61–3; Humphrey Carpenter and Mari Prichard, *The Oxford Companion to Children's Literature* (Oxford, 1984) pp. 150–2.
2. Albert Johannsen, *The House of Beadle and Adams and its Dime and Nickel Novels: The Story of a Vanished Literature*, 3 vols (Norman, 1950, 1962); Alexander Stratton, *The Rise and Fall of the White Republic: Class Politics and Mass Culture in Nineteenth-century America* (London, 1990) pp. 325–6; Christine Bold, 'The Voice of the Fiction Factory in Dime and Pulp Westerns', *Journal of American Studies*, XVII (1983) pp. 29–46.
3. Daryl Jones, *The Dime Novel Western* (Bowling Green, 1978) pp. 75–99; J. Randolph Cox, 'The Detective-hero in the American Dime Novel', *Dime Novel Round-Up*, L (1981) pp. 2–13.
4. D. W. Stevens, 'The James Boys as Guerillas', *The Five Cent Wide Awake Library*, no. 457, 10 Oct. 1881, p. 4; D. W. Stevens, 'The James Boys and the Vigilantes', *The Five cent Wide Awake Library*, no. 462, 18 Nov. 1881, pp. 1–8; D. W. Stevens, 'The James Boys as Train Wreckers', *The Five Cent Wide Library*, no. 474, 24 Feb. 1881, pp. 1–6; Donald Gilmore, 'Revenge in Kansas, 1863', *History Today*, XLIII (1993) pp. 47–53; William A. Settle, Jnr, *Jesse James was his Name or, Fact and Fiction*

Concerning the Career of the James Brothers of Missouri (Columbia, MS, 1966) pp. 187–91.

5. Charles Bragin, *Bibliography: Dime Novels, 1860–1964* (New York, 1964) pp. 1–2; Mary Noel, *Villains Galore: The Heyday of the Popular Story Weekly* (New York, 1954).

Appenix III   Hank Janson Paperbacks of the 1950s

1. Steve Holland, *The Mushroom Jungle: A History of Postwar Paperback Publishing* (Westbury, 1993) pp. 113, 136.
2. Holland, *The Mushroom Jungle*, p. 150; Richard Hoggart, *The Uses of Literacy* (Harmondsworth, 1958) pp. 246–72.
3. Brian Stableford, 'Yesterday's Bestsellers, 7: Hank Janson', *Million*, 7 (1992), pp. 44–9; Steve Holland, *The Trials of Hank Janson* (Westbury, 1991).
4. Holland, *The Mushroom Jungle*, pp. 151–5.

BIBLIOGRAPHY

1. Manuscript Sources

British Film Institute Library, London.
British Theatre Museum Collection, Covent Garden, London.
Burgess, Frederick, 'Penny Theatres', Harvard Theatre Collection, Cambridge, MA (on microfilm).
Children and Young Persons (Harmful Publications) Bill, 1954–55, Home Office Papers, HO 302, Public Records Office, London.
Children's Literature Collection, Library, University of Oldenburg, Germany.
Companies House Records, Returns of Allotments, BT31, Public Records Office, London.
Dime Novel Collection, Rare Books Section, Library, University of Rochester, New York State.
Hearings before the Subcommittee to Investigate Juvenile Delinquency of the Committee on the Judiciary, US Senate 83rd Congress, 1954, J74 A23, Library of Congress, Washington.
Hess Collection, Children's Literature Research Collection, Walter Library, University of Minnesota, Minneapolis.
Johnson, John, Collection of Printed Ephemera, Bodleian Library, Oxford.
London Crime Collection, Bishopsgate Institute, London.
Lord Chamberlain's Day Books, Manuscripts Room, British Library, London.
Newspaper Library, Colindale, London.
New York Society for the Suppression of Vice, Manuscript Room, Library of Congress, Washington.
Ono, Barry, Collection of Penny Dreadfuls, British Library, London.
Opie Collection of Children's Literature, Bodleian Library, Oxford.
Pettingell, Frank, Collection, Osborne Collection of Early Children's Books, Boys and Girls House, Toronto Public Library.
Police Reports on London Theatre Licenses, Greater London Record Office.
Renier Collection of Children's Books, Bethnal Green Museum of Childhood, London.
Tower Hamlets Library, Local History Collection, Stepney Green, London.

2. Parliamentary Papers

Report and Minutes of Evidence, Select Committee on Newspaper Stamps, 1851, vol. XVII (558), 413–15.

Report and Minutes of Evidence, Select Committee on Criminal and Destitute Juveniles, 1852, vol. VII (515), Appendix 2.

Report and Minutes of Evidence, Select Committee on Theatrical Licenses and Regulations, 1866, vol. XVI (373), 7879–82.

Report of the Commissioners of Prisons and Directors of Convict Prisons for 1937, Cmnd 5868, 1938, Appendix.

3. Books and Articles

(a)   General Primary Material

This refers to sources mentioned in text or references that were either the subject of panics or helped to promote them, plus memoirs and autobiographies.

Anon., *The Newgate Calendar, or, Malefactors' Bloody Register*, 5 vols (London, 1773, rev. 1814).

Anon., *The Wild Boys of London: or, The Children of Night. A Story of the Present Day* (London, 1864–6).

Anon., *The Work Girls of London: Their Trials and Temptations. A Novel* (London, 1865).

Anon., *Rose Mortimer; or, The Ballet-Girl's Revenge* (London, c.1865).

Anon., *Tales of Highwaymen or, Life on the Road* (London, 1865).

Anon., *The Jolly Dogs of London or, The Two Roads of Life* (London, c.1866).

Anon., 'The Literature of Vice', *The Bookseller*, CX, 28 Feb. 1867, pp. 121–3.

Anon., 'Mischievous Literature', *The Bookseller*, CXXVI, 1 July 1868, pp. 445–9.

Anon., 'Marihuana of the Nursery', *The Times Literary Supplement*, 25 Feb. 1955, pp. 113–14.

[Bennett, John], *The Life and Career of a London Errand Boy* (London, c.1865).

Blumer, Herbert and Hauser, Philip M., *Movies, Delinquency and Crime* (Chicago, IL, 1933).

'Bos' [T. P. Prest] (ed.), *Oliver Twiss* (London, 1838–9).

Boys of England: A Magazine of Sport, Sensation, Fun, and Instruction (London, 1866–99).

Browne, Matthew, *Views and Opinions* (London, 1866).

Burrage, E. H., *Rags and Riches: A Story of Three Poor Boys* (London, c.1875).

[Byrne, J. C.], *Undercurrents Overlooked*, vol. I (London, 1860).

Catling, Thomas, *My Life's Pilgrimage* (London, 1911).

Charters, W. W., *Motion Pictures and Youth: A Summary* (New York, 1933).

Collins, Wilkie, 'The Unknown Public', *My Miscellanies*, vol. I (London, 1863).

Comstock, Anthony, *Traps for the Young* (Cambridge, MA, 1967 edn).

Day, Samuel Phillips, *Juvenile Crime: Its Causes, Character and Cure* (London, 1858).

Doré, Gustave and Jerrold, Blanchard, *London: A Pilgrimage* (London, 1872).

Ellis, H. H., *My Life* (London, 1940).

Emmett, George, *Charity Joe: or, From Street Boy to Lord Mayor* (London, c.1875).

Ford, Richard, *Children in the Cinema* (London, 1939).

Ford, T. M., *Memoirs of a Poor Devil* (London, 1936).

Forman, Henry James, *Our Movie Made Children* (Chicago, IL, 1933).

Friswell, J. H., *Modern Men of Letters Honestly Criticised* (London, 1870).

Frost, Thomas, *Reminiscences of a Country Journalist* (London 1886).

Godwin, George, 'The Struggling Classes', *The Builder*, XVI, 5 June 1858, pp. 385–6.

Godwin, George, *Town Swamps and Social Bridges* (London, 1859).

Grant, James, *Sketches in London* (London, 1838).

Greenwood, James, *The Seven Curses of London* (London, 1869, new edn Oxford, 1981).

Greenwood, James, 'Penny Awfuls', *St Paul's Magazine*, XII (1873) pp. 154–64.

Greenwood, James, *The Wilds of London* (London, 1874).

Greenwood, James, 'Penny Packets of Poison', in Peter Haining (ed.), *The Penny Dreadful, or Strange, Horrid & Sensational Tales!* (London, 1975) pp. 357–71.

Groser, W. H., *The Opening Life: Studies of Childhood and Youth for Sunday School Teachers* (London, 1911).

Hammerton, J. A., *Books and Myself: Memoirs of An Editor* (London, 1944).

[Handover, P. M.], 'Enough of Blood', *The Times Literary Supplement*, 4 Dec. 1959, pp. i–ii.

Harrison, Jno. Pownall, 'Cheap Literature – Past and Present', *Companion to the [British] Almanac of the Society for the Diffusion of Useful Knowledge or Year Book of General Information for 1873* (London, 1972) pp. 60–81.

[Hazleton, Harry], *Charley Wag: The New Jack Sheppard* (London, 1860–1).

[Hazleton, Harry], *Fanny White and Her Friend Jack Rawlings: A Romance of a Young Lady Thief and a Boy Burglar* (London, c. 1865).

Hitchman, Francis, 'The Penny Press', *Macmillan's Magazine*, XLIII (1881) pp. 395–400.

[Hitchman, Francis], 'Penny Fiction', *The Quarterly Review*, CLXXI (1890) pp. 150–71.

Hotten, John Camden, *The Slang Dictionary* (London, 1874 edn).

[Johns, B. G.], 'The Literature of the Streets', *The Edinburgh Review*, CLXV (1887) pp. 40–55.

Kamen, Jack, 'A Trace of Murder', *Crime SuspenStories*, no. 8, 1951, republished 1990.

Kamen, Jack, 'The Neat Job', *Shock SuspenStories*, no. 1, 1952, republished 1992.

Knight, Charles, *Passages of a Working Life During Half a Century*, vol. 3 (London, 1863).

Leavis, F. R. and Thompson, Denys, *Culture and Environment: The Training of Critical Awareness* (London, 1933).

Legman, Gershorn, *Love and Death: A Study in Censorship* (New York, 1949).

Loraine, Winifred, *Robert Loraine: Actor, Soldier, Airman* (London, 1938).

Macdonald, Dwight, *Against the American Grain* (New York, 1962).

Mackie, John (comp.), *The Edinburgh Cinema Enquiry* (Edinburgh, 1933).

[Martineau, Harriet], 'Life in the Criminal Class', *The Edinburgh Review*, CXXII (1865) pp. 344–50.

Mauger, Peter, 'Should U.S. "Comics" Be Banned?', *Picture Post*, 17 May 1952, pp. 33–5.

Mauger, Peter, 'The Cult of Violence Persists', *Picture Post*, 20 Nov. 1954, p. 12.

Mayhew, Henry, *London Labour and the London Poor*, 4 vols (London, 1861–2 edn, new imp. 1865).

[Mortimer, James], 'Pernicious Literature', *London Figaro*, no. 681, 5 Feb. 1876, pp. 7–8.

Parker, Lieut. [pseud.], *The Young Ladies of London; or, The Mysteries of Midnight* (London, 1867–8).

Pearson, George, *Flashback: The Autobiography of a British Film-Maker* (London, 1957).

Pickard, P. M., *I Could a Tale Unfold: Violence, Horror and Sensationalism in Stories for Children* (London, 1961).

Riesman, David, *The Lonely Crowd: A Study of the Changing American Character* (New Haven, CT, 1950).

Rollington, Ralph [J. J. Allingham], *A Brief History of Boys' Journals, with Interesting Facts about the Writers of Boys' Stories* (Leicester, 1913).

Sampson, George, *Seven Essays* (London, 1947).

Schlesinger, Max, *Saunterings in and about London* (London, 1853).

Sterns, C. M., 'Bloods', *The Library Assistant*, no. 34 (1941), pp. 160–5.

Stevens, D. W., 'The James Boys as Guerillas', *The Five Cent Wide Awake Library*, I, 10 Oct. 1881, pp. 1–16.

Strahan, Alexander, 'Our Very Cheap Literature', *Contemporary Review*, XIV (1870) pp. 439–60.

Thrasher, Frederic M., 'The Comics and Delinquency: Cause or Scapegoat?', *Journal of Educational Sociology*, XXIII (1949) pp. 195–205.

[Trollope, Anthony], 'An Editor's Tales: "The Spotted Dog" ', *Saint Paul's Magazine*, V (1870) pp. 686–90.

Viles, Edward [J. F. Smith], *Black Bess; or, The Knight of the Road: A Tale of the Good Old Times*, 3 vols (London, 1863–8).

Wagner, Geoffrey, *Parade of Pleasure: A Study of Popular Iconography in the USA* (London, 1954).

Waite, A. E., 'By-ways of Periodical Literature', *Walford's Antiquarian*, XII (1887) pp. 64–6.

Warshow, Robert, 'Paul, the Horror Comics, and Dr. Wertham: Communiqué on an Unequal Battle', *Commentary*, XVII (1954) pp. 596–604.

Wells, H. G., *Tono-Bungay* (London, 1909).

Wertham, Fredric, 'What Parents don't know about Comic Books', *The Ladies' Home Journal*, LXX (1953) pp. 50–3.

Wertham, Fredric, *Seduction of the Innocent: The Influence of Comic Books on Today's Youth* (New York, 1954).

Wertham, Fredric, 'Children's Comic Books: Blueprints for Delinquency', *The Reader's Digest*, LXIV (1954) pp. 52–6.

Wood, Wally, 'The Patriots', *Shock SuspenStories*, no. 2, 1952, republished 1992.

(b)   Secondary Material

This refers to books and articles, mostly critical works and histories, not contemporary with the above.

Aldcroft, D. H., 'The Entrepreneur and the British Economy, 1870–1914', *The Economic History Review*, 2nd ser., XXVII (1964) pp. 113–34.

Altick, Richard D., *The English Common Reader: A Social History of the Mass Reading Public, 1800–1900* (Chicago, IL, 1957).

Altick, Richard D., *Victorian Studies in Scarlet* (London, 1972 edn).

Anderson, Patricia, *The Printed Image and the Transformation of Popular Culture, 1790–1860* (Oxford, 1991).

Anglo, Michael, *Penny Dreadfuls and Other Victorian Horrors* (London, 1977).

Arato, Andrew and Gebhardt, Eike (eds), *The Essential Frankfurt School Reader* (New York, 1982).

Armes, Roy, *A Critical History of British Cinema* (London, 1978).

Bailey, Peter, *Leisure and Class in Victorian England: Rational Recreation and the Contest for Control, 1830–1885* (London, 1978).

Bailey, Victor, *Delinquency and Citizenship: Reclaiming the Young Offender, 1914–1948* (Oxford, 1987).

Barker, Martin, *A Haunt of Fears: The Strange History of the British Horror Comics Campaign* (London, 1984).

Barker, Martin, *The Video Nasties: Freedom and Censorship in the Media* (London, 1984).

Barker, Martin, 'Sex, Violence and Videotape', *Sight and Sound*, III (1993) pp. 10–12.

Barker, Martin, and Petley, Julian, *Ill Effects: The Media/Violence Debate* (London, 1997).

Barlow, Geoffrey and Hill, Alison (eds), *Video Violence and Children* (London, 1985).

Barnes, J. J., *Free Trade in Books: A Study of the London Book Trade since 1800* (Oxford, 1964).

Bennett, Scott, 'Revolutions in Thought: Serial Publication and the Mass Market for Reading', in Joanna Shattock and Michael Wolff (eds), *The Victorian Periodical Press: Samplings and Soundings* (Leicester, 1982) pp. 225–57.

Bennett, Tony, 'Introduction: Popular Culture and "the Turn to Gramsci" ', in Tony Bennett, Colin Mercer and Janet Woolacott (eds), *Popular Culture and Social Relations* (Milton Keynes, 1986) pp. xi–xix.

Benton, Mike, *The Comic Book in America: An Illustrated History* (Dallas, 1989).

Benton, Mike, *The Illustrated History: Horror Comics* (Dallas, 1991).

Benton, Mike, *The Illustrated History: Crime Comics* (Dallas, 1993).

Berman, Marshall, *All that is Solid Melts into Air: The Experience of Modernity* (Harmondsworth, 1982).

Black, Gregory D., *Hollywood Censored: Morality Codes, Catholics and the Movies* (Cambridge, 1994).

Bleackley, Horace W. (ed), *Jack Sheppard: Notable British Trials Series* (London, 1933).

Bleiler, E. F., 'Introduction to the Dover Edition', *G. W. M. Reynolds's Wagner the Wehrwolf* (New York, 1975) pp. iii–xx.

Bogdanor, Vernon and Skidelsky, Robert (eds), *The Age of Affluence, 1951–1964* (London, 1970).

Bold, Christine, 'The Voice of the Fiction Factory in Dime and Pulp Westerns', *Journal of American Studies*, XVII (1983) pp. 29–46.

Booth, Michael R., *Victorian Spectacular Theatre, 1850–1910* (London, 1981).

Booth, Michael R., 'The Metropolis on Stage', in H. J. Dyos and Michael Wolff (eds), *The Victorian City: Image and Realities*, vol. I (London, 1973) pp. 211–24.

Booth, Michael R., 'East End and West End: Class and Audience in Victorian London', *Theatre Research International*, II (1977) pp. 98–103.

Bourdieu, Pierre, *Distinction: A Social Critique of the Judgement of Taste* (London, trans., 1984).

Brady, Frank (ed.), *Violence in the Media: Prospects for Change* (London, 1996).

Bragin, Charles, *Bibliography: Dime Novels, 1860–1964* (New York, 1964).

Bristow, Joseph, *Empire Boys: Adventures in a Man's World* (London, 1991).

Brode, Douglas, *Money, Women, and Guns: Crime Movies from Bonnie and Clyde to the Present* (New York, 1995).

Browning, D. C. (ed.), *Everyman's Dictionary of Literary Biography: English and American* (London, 1972 edn).

Buckingham, David, *Moving Images: Understanding Children's Emotional Responses to Television* (Manchester, 1996).

Burke, Peter, 'Revolution in Popular Culture', in Roy Porter and Mikules Teich (eds), *Revolution in History* (Cambridge, 1986) pp. 206–25.

Bushaway, Bob, *By Rite: Custom, Ceremony and Community in England, 1700–1880* (London, 1982).

Calle, Michelle, *Law and Society: An Introduction to Sources for Criminal and Legal History from 1800* (Kew, 1996).

Campbell, Beatrix, 'Moral Panic', *Index on Censorship*, XXIV (1995) pp. 57–61.

Capp, Bernard, 'Popular Literature', in Barry Reay (ed.), *Popular Culture in Seventeenth-Century England* (London, 1985) pp. 198–243.

Carpenter, Humphrey and Prichard, Mari, *The Oxford Companion to Children's Literature* (Oxford, 1984).

Carpenter, Kevin, *Desert Isles and Pirate Islands: The Island Theme in Nineteenth-Century English Juvenile Fiction: A Survey and Bibliography* (Frankfurt, 1984).

[Carpenter, Kevin], *Penny Dreadfuls and Comics: English Periodicals for Children from Victorian Times to the Present Day* (London, 1983).

Caute, David, *The Great Fear: The Anti-Communist Purge under Truman and Eisenhower* (London, 1978).

Childs, Michael J., *Labour's Apprentices: Working-Class Lads in Late Victorian and Edwardian England* (Montreal, 1992).

Clarens, Carlos, 'Hooverville West: The Hollywood G-Man, 1934–1945', *Film Comment*, XIII (1977) pp. 10–16.

Clarens, Carlos, *Crime Movies: From Griffith to the Godfather and Beyond* (New York, 1980).

Clark, Anna, 'The Politics of Seduction in English Popular Culture, 1748–1848', in Jane Radford (ed.), *The Progress of Romance: The Politics of Popular Fiction* (London, 1986) pp. 47–70.

Clarke, W. M., *The Secret Life of Wilkie Collins* (London, 1988).

Cohen, Stan, *Folk Devils and Moral Panics: The Creation of the Mods and Rockers* (Oxford, 1972).

Cohen, Stanley, *Visions of Social Control: Crime, Punishment and Classification* (Cambridge, 1985).

Coleman, D. C., *The British Paper Industry, 1496–1860: A Study in Industrial Growth* (Oxford, 1958).

Cox, J. Randolph, 'The Detective-hero in the American Dime Novel', *Dime Novel Round-Up*, L (1981) pp. 2–13.

Cox, J. Randolph, 'Our Popular Publishers, No. 5: Beadle and Adams', *Dime Novel Round-Up*, LXV (1996) pp. 61–3.

Cumberbatch, Guy, with Howitt, Dennis, *A Measure of Uncertainty: The Effects of the Mass Media* (London, 1989).

Cunningham, Hugh, 'The Metropolitan Fairs: A Case Study in the Social Control of Leisure', in A. P. Donajgrodzki (ed.), *Social Control in Nineteenth-Century Britain* (London, 1977) pp. 163–84.

Cunningham, Hugh, *Leisure in the Industrial Revolution, c.1780–c.1880* (London, 1980).

Denning, Michael, *Mechanic Accents: Dime Novels and Working-class Culture in America* (London, 1987).

Denning, Michael, 'The End of Mass Culture', *International Labour and Working-Class History*, no. 37 (1990) pp. 4–18.

Diehl, Digby, *Tales from the Crypt: The Official Archives* (New York, 1996).

Drotner, Kirsten, *English Children and Their Magazines, 1751–1945* (New Haven, CT, 1988).

Drotner, Kirsten, 'Modernity and Media Panics', in Michael Skovmand and Kim Christian Schrøder (eds), *Media Cultures: Reappraising Transnational Media* (London, 1992) pp. 42–62.

Dunae, Patrick, 'Penny Dreadfuls: Late Nineteenth-century Boys' Literature and Crime', *Victorian Studies*, XXII (1979) pp. 133–50.

Dunae, Patrick, 'New Grub Street for Boys', in Jeffrey Richards (ed.), *Imperialism and Juvenile Literature* (Manchester, 1989) pp. 12–33.

Dyson, Michael Eric, *Between God and Gangsta Rap: Bearing Witness to Black Culture* (New York, 1996).

Easton, Susan, with Alun Howkins, Stuart Laing, Linda Merricks and Helen Walker (eds), *Disorder and Discipline: Popular Culture from 1550 to the Present* (Aldershot, 1988).

Egoff, Sheila A., *Children's Periodicals of the Nineteenth Century* (London, 1951).

Egoff, Sheila A., 'Precepts and Pleasures: Changing Emphases in the Writing and Criticism of Children's Literature', in S. Egoff, G. T. Stubbs and L. F. Ashley (eds), *Only Connect: Readings in Children's Literature* (Toronto, 1969) pp. 419–46.

Emsley, Clive, *Crime and Society in England, 1750–1900* (London, 1987).

Erikson, Kai T., 'Notes on the Sociology of Deviance', in H. S. Becker (ed.), *The Other Side: Perspectives on Deviance* (New York, 1964) pp. 2–20.

Field, Audrey, *Picture Palace* (London, 1974).

Finler, Joel W., *The Hollywood Story* (London, 1988).

Fontana, Biancamaria, 'Thrilling Plots Suspended Over Centuries', *The Times Higher Education Supplement*, no. 956, 1 March 1991, p. 18.

Fowler, David, *The First Teenagers: The Lifestyle of Young Wage-earners in Interwar Britain* (London, 1995).

Frayling, Christopher, *Nightmare: The Birth of Horror* (London, 1996).

French, Karl (ed.), *Screen Violence* (London, 1996).

Fulce, John, *Seduction of the Innocent Revisited* (Layfayette, 1990).

Fullerton, Ronald A., 'Creating a Mass Book Market in Germany: The Story of the "Colporteur Novel", 1870–1890', *Journal of Social History*, XI (1977) pp. 265–83.

Gatrell, V. A. C., 'Crime, Authority and the Policeman State', in F. M. L. Thompson (ed.), *The Cambridge Social History of Britain*, vol. 3 (Cambridge, 1990) pp. 243–310.

Gatrell, V. A. C., Lenman B., and Parker G., *Crime and the Law: The Social History of Crime in Western Europe since 1500* (London, 1980).

Gilbert, James, *Another Chance: Postwar America, 1945–1968* (New York, 1981).

Gilbert, James, *A Cycle of Outrage: America's Reaction to the Juvenile Delinquent in the 1950s* (New York, 1986).

Gillis, John R., 'The Evolution of Juvenile Delinquency in England, 1890–1914', *Past and Present*, no. 67 (1975) pp. 96–126.

Gilmore, Donald, 'Revenge in Kansas, 1863', *History Today*, XLIII (1993) pp. 47–53.

Gledhill, Christine, 'The Melodramatic Field: An Investigation', in Christine Gledhill, *Home is Where the Heart Is: Studies in Melodrama and the Woman's Film* (London, 1987).

Goode, Erich and Ben-Yehuda, Nachman, *Moral Panics: The Social Construction of Deviance* (Oxford, 1994).

Goulart, Ron, *Over 50 Years of American Comic Books* (Lincolnwood, 1991).

Gunter, Barry and Furnham, Adrian, 'Perceptions of Television Violence: Effects of Programme Genre and Type of Violence on Viewers' Judgements of Violent Portrayals', *British Journal of Social Psychology*, XXIII (1984) pp. 155–64.

Haining, Peter (ed.), *The Penny Dreadful, or Strange, Horrid & Sensational Tales!* (London, 1975).

Haining, Peter, *The Legend and Bizarre Crimes of Spring Heeled Jack* (London, 1977).

Haining, Peter, *The Mystery and Horrible Murders of Sweeney Todd, the Demon Barber of Fleet Street* (London, 1978).

Haining, Peter (ed.), *A Pictorial History of Horror Stories: 200 Years of Spine-Chilling Illustrations from the Pulp Magazines*, 2nd edn (London, 1985).

Hall, P. G., *The Industries of London since 1861* (London, 1962).

Hall, Stuart, 'Notes on Deconstructing "The Popular"', in Raphael Samuel (ed.), *People's History and Socialist Theory* (London, 1981) pp. 227–39.

Halloran, J. D., Brown, R. L. and Chaney, D. C., *Television and Delinquency* (Leicester, 1970).

Hannabuss, C. Stuart, 'Nineteenth-Century Religious Periodicals for Children', *British Journal of Religious Education*, VI (1983) pp. 20–5.

Hendrick, Harry, *Images of Youth: Age, Class, and the Male Youth Problem, 1880–1920* (Oxford, 1990).

Hibbert, Christopher, *The Road to Tyburn: The Story of Jack Sheppard and the Eighteenth-Century Underworld* (London, 1957).

Hill, George Birkbeck (ed.), *Boswell's Life of Johnson*, vol. 2 (Oxford, 1934).

Hirschhorn, Clive, *The Warner Bros. Story* (London, 1979).

Hodder, Edwin, *The Life and Work of the Seventh Earl of Shaftesbury*, vol. 3 (London, 1886).

Hoggart, P. R., 'Edward Lloyd, "the father of the cheap press"', *The Dickensian*, LXXX (1984) pp. 33–8.

Hoggart, Richard, *The Uses of Literacy* (Harmondsworth, 1958).

Holland, Steve, *The Trials of Hank Janson* (Westbury, 1991).

Holland, Steve, *The Mushroom Jungle: A History of Postwar Paperback Publishing* (Westbury, 1993).

Hollingsworth, Keith, *The Newgate Novel, 1830–1847: Bulwer, Ainsworth, Dickens & Thackeray* (Detroit, 1963).

Holub, Robert C., *Reception Theory: A Critical Introduction* (New York, 1984).

Hopperton, Tom, 'Two-way Blood Transfusion', *The Story Paper Collector*, IV (1962) pp. 23–7.

Hopperton, Tom, 'Victorian King-Pin', *The Story Paper Collector*, IV (1962) pp. 31–7.

Hughes, Winifred, *The Maniac in the Cellar: Sensation Novels of the 1860s* (Princeton, NJ, 1980).

Humpherys, Anne, 'Generic Strands and Urban Twists: The Victorian Mysteries Novel', *Victorian Studies*, XXXIV (1991) pp. 455–72.

Jackson, Kevin (ed.), *Schrader on Schrader & Other Writings* (London, 1992 edn).

Jackson, Mary V., *Engines of Instruction, Mischief and Magic: Children's Literature in England from its Beginnings to 1839* (Aldershot, 1990).

Jacobs, Edward, 'Bloods in the Street: London Street Culture, "Industrial Literacy", and the Emergence of Mass Culture in Victorian England', *Nineteenth-Century Contexts*, XVIII (1995) pp. 321–47.

Jacobs, Frank, *The Mad World of William M. Gaines* (Secaucus, 1972).

James, Louis, *Fiction for the Working Man, 1830–50: A Study of the Literature Produced for the Working Classes in Early Victorian Urban England* (Harmondsworth, 1974 edn).

James, Louis, 'Tom Brown's Imperialist Sons', *Victorian Studies*, XVII (1973) pp. 89–99.

James, Louis, 'The Trouble with Betsy: Periodicals and the Common Reader in Mid-nineteenth-century England', in Joanna Shattock and Michael Wolff (eds), *The Victorian Periodical Press: Samplings and Soundings* (Leicester, 1982) pp. 348–66.

Jarvis Arthur R., Jr, 'The Payne Fund Reports: A Discussion of their Content, Public Reaction, and Affect on the Motion Picture Industry, 1930–1940', *Journal of Popular Culture*, XIX (1991) pp. 127–40.

Jay, Martin, *The Dialectical Imagination: A History of the Frankfurt School and the Institute of Social Research, 1923–1950* (London, 1973).

Jenkins, Philip, *Intimate Enemies: Moral Panics in Contemporary Great Britain* (New York, 1992).

Jeremy, D. J., 'Anatomy of the British Business Elite, 1860–1980', *Business History*, XXVI (1984) pp. 1–15.

Johannsen, Albert, *The House of Beadle and Adams and its Dime and Nickel Novels: The Story of a Vanished Literature*, 3 vols (Norman, 1950, 1962).

Jones, Daryl, *The Dime Novel Western* (Bowling Green, 1978).

Jones, Gareth Stedman, *Outcast London: A Study in the Relationship Between Classes in Victorian Society* (Harmondsworth, 1976 edn).

Jowett, Garth S., Jarvie, Ian C. and Fuller, Kathryn H., *Children and the Movies: Media Influence and the Payne Fund Controversy* (Cambridge, 1996).

Judd, Mark, ' "The Oddest Combination of Town and Country": Popular Culture and the London Fairs, 1800–1860', in John K. Walton and James Walvin (eds), *Leisure in Britain, 1780–1939* (Manchester, 1983) pp. 10–30.

Kidd-Hewitt, David and Osborne, Richard, *Crime and the Media: The Post-modern Spectacle* (London, 1995).

King, Elspeth, 'Popular Culture in Glasgow', in R. A. Cage (ed.), *The Working Class in Glasgow, 1750–1914* (London, 1987) pp. 142–87.

Landes, David, *The Unbound Prometheus* (Cambridge, 1969).

Lang, Marjory, 'Childhood's Champions: Mid-Victorian Children's Periodicals and the Critics', *Victorian Periodicals Review*, XIII (1980) pp. 15–24.

Leach, Clifford and Craik, T. W. (eds), *The Revels History of Drama in English*, vol. 3 (London, 1975).

Levidow, Les, 'Witches and Seducers: Moral Panics for Our Time', in Barry Richards (ed.), *Crises of the Self: Further Essays on Psychoanalysis and Politics* (London, 1989) pp. 181–215.

Levine, A., *Industrial Retardation in Britain, 1880–1914* (London, 1967).

Levine, Lawrence, *Highbrow/Lowbrow: The Emergence of Cultural Hierarchy in America* (Cambridge, MA, 1988).

Linebaugh, Peter, *The London Hanged: Crime and Civil Society in the Eighteenth Century* (Harmondsworth, 1993 edn).

McBride, Joseph, *Frank Capra: The Catastrophe of Success* (London, 1992).

McCarty, John, *Hollywood Gangland: The Movies' Love Affair with the Mob* (New York, 1993).

MacKenzie, John M., *Propaganda and Empire: The Manipulation of British Public Opinion, 1880–1960* (Manchester, 1984).

McKernan, Luke, 'The Arrival of British Movies', in Colin Sorensen (ed.), *London on Film:100 Years of Filmmaking in London* (London, 1996), pp. 17–25.

McLynn, Frank, *Crime and Punishment in Eighteenth-century England* (Oxford, 1991).

McRobbie, Angela and Thornton, Sarah L., 'Rethinking "Moral Panic" for Multi-mediated Social Worlds', *The British Journal of Sociology*, XLVI (1995) pp. 559–74.

McWilliam, Rohan, 'The Mysteries of G. W. M. Reynolds: Radicalism and Melodrama in Victorian Britain', in Malcolm Chase and Ian Dyck (eds), *Living and Learning: Essays in Honour of J. F. C. Harrison* (Aldershot, 1996) pp. 182–98.

Malcolmson, R. W., *Popular Recreations in English Society, 1700–1850* (Cambridge, 1973).

Manvell, Roger and Low, Rachael, *History of the British Film*, vol. 1 (London, 1949).

Martin, John, *The Seduction of the Gullible: The Curious History of the British 'Video Nasty' Phenomenon* (Nottingham, 1993).

Mathews, Tom Dewe, *Censored* (London, 1994).

Matthews, Glenna, *'Just A Housewife': The Rise and Fall of Domesticity in America* (New York, 1987).

Medcraft, John, 'Newagents' Publishing Company', *Collector's Miscellany*, 5th ser., no. 2 (1945) pp. 23–6.

Medcraft, John, 'The Rivalry of Brett and Emmett', *Collector's Miscellany*, 5th ser., no. 7 (1947) pp. 103–5.

Medved, Michael, *Hollywood vs. America: Popular Culture and the War on Traditional Values* (London, 1993 edn).

Meisel, Michael, *Representations: Narrative, Pictorial, and Theatrical Arts in Nineteenth Century England* (Princeton, New Jersey, 1983).

Miller, David and Philo, Greg, 'The Media Do Influence Us', *Sight and Sound*, VI (1996) pp. 18–20.

Mitchell, B. R. and Deane, P., *Abstract of British Historical Statistics* (Cambridge, 1962).

Mitchell, B. R. and Deane, P., *Second Abstract of British Historical Statistics* (Cambridge, 1971).

Mitchie, R. C., *The City of London: Continuity and Change, 1850–1900* (London, 1992).

Murdock, Graham, 'Disorderly Images: Television's Presentation of Crime and Policing', in C. Sumner (ed.), *Crime, Justice and the Media* (Cambridge, 1982) pp. 104–21.

Neuberg, Victor, *Popular Literature: A History and Guide: From the Beginning of Printing to the Year 1897* (Harmondsworth, 1977).

Noel, Mary, *Villains Galore: The Heyday of the Popular Story Weekly* (New York, 1954).

Partridge, Eric, *A Dictionary of the Underworld*, 3rd edn (London, 1968).

Pearson, Geoffrey, *Hooligan: A History of Respectable Fears* (London, 1983).

Plant, M., *The English Book Trade: An Economic History of the Making and Sale of Books* (London, 1974 edn).

Plumb, J. H., *The Commercialisation of Leisure in Eighteenth-century England* (Reading, 1973).

Quinn, Laura, *Victorian Popular Fiction: Penny Dreadfuls, Boys' Weeklies and Halfpenny Parts* (Minneapolis, 1974).

Rahill, Frank, *The World of Melodrama* (Pennsylvania, 1967).

Rawlings, Philip (ed.), *Drunks, Whores and Idle Apprentices: Criminal Biographies of the Eighteenth Century* (London, 1992).

Reid, Douglas A., 'Popular Theatre in Victorian Birmingham', in David Bratby, Louis James and Bernard Sharratt (eds), *Performance and Politics in Popular Drama: Aspects of Popular Entertainment in Theatre, Film and Television, 1800–1975* (Cambridge, 1980) pp. 65–89.

Reid, J. C., *Bucks and Bruisers: Pierce Egan and Regency England* (London, 1971).

Reidelbach, Maria, *Completely Mad: A History of the Comic Book and Magazine* (Boston, MA, 1991).

Richards, Jeffrey, *The Age of the Dream Palace: Cinema and Society in Britain, 1930–1939* (London, 1984).

Richards, Jeffrey, 'The Cinema and Cinema-going in Birmingham in the 1930s', in John K. Walton and James Walvin (eds), *Leisure in Britain, 1780–1939* (Manchester, 1983) pp. 31–52.

Richards, Jeffrey, 'The British Board of Film Censors and Content Control in the 1930s: Images of Britain', *Historical Journal of Film, Radio and Television*, I (1981) pp. 95–116.

Richards, Kenneth and Thomson, Peter (eds), *Nineteenth-century British Theatre* (London, 1971).

Ridgewell, Stephen, 'The People's Amusement: Cinema and Cinema-going in 1930s Britain', *The Historian*, no. 52 (1996) pp. 18–21.

Ringgenberg, S. C., 'Oh . . . the HORROR! A Capsule History of American Horror comics', *Comic Book Marketplace*, no. 41 (1996) pp. 20–6.

Roberts, M. J. D., 'The Society for the Suppression of Vice and its Early Critics', *The Historical Journal*, XXVI (1983) pp. 159–76.

Robertson, James C., *The British Board of Film Censors: Film Censorship in Britain, 1896–1950* (London, 1985).

Robertson, James C., *The Hidden Camera: British Film Censorship in Action, 1913–1976* (London, 1989).

Roddick, Nick, *A New Deal in Entertainment: Warner Brothers in the 1930s* (London, 1983).

Rose, Lionel, *'Rogues and Vagabonds': Vagrant Underworld in Britain, 1815–1985* (London, 1988).

Rosenberg, Bernard and Manning, David (eds), *Mass Culture: The Popular Arts in America* (New York, 1957).

Rosow, Eugene, *Born to Lose: The Gangster Film in America* (Oxford, 1978).

Sabin, Roger, *Adult Comics: An Introduction* (London, 1993).

Sarris, Andrew, 'Big Funerals: The Hollywood Gangster, 1927–1933', *Film Comment*, XIII (1977) pp. 6–9.

Savage William W., Jr, *Comic Books and America, 1945–1954* (Norman, 1990).

Schaller, Michael, Scharff, Virginia and Schulzinger, Robert D., *Present Tense: The United States since 1945* (Boston, MA, 1996 edn).

Schlicke, Paul, *Dickens and Popular Entertainment* (London, 1985).

Selwood, Sara and Irving, Diana, *Harmful Publications: Comics, Education and Disenfranchised Young People* (London, 1993).

Server, Lee, *Danger is My Business: An Illustrated History of the Fabulous Pulp Magazines, 1896–1953* (San Francisco, CA, 1993).

Sheppard, Frederick, *London, 1808–1870: The Infernal Wen* (London, 1971).

Sheridan, Paul, *Penny Theatres of Victorian London* (London, 1981).

Shindler, Colin, *Hollywood in Crisis: Cinema and Modern Society 1929–1939* (London, 1996).

Simon, Joe, with Simon, Jim, *The Comic Book Makers* (New York, 1990).

Sindall, Rob, *Street Violence in the Nineteenth Century: Media Panic or Real Danger?* (Leicester, 1990).

Skinner, James M., *The Cross and the Cinema: The Legion of Decency and the National Catholic Office for Motion Pictures, 1933–1970* (Westport, CT, 1993).

Smith, Henry Nash, *Virgin Land: The American West as Symbol and Myth* (Cambridge, MA, 1970 edn).

Sparks, Richard, *Television and the Drama of Crime* (London, 1992).

Speaight, George, *Juvenile Drama: The History of the English Toy Theatre* (London, 1946).

Springhall, John, 'Leisure and Victorian Youth: The Penny Theatre in London, 1830–1890', in John Hurt (ed.), *Childhood, Youth and Education in the Late Nineteenth Century*, History of Education Society (Leicester, 1981) pp. 101–24.

Springhall, John (ed.), with Brian Fraser and Michael Hoare, *Sure and Stedfast: A History of The Boys' Brigade, 1883 to 1983* (Glasgow, 1983).

Springhall, John, *Coming of Age: Adolescence in Britain, 1860–1960* (Dublin, 1986).

Springhall, John, ' "Healthy Papers for Manly Boys": Imperialism and Race in the Harmsworths' Halfpenny Boys Papers of the 1890s and 1900s', in Jeffrey Richards (ed.), *Imperialism and Juvenile Literature* (Manchester, 1989) pp. 107–25.

Springhall, John, ' "A Life Story for the People"? Edwin J. Brett and the London "Low-Life" Penny Dreadfuls of the 1860s', *Victorian Studies*, XXXIII (1990) pp. 223–46.

Springhall, John, ' "Boys of Bircham School": The Penny Dreadful Origins of the Popular English School Story, 1867–1900', *History of Education*, XX (1991) pp. 77–94.

Springhall, John, ' "Corrupting the Young"? Popular Entertainment and "Moral Panics" in Britain and America since 1830', *Journal of the Institute of Education: The University of Hull*, no. 50 (1994) pp. 95–110.

Springhall, John, 'Horror Comics: The Nasties of the 1950s', *History Today*, XLIV (1994) pp. 10–13.

Springhall, John, 'The Dime Novel as Scapegoat for Juvenile Crime', *Dime Novel Round-Up*, LXIII (1994) pp. 63–72.

Springhall, John, ' "Disseminating Impure Literature": The "Penny Dreadful" Publishing Business since 1860', *The Economic History Review*, XLVII (1994) pp. 567–84.

Spufford, Margaret, *Small Books and Pleasant Histories: Popular Fiction and its Readership in Seventeenth-century England* (London, 1981).

Stableford, Brian, 'Yesterday's Bestsellers, 7: Hank Janson', *Million*, no. 7 (1992) pp. 44–9.

Starker, Stephen, *Evil Influences: Crusades against the Mass Media* (New Brunswick, NJ, 1991 edn).

Stephens, John Russell, '*Jack Sheppard* and the Licensers: The Case against Newgate Plays', *Nineteenth-Century Theatre Research*, I (1973) pp. 1–13.

Stephens, John Russell, *The Censorship of English Drama, 1824–1901* (Cambridge, 1980).

Stephens, John Russell, 'Thespis's Poorest Children: Penny Theatres and the Law in the 1830s', *Theatre Notebook*, XL (1986) pp. 123–30.

Stephens, W. B., *Education, Literacy and Society, 1830–70* (Manchester, 1987).

Suleiman, Susan, 'Varieties of Audience-Oriented Criticism', in Susan Suleiman and Inge Crossman (eds), *The Reader in the Text: Essays on Audience and Interpretation* (Princeton, NJ, 1980) pp. 3–45.

Surette, Ray, *Media, Crime, and Criminal Justice: Images and Realities* (Pacific Grove, CA, 1992).

Taylor, John Russell (ed.), *The Pleasure Dome: Collected Film Criticism of Graham Greene* (Oxford, 1980).

Tobias, J. J., *Crime and Industrial Society in the Ninteenth Century* (Harmondsworth, 1972 edn).

Toulet, Emmanuelle, *Cinema is 100 Years Old* (London, 1995).

Touraine, Alain, trans. David Macey, *A Critique of Modernity* (Oxford, 1995).

Turner, E. S., *Boys Will Be Boys: The Story of Sweeney Todd, Deadwood Dick, Sexton Blake, Billy Bunter, Dick Barton et al.* (London, 1948).

Twitchell, James B., *Dreadful Pleasures: An Anatomy of Modern Horror* (New York, 1985).

Twitchell, James B., *Preposterous Violence: Fables of Aggression in Modern Culture* (New York, 1989).

Vincent, David, *Bread, Knowledge and Freedom: A Study of Nineteenth-Century Working-Class Autobiography* (London, 1982 edn).

Vincent, David, *Literacy and Popular Culture: England, 1750–1914* (Cambridge, 1989).

Walsh, Frank, *Sin and Censorship: The Catholic Church and the Motion Picture Industry* (Cambridge, 1994).

Waugh, Coulton, *The Comics* (Jackson, 1991 edn).

Webb, W. L., 'Working-class Readers in Early-Victorian England', *English Historical Review*, LXV (1950) pp. 333–51.

West, Mark I., *Children, Culture and Controversy* (Hamden, CT, 1988).

Wilson, J. J., 'Some of the Old "penny dreadful" Newsvendors', *Collector's Miscellany*, I (1928) pp. 15–16.

Winskill, B., 'The Penny Dreadful Offices', *Vanity Fair* [Saltburn-by-Sea], no. 2 (1925) pp. 47–8.

Winskill, B., 'Publishing Offices of the Old Boys' Papers that are Gone', *Collector's Miscellany*, 4th ser., no. 4 (1942) pp. 44–6.

Young, Jock, *The Drugtakers: The Social Meaning of Drug Use* (London, 1971).

Zone, Ray, '4-Color Frenzy: The Rise and Fall of the Crime Comic Book', *Blab*, no. 5 (1990) pp. 46–65.

Zweig, Paul, *The Adventurer* (London, 1974).

4. Unpublished Theses

Barnett, Patricia Mary, 'English Boys' Weeklies, 1866–1899', DPhil thesis, University of Minnesota, 1974.

Boyd, K. K., '"Wait Till I'm a Man": Manliness in the English Boys' Story Paper, 1855–1940', PhD thesis, Rutgers University, 1991.

Dunae, Patrick, 'British Juvenile Literature in an Age of Empire, 1880–1914', PhD thesis, University of Manchester, 1975.

INDEX